William Icrin Gill

Philosophical Realism

William Icrin Gill

Philosophical Realism

ISBN/EAN: 9783337072698

Printed in Europe, USA, Canada, Australia, Japan

Cover: Foto ©Thomas Meinert / pixelio.de

More available books at **www.hansebooks.com**

PHILOSOPHICAL REALISM

BY

WILLIAM ICRIN GILL, A.M.

AUTHOR OF "EVOLUTION AND PROGRESS" AND "ANALYTICAL PROCESSES"

BOSTON
INDEX ASSOCIATION, 44 BOYLSTON STREET
1886

CONTENTS.

PREFACE, ... ix

I.
EVOLUTION, OBJECTIVE AND SUBJECTIVE.

Grandeur of Objective Evolution, ... 1
Its Defective Psychology, ... 2
All Phenomena and therefore all Evolution Subjective, 2
Nature of the Supposed Material World, ... 4
This View is only a Metaphysical Theory, ... 6

II.
NO SUPERSENSIBLE MATTER.

Experience our Base, and all Postulates discarded, . . 8
The World known to Different Men is a Different World, 9
Self-consciousness no Proof of Non-ego, ... 9
If Matter is Supersensible, our Real Organism is Unknown, ... 9
That makes our Real Bodies Non-ego and Dual, . . . 10
It gives a Double twice over to All Things, ... 11
Its False Etiology, ... 11
Its Various Inconsistency, ... 13
Its Intrinsic Improbability, ... 15
Supposed Possibility as an Argument, ... 15
Dualistic Vacillation, ... 16
Sundry Logical Points, ... 18

III.
SCIENTIFIC PHILOSOPHY.

Relation of Nominalism to Modern Subjectivism, . . 22
Substitution of Relations for Universals, ... 26
Subjective Relations, ... 27

Identity and Difference of Method in Science and Philosophy, ... 28
Scope of Science and Philosophy, ... 31

IV.
THE BLACK HOLE — SOLIPSISM.

Involuntary Action, ... 35
Alleged Necessary Belief, ... 36
Spencer's Negative Proof of Transfigured Realism, . . 36
Spencer's Positive Proof of Transfigured Realism, . . 37
The Subjective World a Real World, ... 40
Nature and Evolution shut us up in the Ego, ... 42

V.
REFLECTIONS ON THE SITUATION.

Individualism of All Evolution, ... 47
The Pre-animal World a Sentient World, ... 49
This Sentient Being or World is a Force, ... 53
This Sentient Being or World is One with the Alleged Great Unknown, ... 54
Both the Known and Unknown of this Universe are One with the Ego, ... 55
Sublime Representation of Man, ... 56
Relation of Ego to Organism and Environment, . . . 57
Relation between Thought and Brain, ... 58
Relation between Organic and Extra-organic Phenomena, ... 59

VI.
SUPERFICIAL EXPOSITIONS OF OBJECTIVE REALITY.

VII.
THE ABSOLUTE AND RELATIVE.

Mephistopheles on Verbalism, ... 72
Verbalism on Substance and Noumena, ... 73
Its Generation of an Impossible Absolute, ... 75
An Erroneous Notion of Relativity, ... 77
Source of this Error,—Fossil Metaphysics on Matter and Mind, ... 78
Confusion of Identity and Similarity, ... 83
Cause of Relative Sensitive Variation, ... 84
No Unknowable Absolute, ... 86

VIII.
THE EGO.

What is Ego, and its Proof?	87
Personality and Individuality,	89
Alleged Obscurity of this Doctrine,	90
Whence the Apparent Clearness of the Vulgar Notion?	91
Two Exclusive Conceptions of the Ego,	91
Mutual Destruction of the Organicists,	93
Superior Clearness of Extra-organicism,	93
Unrecognized Prevalence of Extra-organicism,	94
Ultimacy of our Doctrine,	95
Environment of Organism not Environment of Ego,	96
Argument of Comicality,	97

IX.
PERMANENCE AND SIMPLICITY OF THE EGO.

The Constant and Perduring Ego,	99
Its Immortality,	100
The Aggregated Monadism of Leibnitz,	105
Organic Atomism,	107
Dichotomy,	110
Trichotomy,	112
Logical Difficulties of all forms of Pluralism,	113
The Ego of Philosophical Realism a Pure and Simple Unity,	114

X.
THE ABSOLUTE AND LOCAL EGO.

The Absolute Ego,	117
The Local Ego,	120
The Local Ego defined as Transphenomenal and all Phenomena as Non-ego,	120
The Local Ego conceived as Supersensible and Sensible Phenomena as Non-ego,	123
The Local Ego defined as Organic, which gives the Physiological Ego,	125
The Panheisenist Ego,	131

XI.
INDUCTIVE METHOD OF TRANSCENDING THE EGO.

Fichte's Effort to transcend the Ego,	133
Sematism the Base of Induction,	138

Sematism on the Relations of the Several Senses, . . 142
Sematism between the Senses and their Common Subject, ... 142
Sematism between the Ego and its Organism, ... 143
Sematism between our Organism and Other Organisms, 144

XII.
PSYCHE-MORPHISM.

Problem of Permanence and Change in Causation, . . 148
Probable Pre-existence in other Forms, ... 150
Pre-existence in Human Form, ... 152
Number and Duration of Psyche-morphisms, ... 153
A Method of Evading Psyche-morphism, ... 155
Objections to this Method, ... 156
Limitation of Psyche-morphic Changes, ... 160
Dignity and Significance of the Lower Animals, . . . 160
Reality and Thoroughness of Subjective Evolution, . . 161
Universality of Evolution, ... 162

XIII.
HUMAN INTERCOURSE.

Collateral Testimony, ... 168
Conditions of Intercourse, ... 170
Demand for a Method or Medium of Intercourse, . . 171
Method not explained by Sematology, ... 171
No Medium in Non-egoistic Matter, ... 172
Nor in the Forms of Sensible Matter, ... 173
An Impassable Gulf between Different Minds, ... 173
A Supernatural Appointment to be inferred, ... 173
Pre-established Harmony, ... 174

XIV.
THEOLOGY DEMANDS A PHILOSOPHY.

Theism and Agnostic Deism, ... 175
God's Existence to be proved, not postulated, ... 176
Penumbral Metaphysics no Refuge for Theology, . . 177

XV.
METHOD OF CONCEIVING AND PROVING CREATION.

Conception of Deity, ... 179
On Conceiving Creation, ... 183

Logical Methods and Demands in Proof of Deity, . . 193
The Positive Method must supersede the Old Metaphysical Method, ... 195

XVI.
ORIGIN OF MAN.

Not Known Directly, ... 199
Our Alleged Parents not our Authors, ... 200
Knowable Nature not our Author, ... 203
Universal Symbolism of Successive Changes, ... 203
Creation at the Lowest Point (if at all), ... 204
Proofs of Creation summed up, ... 208
Our Creation in the Preorganic State, ... 209
Creation and Evolution distinguished, ... 213
Man an Intrinsic Force, Individualistic, ... 214
Divine Immanence in Nature, ... 214
Immanence in Nature is Immanence in the Ego, . . . 216
Creation Instantaneous, not Continous, ... 216
The Soul evolves its own Organism, ... 216
The Soul's Transcendence of the Material Universe, . 217

XVII.
PHILOSOPHY OF ETIOLOGY.

Designing and Undesigning Causes, ... 218
Causes in Science and in Philosophy, ... 218
Etiology Relative to Matter and Force, ... 219
Alleged Forcelessness of all Creation, ... 220
Paralogism of the Old Metaphysical Principle of Causality, ... 222

XVIII.
ETIOLOGY AND OBJECTIVE EVOLUTION.

Nature's Panheisenism, ... 225
Immutability of Gravity, ... 227
Dissipation and Equilibration of Heat, ... 228
Autonomy and Eternity of Gravity, ... 230
Doctrine of Chances, ... 231

XIX.
ETIOLOGY AND SUBJECTIVE EVOLUTION.

Subjective and Objective Autonomy of the Universe, . 233
Relation of Science to Supernaturalism, ... 235

Unity of God, ... 236
Unceasing Creation, ... 236
Importance of the Supernatural, ... 236
Importance and Moral Need of its Manifestations, . . 237

XX.
Presuppositions of Teleology.

Relation of Teleology to Etiology, ... 239
Design no Proof of Creation, ... 240
Design no Proof of Supernatural Agency, ... 240
Design not certainly Manifest in Nature, ... 241
Nature a Designless, Unconscious Combining Force, . 243
Designless, ... 244
Variableness of Volition, ... 245
Adaptations, Good and Evil, ... 247

XXI.
Sphere of Teleology.

Foundation of Teleology, ... 249
Teleology Relative to other Men and Animals, ... 251
Teleology Relative to Nature and God, ... 252
Exalted Place of Design in Philosophical Realism, . . 253
Limitations of Teleology, ... 255

XXII.
Assimilation of Science.

Tests of a True Philosophy, ... 257
Assimilation of Kosmogeny, ... 257
Assimilation of Phylogeny, ... 263
Assimilation of Ontogeny, ... 265
Useless Organs, ... 267
Prefossil Phenomena, ... 268

XXIII.
Summary and Conclusion.

The World as Sensation, ... 272
Its Cause or Origin, ... 273
How to transcend the Ego, ... 274
Theistic Conclusion, ... 274
Prospective Working of this Theory, ... 277

PREFACE.

IN his *Analytical Processes*, the author made some liberal promises for which this book is only an apology, because the public cares little for the fulfilment of the promises of metaphysicians. This miniature of a larger labor indicates a line of thought which, it is hoped, may be found of some value as a distinct contribution to philosophy, which is now at a stand-still. The prolonged cry, maintained in some quarters, of "Back to Kant!" is a confession of hopeless defeat and confusion; while the weaker sort of minds, wearing the airs of mental omnipotence, resort to physics for the solution of metaphysical problems. Never was there greater need of something to reanimate the despairing spirit of Philosophy. Her votaries, therefore, may possibly be induced, some of them, to look into even this small and unattractive volume, to see if, perchance, they may find an atom of comfort and support.

Philosophical Realism, here briefly expounded, has no affinity with scepticism. It eschews negations, and abhors abstractions substituted for concretes. It is positive and constructive in its method and object and conclusion. It believes in the attainability of philosophic truth, which is a unity of thought concordant with and expressive of the unity of all possible experiences and their causes and relations. Nothing can go further than this, and nothing can be more comprehensive. Besides, in all experiences and all thought, Philosophical Realism finds substance and essence and reality, so that the unity which is here discovered in the manifold is an ultimate and all-embracing unity. At least, this is the author's aim and his notion of his work.

Philosophy, not theology and religion, is the writer's quest; and an argument on God and creation is introduced only for the sake of philosophy, which required it as a condition of intellectual continuity and final unity of conception.

As it is a beautiful custom for authors in their preface to designate the sources and lines of light whence their own radiance, which might not else be clearly seen in some cases, the present writer wishes to say that he is indebted to all thinkers who have gone before him, both the known and the (to him) great unknown; and he sincerely thanks them for their inestimable benefactions, of the value of which to him, as indicated in this volume, he invites the philosophic public to judge, if it can find time, now or in the future.

Copernicus, it has been said, changed for man the front of the universe. Before his time, our earth had been conceived as the front, with sun, stars, and planets in the background,— we the centre, they our satellites. This order being reversed by Columbus, the dignity and importance of man seemed to be relatively depressed; but, on further thought and knowledge, we see that this elevates man by showing him as the known conscious constituent of a far grander universe, every part of which becomes his servitor. The doctrine of evolution operates in a similar way. Its first effect is, apparently, to belittle man, by showing him to have a very humble ancestry, though a very ancient one. Where is the dignity of a race born of an ascidian? But, as we study the subject more thoroughly, we begin to see a fresh light. We see that the law of evolution exalts man, and crowns him with peculiar glory as earth's proper king and lord, the evident final cause of the world, the great grand end toward which all things have been always tending in all their combinations, and that beyond man our kosmic forces can never go; that in man they have achieved their highest physical result; and that henceforth it is their function to develop man's spiritual nature, and thus apparently fit him for a higher sphere when he shuffles off this mortal coil.

The doctrine of Philosophical Realism expounded in the following pages presents man and the universe in a still grander aspect. It exalts the universe by making it spiritual,—the lower and preliminary modes of a being capable of evolving the highest spiritual agency. The universe is the lower part of man; and he, as a spiritual being, is its all and in all,—not merely its end, but its intrinsic nature, substance, and force. Not from the sun derives he his nourishment and existence. The sun and all the stars and their satellites are but the fainter gleams of his brightness, for of him and for him are all things knowable. Nay, they are he himself, modes of his action and expressions of his nature; and they are only the lower parts of his ways, which in the change which we call death give place to a higher universe, a higher order of psycho-sensible experiences, the present universe being the correlate of the succeeding universe, one ceasing that the other may begin.

While arguing in one chapter in favor of extra-organic spirit agency, the author is not responsible for more than he affirms.

The *unity* which Hegel makes such monstrous efforts to attain is the natural heritage of Philosophical Realism. Conceive the problem aright and stick to the declared meaning of its terms, then the solution follows as surely and readily as steam rises from heated water, just as the Chinese puzzle appears simple enough when we have got the key. The author's primary principle is simply, "Cover all facts, and be consistent." Our little scheme may be wrong, though self-consistent; but, if not self-consistent, it is no system at all, but only an aggregation, and is certainly wrong somewhere. Facts are always necessarily consistent because existent. We have only to take account of them and of their relations and logical implications. It is here only where inconsistency is possible, arising from the omission or misinterpretation of some of the facts or of their relations and logical implications. If on any of these points we are wrong, we shall probably somewhere be involved in inconsistencies. On the other hand, if we have all the facts and nothing but the facts,— that is, no inventions and fantasies,— and these facts and their relations rightly conceived, there cannot possibly be any self-contradiction, total or partial, real or apparent; and our theory is then certainly true.

The task of philosophy has been magnified by a confusion of opposition with contradiction or by the inclusion of them under the same category, as requiring the same treatment. Nearly all the German philosophers have been guilty of this in some degree, and with more or less of conscious articulateness. Hegel, for the first time in the history of philosophy, did it deliberately, and made it one of the corner-stones of his theoretic fabric. Opposition is of forces: contradiction is of conceptions. Opposing forces are all equally real, and propositions affirming them are all perfectly true. Opposing conceptions are equally real as conceptions, as conceptual forces; but they cannot all be true. So far as any one is affirmed, the others are by implication denied; and, so far as any proposition is true, all opposing propositions are false. If we allow that there is an ultimate unity in the opposing forces of nature, that does not justify or in any wise connect with the inference or assumption that there is an ultimate unity of contradictory propositions. The latter is an ultimate self-contradiction, and so destructive of the alleged unity. Nothing but fundamental error somewhere could ever make this seem necessary or justifiable.

Another difficulty has arisen from the identification of the abstract and concrete. Pure being, from which all quality is abstracted, is nothing, as

Hegel truly says. But, because it is nothing, it is not being at all, but simply no being and no thing, — no think, the negation of thought and reality. If we choose perversely to call this a thing or being, then it will be perversely consistent in us to say that thing and being are equal to nothing and no being. But that is only a wretched play on words; and, if that is put forth and received as the profoundest thought in the very centre of philosophy, philosophy then wears, to the normal vision, the most sardonic aspect ever presented to the eye. The real being or thing, that which all men mean when they use the word, includes quality, a concrete reality, which is not equal to nothing, or, rather, to which nothing is not equal. Surely, a philosophy whose foundations consist in such identification of the concrete and abstract can never be accepted as a whole, however powerful and helpful it may be in parts, as the result of a historic crisis in the history of human thought. Hence, the author's justification of his attempt to expound Philosophical Realism. Philosophical progress and intellectual unity are not to be attained by confounding things which differ, but by conceiving them in their true logical distinctions and relations.

A corresponding error has been perpetrated in the confusion of logical correlatives. While these are necessarily thought together, they are conceptually contradistinguished from each other, as not only different, but as opposites and incompatibles. Each term is conceived as excluding absolutely the other term from its sphere. Finite cannot be conceived except as excluding infinite, and *vice versa*. So of being and non-being. This is a perfect description of all contradictory and many contrary correlatives. The law of non-contradiction is thus absolutely unmodifiable; and Philosophical Realism feels that its command is not grievous, but rather conceives it is the electric light of the universe, which it is always safe to follow, and by which it can ultimately explore all things to the very centre.

The much-mooted ultimate unity which philosophy properly seeks is not to be confounded with simplicity. Here Hegel has done valuable service in opposing the pure substance of Kant and other philosophers, and the pure absolute of Schelling, by showing that the ultimate unity is a plurality; though he is himself very unfortunate in his attempt to limit the plural modes to three and in his definition of these three, whether as being, non-being, and becoming, or as being, essence, and notion, which is artificial and constrained.

Neither is the unity which philosophy rightly seeks an individual or numerical oneness, as opposed to a duality of individuals. We have no right to start with the assumption that all existing forces are ultimately modes of one individual reality, whether, with Spinoza and others, we call it substance, or whether, with Hegel, we call it spirit. There may be many ultimate substances or spirits for aught we know or have a right to say till we have found it out by a philosophic investigation, and the interaction of these may be the causes of the phenomenal universe. To assume either this or the contrary at the outset, and then on such assumption to go about deducing explanations of opposing phenomena and self-contradictory notions as the chief end of philosophy, is surely a method which ought to have a short life.

Philosophical Realism assumes nothing on this question or any other, but it easily proves the unity of the known universe by holding steadily to the oft admitted and expounded doctrine that all known phenomena are subjective states. They have thus very clearly their unity in the ego, which is a unity of spirit, and includes a variety of vast and indefinitely progressive extent.

The author attaches great importance to a rigid adherence to a correct method. Eclecticism is not philosophy. We are not to pick and choose according to our predilections, but to prosecute undeviatingly a scientific method, and take what comes of it. This is the spirit of the author's work, and his excuse for presenting what seems so far a departure in some points from common sense, which has a province, but not in philosophy.

Philosophy may not say that all interest is in the pursuit, indifferent to results, or, with the old theology, Believe or be damned, indifferent to rational proofs. Both are paradoxes, and they are related to the truth as the poles to the equator and as the horizons to the zenith. Philosophy cannot be indifferent to results, else the alleged pursuit is only a pretence. Nor, on the other hand, can it be indifferent to the method of pursuit, whether it be rational and logical, else we can have no guarantee that the results are rational, as this can often be seen only in the light of its connections and supports, or the method by which the results are attained, so that we have no evidence whatever, unless this method is self-justified. A correct method is, therefore, essential in philosophy.

As the means are always subservient to the ends they seek, there is an aspect in which results are supreme, and the method of comparative insignificance. This is true in all purely practical matters. It is very important that a man finds out what diet and regimen are healthful for him, but of no consequence how he attains it. A good medicine is none the less valuable to those who know it, whether they can give a scientific account of it or not. Truth and virtue are of practical value, even though they are advocated by a false method.

In theoretic pursuits and in all pure science and philosophy, the case is entirely altered. Here the method is everything, because it includes and guarantees the end ; and, if we fail to appreciate here the supremacy of the method, we shall be likely to fail in regard to the end. We shall be tempted impatiently and blindly to adopt agreeable results, in opposition to rational evidences of their untruth. I regard this state of mind as so very strong and prevalent even now as to constitute the great philosophical misery and degradation of our times. I regard this as the only, or chief, source of the monstrous inconsistencies everywhere manifest in speculative thought, the parent of "the riddle of body and mind," and the blind clashing and revolting of materialism, dualism, and half-fledged idealism against the results of a consistent procedure in psychological and metaphysical studies. Hence, the lofty though partial jealousy of Plato concerning the practical uses of geometry. He saw, as all ages have seen, men interested in geometry and in all intellectual pursuits only for certain practical, material, and social results which they may be made to yield; and he knew that the higher advances of the mind could not be made in that spirit. He, however, was, no doubt, a little narrow at the bottom, too little in sympathy with the necessities of inferior minds and with the idea now dominant, that scientific truth should be made to yield practical fruit,— a demand which was emphasized by Bacon, till he came near merging science into an art, as merely the mistress of artisans, as a large portion of moderns have done.

Philosophy cares for results, not as practical forces, which is only art, nor as beautiful combinations, which is only poetry, nor as promisingly helpful to the spiritual life, which is morals and religion, but simply as logical consequences of a rational and scientific method. It cares supremely for correct processes, for rational methods, because these justify themselves, and they constitute the true guarantee of correct results. Philosophy has no thesis primarily to maintain, but only a rational course to pursue, confident that that, and that only, can assure us that we shall reach the right point all along the endless route. Hence, philosophy acknowledges no other obligation than the honest prosecution of such a method.

This is the only obligation the author has

recognized. The result is therefore not the echo to a popular call, but the evolution of a philosophical product, which at first sight is always pronounced a monster, and by propagation it becomes normal. This will doubtless be the first fate of Philosophical Realism, and after that it is believed it will have an authentic history.

The various schools of mental healing will see that Philosophical Realism is the common foundation of all their theories, and an argument in their favor; and here "Christian Science" especially will see its corner-stone.

I.

Evolution Objective and Subjective.

Grandeur of Objective Evolution.

The theory of Evolution is the grandest and promises to be one of the most enduring monuments of the human intellect. It has opened up a field of thought and research which is literally boundless. It has fused the universe into a clear, intelligible unity, here meeting the utmost hope and want of science and philosophy, and with more thoroughness and apparently with closer approximation to ultimacy than they had ever anticipated. It avails itself to the utmost of the methods and results of physical science; and thence in a marvellous way, which cannot be controverted, it identifies matter and mind. It furnishes a scope for inductive reasoning never before known or conceived in connection with the pursuit of an ultimate and all-comprehending philosophy, and it is all along giving increasingly admirable exemplifications of the inductive method and spirit. By this method, it has made an utter end of the old, disjointed, science-repelling dualism, so that the only possible, effective enemy which remains to contest the supremacy of evolution is some form of idealism; and that cannot do it, for, to be true and effective, that must be evolution and make evolution paramount.

Evolution gives us a philosophical history of the universe, with the causes and connections of its successive changes. In all this wide field, it has the merit which belongs to physical science, the ability to unite many minds in the harmonious though emulous pursuit of the same end. As a consequence, it has already become the source of more positive intellectual wealth than accrued from all the labors and acquisitions of the world before it began its course.

Its Defective Psychology.

There is one department of research in its all-embracing field in which it is less advanced than the rest. That department is the psychological, the most important of all. Before the work of evolution is complete, all psychological phenomena must be duly registered, and their relation to each other and to the external world as a whole exhibited, and the perfect *egoistic* unity of the inner and outer worlds must be philosophically expounded. Here, as elsewhere, Mr. Spencer has done much; and his Principles of Psychology is his ablest work. But, as this department is the most difficult and profound, it should be expected to lag behind.

All Phenomena and therefore all Evolution subjective.

Growing out of this, the great defect of evolution in its present stage of development consists in its being too exclusively objective in its course and character. While evolution is objective, it is also subjective; and the question concerning their respective spheres has yet to be considered. A proper answer to this question, I believe, will give to evolution all it has ever claimed, and much more, and all more philosophically expounded and scientifically classified; will therefore make evolution more thorough and comprehensive as a theory, and may radically change its religious aspect without calling in question a single fact or principle or process which has been verified.

When the advocates of objective evolution begin to carry their researches into psychology, to study external phenomena in regard to their ulterior nature and origin and their relation to their subject, and then to analyze them to the utmost, they find (with all psychologists of modern times) that all the external world known or knowable, in every form, is purely subjective, a congeries of experiences, feelings, or modes of consciousness. These feelings imply a subject, whatever that may be and whatever its powers or origin, if origin it had. We know it as the power to have all these experiences, and we name it self or *ego* or me; and, relative to it, we say or it says, "I," or "I feel," "I think," "I will." This *ego* is the subject of all known phenomena, which is to say, simply, that they are phenomena or modes of the *ego*. The *ego* thus spreads itself over all the known universe, and says of every form and object or motion, "It is I, a mode of myself." Once clearly understood, this fact will give a sudden metamorphosis to evolution, making it dominantly subjective.

Relative to its subjective aspect, the new exposition will be generally designated by the objectionable, because partial and much ridiculed term, idealism, since it resolves all known and knowable things into ideas, using that term in the old meaning in which it was employed by Descartes, Locke, Berkeley, and other of the earlier writers. Mr. Spencer considers idealism and evolution as antagonistic to each other; and, on this ground, he makes very elaborate efforts to refute idealism, and to establish a dualism of the *ego* as unknown and some sort of an unknown external world. This betrays an incomprehension of both theories. Nothing can antagonize evolution, because evolution is a fact of indubitable experience; and, for the same reason, nothing can philosophically antagonize idealism as an assertion of the subjective nature of all phenomena. Evolution is as extensive as Mr. Spencer conceives it, and I think indefinitely more so; but it is always a subjective process, even where it is external to the organism. No one has ever attempted to carry evolution beyond the knowable universe; but all that universe is never more than the modes of one individual, *ego*. I allow that in all that universe the law of evolution reigns. But subjective evolution multiplies universes and all their evolutionary processes by the number of souls or subjects, and thus makes evolution, so to speak, infinitely more extensive and multifarious. Subjective evolution includes objective evolution, as the greater the less, as the temple includes all its parts, the grand façade, the lofty tower and pinnacle, the majestic dome, the pillared arches and every angle and curve and sculptured form in the great building.

What is called my organism is only an infinitesimal fraction of the sensible phenomena of which I am the subject. Of known and knowable objects beyond my organism, there is almost an infinite number. They are not a part or mode or product of my organism. They are not even objects of my organism, as sensible phenomena or organic precepts. My organism does not perceive them, for it perceives nothing. I perceive it, and so it is a mode of me. All extraorganic objects are modes of the *ego*, but not of the organism. They transcend the organism, but not the *ego*. It is logically possible for these to exist without the organism, or for the organism to exist without them. But, in point of fact, they begin and run their course together. On the other hand, it is a logical necessity that the *ego* exist as a condition of the existence of any phenomena, organic or extraorganic or superorganic, because these in all cases are *ego*, and nothing else. It is clearly possible that the *ego*, the essential being we now so designate, may exist before any of the phenomena of which we speak, and may then evolve phenomena in and of itself, according to laws which we may discover. That this possibility is the fact, all experience, informed by the light of modern psychological analysis, conspires to say and prove. The doctrine of the subjective nature of all phenomena logically necessitates this conclusion, as we shall see.

Nature of Supposed Material World.

That all phenomena are subjective, that all the sensible realities of heaven and earth are *ego*, I shall assume as having been sufficiently proved and generally accepted. Hence, if there is any non-egoistic material world, it is a thing which transcends all sensible experience and all direct knowledge. Nearly all German philosophers have affirmed the existence of such a world, admitting that the *non ego* can be known only indirectly. But they are singularly illogical. They offer no proof of its existence, deeming the fact that it can be known mediately only to be sufficient proof. That is no proof or argument at all. Whoever thought that the mere fact that we cannot know Cæsar or Mohammed directly is proof of their existence? It is that fact which makes proof necessary as a condition of a rational affirmation. That proof is therefore called for. Can it be furnished?

The English-speaking mind, from its more scientific habit, is more exacting concerning proof than the German mind. Here, it recognizes the need of proof, and that it needs to be good and strong, and endeavors to furnish it. We should have a good, if not sufficient, proof, if it were shown that such a world would be very useful, still more if it were really a necessary condition of experiences of which we are the subject; and this is supposed to be exhibited. Mr. Spencer says: "Not a step can be taken toward the truth that our states of consciousness are the only things we can know, without tacitly or avowedly postulating an unknown something beyond consciousness. The proposition that whatever we feel has an existence which is *relative to ourselves only* cannot be proved, nay, cannot be intelligently expressed, without asserting, directly or by implication, an *external existence which is not relative to ourselves.*" What is logically implied in the phenomena of consciousness cannot surely be justly described as "*not relative to ourselves.*" It may not be ourselves, but it is relative to ourselves always. Whether it is true that the proof of egoistic phenomena is impossible without implying a *non ego*, we shall consider in its place.

In the mean while, let us make very clear to ourselves our acknowledged position and what must be the external world which would thus be proved. If all phenomena are *ego*, then the *non ego*, called the material world, if it were thus proved, is supersensible and transphenomenal. Sometimes such a thing is boldly affirmed, and called the material world. This supersensible world is supposed, in some inconceivable way, to answer to sensible phenomena, and is explanatory of them as their cause. Judging from sensible phenomena, it is supposed to operate with lexical regularity, and thus reveals its existence and action and nature in its effects. Thus, while the visible sun is only a mode of mind, it is an effect and sign of a non-egoistic, material sun, which is invisible, inaudible, intangible, and every way supersensible. Similarly of all other sensible objects. All are *ego*, and all are effects and proofs of supersensible, non-egoistic, material causes variously differing from each other in correspondence with the phenomena.

This View is Only a Metaphysical Theory.

This is a view (if we may speak of a view of the viewless) of the material world which at every point is utterly at variance with both the popular and scientific notion. All men engaged in the pursuit of physical science assume that the realities of the world are sensible; and it is only the *sensible* forms, motions, and forces of the universe that they ever contemplate, and they never think of any other universe than this same sensible universe. Never do they conceive the material universe, whose laws they are supposed to study, to be utterly beyond their senses and all direct knowledge, and so void of all qualitative differentiation as to be also entirely inconceivable. Whatever assent they give to the psychologist's assertion that all phenomena are *ego*, they none the less always speak and think of the sensible universe as the real material universe. They are inconsistent and superficial; but they are right in assuming that the sensible world is the material world, and the only material world of interest to science or practical life. Of the material world of the metaphysician they never think or feel the need, thus contradicting Spencer's alleged intellectual necessity for it in conceiving phenomena.

If the material world of the metaphysician has an existence, it follows that either there are two material worlds—the sensible and the supersensible—or that the sensible world is not material, neither of which accords with any accepted notion of the material world or is likely to find any acceptance among the living convictions of mankind. At the best, they can only be like Hume's philosophical scepticism, effective in the study, but not in the saloon, the drawing-room, or the place of business. The theory of the two worlds, one of which—and that the real one and the effective one—is absolutely unknown and unimaginable, will surely require much in the way of exposition and argument to make it intelligible, and to prove that it is neither an empty verbalism in part nor a false because a needlessly cumbersome complication, like the old Ptolemaic system of astronomy. The alternative, which denies the sensible world to be the material world and affirms that the real material world is wholly supersensible, contradicts all human thought and expression. It says that material science never is material science; that of all its objects, from nebulæ, comets, and globes to whales, animalculæ, and atoms, not one is material. But, while the ultimate nature and distinction of mind and matter are not yet agreed on, one thing is universally agreed on,—to call the sensible the material, whatever be the immaterial, or whether there be anything immaterial. The position, then, of our objective evolutionists is itself very unenviable, and of a kind which will be very difficult, if not impossible, to defend against an enemy.

II.

NO SUPERSENSIBLE MATTER.

Experience our Base, and All Postulates discarded.

Perhaps it will prevent some misapprehension if I pause here to say that I make no assumptions or postulates, only that science has already clearly and abundantly proved that all sensible phenomena are subjective states. If this has not been done, my foundation is imperfect; but I can make it good, if necessary. I resort to no transcendental metaphysical principles to start with or to cover my track anywhere. Experience, and the logical implications of experience, are the beginning, middle, and end of my philosophy; and the experience must be scientifically sifted and rectified. We are told that "it is the favorite *postulate* of the idealist that matter—the external universe—is an *illusion*, a subjective creation of the mind: it possesses no *objective reality*." As a description of my method, this would be very erroneous. I hold that the material universe is egoistic; but I do not *postulate* that, but verify it scientifically as an experience, or assume that it has been done by others. I do not, however, affirm that this universe is an *illusion*, without *objective reality*,—just the contrary. *I know it as real, because I know it as an experienced fact*, and an objective reality, because external to my organism and an object of knowledge or experience; and, if ever we are the subjects of illusion, that is only through a false inference from a real experience.

The World known to Different Men is a Different World.

As a subjective state, however real and objective as well as subjective, the same thing, whether it be a mouse or a world, can never be known to more than one person,— its affected or experiencing subject. Hence there must be as many worlds of the same kind as there are world-sensations and subjects thereof of the same kind, and it is utterly erroneous to say that "the appearance is essentially identical to different persons." That is one of the certain impossibilities, because it is self-contradictory. The appearances to different persons may be alike or similar, but even that we can never directly know. We can only infer it, as we do on the basis of a natural and spontaneous system of symbolism, which I propose hereafter to explain.

Self-consciousness no Proof of non-Ego.

I call attention to an important distinction often overlooked, that between conception and experience. On this confusion, we are often told that self implies a not-self, and that neither can be known without the other. I allow that neither can be *conceived* without the other, because they are logical counterparts. But that proves nothing concerning experience and non-egoistic reality. That we can or must conceive a thing is no proof of experience or reality. Such a supposition would prove too much by involving us in endless absurdities. Therefore, self-consciousness and the conception of a *non-ego* are no proof of the existence of the *non-ego*. We must find some other proof than this.

If Matter is Supersensible, our Real Organism is Unknown.

As all sensible things are egoistic, it follows, of course, that, if there is any non-egoistic matter, it must be supersensible. Some objections to the unrecognized yet tacitly prevailing theory, that matter and all the material universe are supersensible, I propose now to mention. In stating the theory, I am impressed with its intellectual repulsiveness as a whole; but this impression will become deeper and more distinct in proportion as it is contemplated in detail. If we look at it relativé, for instance, to our organism, it becomes ludicrous. It implies that my own body is always entirely unknown to me. As there is a sensible world external to my organism and its supersensible counterpart, so there is a sensible object called my body, which is not my body, but my mind; and it has its supersensible counterpart, which is my real body, and which is unknown and inconceivable, except as a thing conjectured or inferred as being someway the cause of the sensations which constitute my phantom body. Here, as everywhere, the theory makes the experiential to be the unreal and the metempirical to be the real, and makes the material to be supersensible and the immaterial to be sensible, contrary to all the wonted judgments of mankind, popular or philosophical.

That makes our Real Bodies non-Ego and Dual.

As the sensible world is *ego* and the supersensible world *non-ego*, so my sensible organism is *ego*, and the real organism which it represents is *non-ego*.

Every man not blind has two sensible organisms,—the visible and the tangible,—which have no unity except in the conscious subject, of which they are simply two complex sensations utterly unlike each other. According to the theory in question, each of these organisms must be the representative of a distinct supersensible, non-egoistic organism. There may be dualists who may be pleased with even this, as there never was an unfortunate intellectual waif found adrift upon the world but some one was ready to give it a hospitable reception.

It gives a Double twice over to All Things.

It follows that every sensible object is of two sensible forms to all men who are not blind; and that, corresponding to each of these, there is a supersensible body. This pen, this paper, this flowing ink, *as seen and as felt*, are each dual; and each has two supersensible counterparts, which are the real pens, the real papers, and the real inks. Thus, all things are quadruple,—double as sensible, and again double as supersensible. Such a philosophy reminds us of Tam O'Shanter's vain attempt to count the horns of the moon, as he could not be sure whether they were six or seven.

Its False Metiology.

Such a theory refutes itself as soon as it is stated with any degree of clearness and fulness, so that an adequate conception of its import is proximately attained. And, as it is constructed of opposing elements, it can make but a poor showing in the formation and support of its outward defences. When we demand the evidence of the existence of this supersensible matter, and inquire as to what necessary purpose it serves, it gives us a verbal answer which is a mental blank. To the apparently intelligible plea that it must be inferred as the necessary cause and explanation of sensible phenomena, there are several answers.

In the first place, the plea is based on a method which is not justified by what in these days has received the name of "science." All strict science of modern times treats only of phenomenal causes and effects, antecedent and subsequent phenomena lexically related to each other. It is purely by this method that all the sciences, from physics to psychics, have made all their conquests. And it will be so forever. We can never investigate and discuss the unphenomenal, because it is without any qualitative marks, and all our terms are void of meaning; and the alleged supersensible world in question is of this class.

If we attempt to rise from science to philosophy, and seek an explanation of phenomena in a cause which lies back of them, the right to this may be conceded; but we must see to it that it accord with science and that the mental process be a real one, and not merely verbal, which is the character of the process in question. According to all objective evolutionists, sensible experience is the source of all real mental forms, and all are traceable back to sensible experience. But that is clearly impossible concerning supersensible matter. It is not only unsupported by experience, but it is opposed to experience, since all experience is phenomenal, conscious; while that is neither, and never can be. The final reply of the objective evolutionist is that this inference is an intellectual necessity, that all experience leads up through a narrow gateway to a transcendent reality which is knowable and conceivable only as cause and fount of the known. This example, of course, is not that which alone is recognized in science, an experiential antecedent. It is a cause which was precedent of all experience, and is now concomitant with all. Thus, it is always the same infinite causation, without change even in mode; for it has no modes, modes belonging only to its effects. And so there is no conceivable reason for the variety of its causal action, that reason being found in its effects in the uniform antecedent of other phenomena. It ultimates in self-contradiction and the abdication of ultimate philosophy in the attempt to establish such a philosophy. Its agnosticism is here sufficiently obvious.

But that is not all. The theory cannot be permitted the poor privilege of creeping mortally wounded within the veil of ultimate mystery, the last refuge of all craft and mental impotence. This ultimate refuge of the unknowable is absolutely one and unvarious, without any possible distinctions of mode or form or condition. But this is utterly inapplicable to the question at issue. Here, we are criticising a theory of supersensible matter, matter which is alleged to exist in countless various forms or modes answering to the infinitely multifarious forms of the sensible world; and these supersensible material forms are supposed to be temporal, and their duration commensurate with their sensible representatives. These are not therefore to be identified with the great only One, the absolute undifferentiated unknowable; and from this they can find no countenance or explanation. They have no support from either science or philosophy. They are metempirical, intrinsically inconceivable, and utterly incapable of explaining the phenomena of sense; while their alleged existence and action furnish new elements and a new complication (verbally, at least), which demand further explanation as to whence they came and what is the law of their operation, and their relation to the One unknown and the known many or sensible things, and they can explain nothing.

Its Various Inconsistency.

By way of carrying this theory still nearer to an ultimate and all-sided analysis, I would now ask its abettors whether they consider their supersensible matter to be spacial or non-spacial. I see not how it can be spacial or extended, since it has no points of difference or distinction, being unphenomenal; yet it were a singular matter that were unextended, since extension has always been considered its most characteristic quality. On the other hand, since it is supposed to be specially related in its parts and forms to the parts and forms of the sensible world, it must be supposed to be extended. Hence, we have two classes of extended things or matter (besides pure space itself), the sensible and supersensible; and they are supposed to be coextensive. The theory affirms that, wherever there is an external or sensible phenomenon "*there*," there is a supersensible material thing as its cause and explanation, and of which it is the representation. But this again is nullified by the doctrine in which all parties agree, though blindly, that all phenomena are *ego*. For, according to that doctrine, "here" and "there" and all local or spacial designations in the known universe are of the *ego* and within the *ego*. Hence, it makes all the forms of this same supersensible matter, though non-egoistic, to be entirely within the bounds of the *ego*, so that it is conceived of as existing only where the *ego* is, and it is indiscriminable from the *ego*, and we are logically compelled to identify it with the *ego*; and, as all spacial discriminations are of the *ego*, to apply these discriminations to it is to make it sensible and to identify it with the sensible. Thus, the theory is again self-destroyed, and its verbal dualism is metamorphosed into a pure senseism, or into Philosophical Realism which makes the permanent cause and substantive base and background of all phenomena to be the known *ego*, which is known in consciousness as both sensible and supersensible. This subjective ground and cause is complete, consistent, and self-sufficient. It leaves no unexplored or unexplained remainder, no relation which it does not so far find in itself in the comparative forces and distinctions of its own qualities.

This leads me to observe that, if force is demanded as the correlate of these phenomena, that force need not be non-egoistic force, and ought not to be. As all being is force, the *ego* is force. It is this force which evolves all the phenomena of consciousness, and it constitutes their ultimate and all-sufficient explanation. On this score, therefore, we are prohibited from passing beyond self. Thus far, we have come by clear logical necessity; and here at the same time ends the possibility of further progress and the intellectual motive to attempt it, because here all logical avenues are now closed up and every logical question is logically answered.

Its Intrinsic Improbability.

Another aspect of the doctrine of supersensible matter impresses us with a sense of its intrinsic improbability, if not absurdity. In affirming that the sensible world is only a seeming world and that the real material world is supersensible, it implies that the real light and colors are dark and invisible, that the real heat and cold are neither one nor the other, that the real odors are odorless, that all real tastes are tasteless, that all the real hardness and softness and other allied qualities are utterly other and different from what they are described and designated, and that even the real extension is unextended. Thus, all our language, with all the thinking it implies, is entirely false. We have a system of simulacra which are the opposite of the things they simulate. The lamp and its light, so called, it is allowed are simply sensations; but it is said there are a real lamp and light, which are dark and invisible, and the cause of the phenomenal lamp and light. Of this, science knows nothing; for its causes of the known light and lamp are other phenomenal antecedents, all of which are modes of the *ego* or sensations, and philosophy can find a possibly sufficient cause of phenomena in their subject, so that to go further is inadmissible, because so much is necessary and no more.

Supposed Possibility as an Argument.

'Tis said a drowning man will catch at straws; and the baffled dualist, persistent in his faith, catches at a supposed possibility, and on this he suspends his material worlds. He asks, as if that were enough for his faith, whether it is not possible for the sensible and supersensible to coexist in such relation to each other, and yet be numerically different. Allowing the possibility, that is no proof whatever to a logical or scientific mind. It is possible for the story of Bluebeard to be true, and no one can prove the abstract impossibility of the existence of centaurs, hippogriffs, and flying dragons; and, on this ground, these fantasies and the old dualism are worthy of equal credit with the theory in question.

But the possibility of the truth of such a theory cannot be allowed, because of its intrinsic inconsistencies. On the theory of a non-egoistic matter and space, sensible or supersensible, there can never be a notion of motion or rest, or here or there, a whole or part or division which does not involve insoluble contradictions. It is impossible for any theory to be true which does not reconcile all facts in a logical unity of conception. This unity, the simplest possible, is found in Philosophical Realism, which drops the supersensible matter as unsupported by experience and contradicted by logic, and explains known phenomena by referring them solely to the known *ego* as their subject, substance, and cause. This is a logical possibility and necessity, and neither can be said of any form of dualism yet invented.

Dualistic Vacillation.

Philosophical progress is not to be effected by denying or evading well-ascertained facts, the results of long and laborious research and reflection. One of these facts is the egoism of all the known. By this and on this, we must stand and advance. All our thinking must be made to square with it, because it is indubitably true; and, therefore, whatever conflicts with it must be false. Here is the great failure of objective evolution. While it affirms or admits the subjectivity of all phenomena, and makes them at most to be symbols of an unknown force, it perpetually confounds the symbol with the thing symbolized, and talks as if the sensible kosmos were something more than a complexus of subjective states, as if the known external worlds of the heavens and earth were *non-ego* and the preorganic source whence our conscious individuality was evolved. Then, with a vague, uneasy consciousness, its advocates endeavor to cover their track by saying that, when they speak of kosmic evolution, they say they mean supersensible processes. This is the confession of a fatal error. They ought to mean sensible processes. Without question, it is the sensible world and its processes which concern our inquiries in all the physical sciences, as, for example, astronomy, geology, physiology, anatomy, histology, etc. .

There is, indeed, a supersensible which is superphysical, and which, relative to physical science, is superscientific. This is exemplified in all abstract thought and all moral feeling and conviction. These cannot be the object of any of the senses. Now, the supersensible pertaining to the physical sciences is not of this character. What is supersensible to one sense is phenomenal to another sense. Not one of the senses is cognizant of what is the real and proper object of any other sense. So, also, what is supersensible to one man is sensible to another, who has better trained and more fully developed faculties.

Yet the same physical properties or processes, which are known by the one man and unknown by the other, are equally and wholly either ego or non-ego. So, also, the invisible forms and the alleged pre-visible motions of the light, before it shivers the ether on the eye, are both equally egoistic or non-egoistic; and, as it is agreed that the visible forms are all subjective states, the same must be allowed of the other, though this other may not have entered the sphere of consciousness.

It is true that no small proportion of what is included in the compass of physical science is not directly known by the senses; but, in all cases, it is conceived that that is only because of the limitation in the degree of the power of our sensitive faculty, not because the objects are qualitatively foreign to that faculty; and that, if this faculty were exalted, intensified, or enlarged, it would bring within its immediate range as sensible phenomena a vast area of what is now only inference. It is, therefore, a poor evasion to say that, by kosmic evolution and the evolution of the senses, they mean those unknown events or processes which are symbolized by the known. According to this, the real evolution is unknown; and the evolution, so called, which is known to us, is only apparent, phantasmic, symbolical of the unknown real. They have now entered a tenebrious region, which they do not much enjoy, and which to the unmetaphysical minds to which they chiefly appeal appears unreal and ghostly; and so they hie away again with unphilosophical haste, and they refer to this region again only with the dubious and solemn brevity with which the ancients spoke of their visit to the shades of Proserpine. They ought now to tell us what is the mutual relation of these two sets of evolution, and how they know the unknown, and on what ground they affirm that the known is symbolic of the unknown.

Sundry Logical Points.

Allowing that there is an unknown which is manifested by the known, we ought not without special reasons of insuperable force to affirm that it is *non-ego*. And no such reason has ever been assigned or is assignable, as far as I can see; while there are very cogent reasons for referring it to the *ego*. It ought to be considered as egoistic, because the *ego* we know as a conscious subject; and we know nothing else, so that any other reference of it is a blind action. It ought to be so considered, because we ought not to multiply entities without necessity; and here there is no necessity, either logical or experiential, for more than one. It ought to be so referred, because there is, it is assumed, a lexical connection of natural cause and effect between it and the known *ego*; and, as this causal connection is one of evolution (not creation), the known and unknown are but different modes in which exists the same one being. We thus reach the conclusion that all evolution and evolving force and being known or unknown is purely subjective or egoistic, and all evolution is limited in its operation to the one subject. We are as yet, therefore, absolutely confined within the bounds of self; and no avenue of egress opens up to us. On the other hand, against the theory of supersensible matter, in addition to what has been already said, we are obliged to make the following points:—

1. We have no proof of its existence.
2. We have no conception of it. It answers to nothing that has ever come within the range of experience.
3. We can explain all material phenomena without having recourse to this hypothesis, and by an infinitely simpler hypothesis,—that they are all the necessary product of the inherent force (created or not) of the *ego;* and the *ego* is known in consciousness.
4. This hypothesis is therefore also utterly useless as well as proofless. Neither logic nor practical life makes any demand for it.
5. None but theorists care anything about it. It is only the sensible world men care for, or that they contend for, when they affirm the existence of matter.
6. The vacillation of philosophers between the known and unknown is the cause of all the trouble. It is under the illusion of the known that they fight for the unknown. Their zeal would rapidly abate and their following would rapidly diminish, were it always clearly and distinctly kept in view that it is not the known world they contend for, but a world which is unknown, unknowable, indescribable, and inconceivable.
7. Therefore, I think it is equal philosophy and modesty not to assert, and to deny the right of any one to assert, its existence.

Dualists often tell us that the idealist must "show that the affirmation of things, in the common sense of the term, is not only not necessary, but is inconsistent, or *that the so-called world* is seen, upon reflection and analysis, to be incapable of existence apart from thought." This has already been abundantly shown concerning "the affirmation of *things, in the common sense of the term*"; for all these things are *nothing else than thought* (and feeling), and it is therefore a contradiction to suppose *these* can exist except as thought and feeling. This has indeed been long settled among the first thinkers; and the only point of controversy now remaining concerns the existence of a transphenomenal world.

Since an able contributor to *The Index* has already shown that I am very likely to be misapprehended, I must endeavor to be perspicuous, though at the expense of terseness. I will therefore adopt the language of my critic: "Every act of consciousness is as truly objective as subjective. The external universe ... is therefore known to us as directly and immediately as the workings of our own minds." In this passage, the author inserts the phrase "the *non-ego*," as in apposition with "the external universe." That is his mistake, the head and front of his offending; and, in that, he differs from Spencer, Lewes, Huxley, Hamilton, and Mansel, and all the great host of modern psychologists, beginning with Descartes. The known external universe, all the *ensemble* of sensible things, is known as directly and immediately as the working of our own minds, because they are known as being the working of our minds solely and simply. If this is true, it is surely very important that it be fully understood and its logical implications traced out, as that would form the true and philosophical realism.

Because I thus identify the known universe with the *ego*, and yet make it evolve from the *ego*, I am charged with the self-contradiction of creating myself. If so, I only logically follow out the modern psychological doctrine affirming the egoistic nature of all phenomena. But my position involves no such absurdity. Evolution is not creation. Every one knows or believes that thoughts are evolved from the *ego* and are modes of the *ego*. What is thus unquestioned concerning our inner modes or phenomena I affirm concerning all the phenomena of the external world, that they are modes of the mind involuntarily and lexically evolved from the mind.

I wish my readers to remember that, when I call any party materialist, I use the word in a meaning worthy of the modern conception of matter. This I indicated seven years ago in my *Evolution and Progress*. By "material monist," I mean those who hold that there is, in the last analysis, no evidence of more than one substance, which through the external, material world generates all forms of conscious beings.

III.

SCIENTIFIC PHILOSOPHY.

A boulder has just been rolled onto my track, and I must halt a little while to blast it. All over the world, men are seeking a rational escape from the toils of solipsism. The British quarterly review, *Mind*, for October, 1882, has two articles seeking this result. One of these is too abstract and obscure to need much refutation. The other is clear and able, well suffused with the spirit of modern physical science, and its learning is quite imposing. Its first title is "Scientific Philosophy," which it expounds under the designation of "Relationism," which is the ancient and mediæval realism improved, which refutes nominalism, now dominant, and its alleged consequent, idealism, and makes philosophy scientific by confounding it with science. As this coincides with a strong tendency of the age an with a style of thinking prevalent always, it is likely to find adherents among a class of desultory psychologists who are ardent theorizers. It therefore demands attention.

Relation of Nominalism to Modern Subjectivism.

The first step in the process by which this is accomplished is to show that modern psychological subjectivism is only a more subtle and comprehensive form of the old nominalism, and is therefore the child of mediæval scholasticism. This is certainly fresh enough to be interesting. Whether it is true, we will proceed to inquire.

A genus comprises such, and only such, qualities as are common to all the individuals of the genus. If the genus is an objective reality, and therefore a single individual, it cannot be of any particular color, form, odor, weight, taste, or subjective states peculiar to any one; for, then, it would exclude every other, and every individual would be a genus, which is contrary to the hypothesis. And it is a contradiction in terms to say that it objectively exists and yet is void of all particular and distinct quality, as that were to be void of all quality. Hence, real genera and species are an impossibility. They are only mental and verbal expedients and symbolical designations for scientific convenience. Such are, in brief, the doctrine and proof of nominalism.

This does not, as alleged, logically involve idealism, nor the invention of noumena as the unknown real in distinction from phenomena as subjective states, nor the denial of relations or the knowledge of relations; and it leaves entirely untouched the whole question of egoism and altruism. It is therefore utterly erroneous to assert that all our modern psychological subjectivism is derived from the acceptance of nominalism. Modern philosophy holds to nominalism, because it is a logical necessity from the very notion of a genus and an individual, because thus only can it escape self-contradiction. Not one of its adherents has ever in any wise connected it with his subjective psychology. Surely, if there were a vital and universal connection between nominalism and subjectivism, some, if not all, of the great subjectivists would have seen and announced it and drawn additional support from it, which none of them has ever done, so far as I am aware.

The irrelevance of nominalism as either reason or cause for psychological subjectivism is further seen from the fact that it is held by those who are not purely subjectivists. Bishop Berkeley is of this class. Though he held to a species of idealism, it is a serious historical error to number him among pure psychological subjectivists. He had in his composition exceedingly little of subjectivism. In his theory, the objective and the *non-ego* were conspicuous and paramount. With him, everything sensible was objective and *non-ego*, and no objectivism, it would seem, could go beyond that; though I believe that of Berkeley did, by making even our reflective mental processes to be non-egoistic objects. Yet he was one of the most ardent and iconoclastic of nominalists. Berkeley reminds us of what the most cursory student of philosophy should understand, that there is an objective as well as a subjective idealism, and that the former, which had its most conspicuous development in India, is far the older of the two, and still survives in the East as well as in the followers of Berkeley in the West, of whom in England some command a respectable hearing. This double form of idealism is of itself a disproof of the alleged idealistic influence of nominalism, especially as the objective idealism of India was matured before nominalism was formulated or before the intellect of Greece had entered on its highest course. All the prominent Scotch philosophers — Reid, Stewart, Brown, Hamilton — were objectivists more or less; and all were decided nominalists or conceptualists, which are logically one, as the names must have some meaning.

On the other hand, there is also a class of realists which is not only idealistic, but, in the main, objectively idealistic. One of the most pronounced of these is the amiable and eloquent author of *Recherche de la Vérité*. In this work, Malebranche makes a distinction between sentiments and ideas. Sentiments, he says, are egoistic, modes of mind, and that the ideas are not, but primary necessary forms which cannot exist in us nor subsist of themselves, and therefore must exist in God. In God, we see them. And this species of idealism he connects with the old realism. Besides these ideas and sentiments, he holds that there is an unknown world whose unknown action is made the occasion of God's presenting these ideas to us in their order, whence follow those sentiments, or mental modifications, in the order in which they occur. In these views, Malebranche is followed by Fénelon, Bossuet, and even by the great Leibnitz.

Further, and finally on this point, there is a long line of antagonism between an allied realism and subjective idealism (total or partial) on the one side, and an allied nominalism and objective sensism on the other side. Plato was the Greek originator of the realism of generals, and he is sympathetic with the Eleatic sceptics, or idealists. He treats the sensible world with much contempt; and, because of the evanescence and instability of its forms, he almost denies it existence. The Academics, who claimed him as their master, were realists, and yet very sceptical concerning the sensible world, and tended to the reduction of its forms to subjective states or impressions, as Hume did, who called himself an Academic, though he was a broader sceptic than they, as they, like good realists, held to the stability and supersensible origin of the higher intellectual world. Aristotle and his adherents took a different and rather antagonizing position on both these points; and the two parties fought a languid battle till in the Middle Ages (through Porphyry) the question took no a new form, and Aristotle's own disciples were divided into hostile camps, and for some four centuries the fiercest of all intellectual contests raged throughout Europe. The realists were always the orthodox and the high and *a priori* metaphysicians, who made much of the inner consciousness and little of sense; while the nominalists were just the opposite. Hence, M. Cousin, who is one of the best informed historians on this subject, says that the contest was virtually a contest between sensism and idealism, nominalism being the sensist party and realism the idealistic party. He tells us that Duns Scotus was for that age a great student of the material world, and held to an immediate knowledge of it as *non-ego*, and that Occam inherited his views and tastes.*

M. Cousin is himself a striking illustration of the point I am endeavoring to make, that nominalism is not the father of modern subjectivism. Cousin is a strenuous realist; and from this he forges weapons against sensism, and maintains that by none of the senses can we transcend the *ego*, and that the knowledge of the *non-ego* is attainable only through the medium of a principle of causality which can be explained and vindicated only on the theory of realism, just such a realism as this which affirms that universals cannot subsist of themselves, but in connection with all the individuals, finite and infinite.

Substitution of Relations for Universals.

The theory in question is not, as its author supposes, inconsistent with nominalism. It expressly identifies relations with universals, and then substitutes the former term for the latter, and then proceeds to show the serviceableness and objective character of relations as therefore reals and universals (pp. 476–478). This is all erroneous,—an unconscious intellectual jugglery. Relations and universals are not the same. Relations of external objects are objective, inhere in objects as members of a group, and are the special and variable modes of the members of said groups; and *because they are variable, indefinitely, they are not universals. Some relations always exist, but not the same relations. The real and active objective relations are therefore not universal.* Indeed, they are not at all

---

* See his *History of Modern Philosophy*, vol. ii., Lect. ix.

the expression of genera and species, and have no manner of connection with the question of nominalism and realism on that subject; and so the existence of these relations is nothing against nominalism. Nominalism admits and assimilates them with so much ease and comfort as not to know that it has any digestion. As a nominalist, I accept them as indubitably true. Thus, nominalism is the maelstrom which swallows up the great new theory of relationism, instead of being logically extinguished by it.

Subjective Relations.

We must here call attention to an important fact, which has been overlooked, that there are subjective as well as objective realities and relations. There are logical relations, very many: relations innumerable in the field of abstract or pure mathematics in all its many branches; relations between all the sensations, between other feelings, and all the moral conceptions, and between all these classes. These relations of the subjective world involve an infinity of possible detail and modification. Now, these relations are certainly not "reals" in the sense of external and non-egoistic, which is the kind of real and universal we are discussing. They are real facts, and real relations as subjective states, and nothing more. Neither are these relations universals. We can classify them; but the result is only so many classes of particular experiences, which are so much alike in each class that they are put together, and so separated as a class from others because of their relative unlikeness. Myriads of sensations related to each other are brought under five different classes or senses; but there is no general sensation which combines or concentrates or represents or constitutes the generic class sensation, or the specific class of each sense and including all special experiences of that sense. Relations we have in abundance, but no general or universal reals; and relations cannot be substituted for universals, as if they were the same.

Identity and Difference of Method in Science and Philosophy.

A striking contrast is drawn between the successful method of science and the barren method of philosophy, as the latter is represented by Kant's metaphysics. Science, it is said, teaches that cognition conforms to things, not things to cognition, and metaphysics just the opposite. But this is an inadequate representation of modern philosophy. When Kant speaks of making the objects conform to cognition, he confessedly designs to speak under the limitations of science and in conformity with the method of science; and he mentions a great scientific fact and name in illustration of his object, Copernicus and his procedure. It was experience, the experience of sensible disharmony and mental confliction, which led Copernicus to transfer his theoretic stand-point of observation from our planet to the sun. In like manner, it was a corresponding disharmony of experience, outer and inner, which led Kant to change conversely his theoretic stand-point. Copernicus endeavored (successfully) to give a theoretical unity to the known facts or objects of the material universe by supposing that we revolve around the sun and not the sun around us. Kant endeavored to furnish a theoretical unity to the known facts or objects of the psychological world, inner and outer, by supposing that our faculty of cognition shapes the outer world instead of being shaped by it. This is inadequate and partially erroneous, but it is not contrary to the method of science. It does not ignore or depreciate sensible objects or experience, any more than Copernicus did. Kant is wrong in his whole system, nearly,—wrong in his method of deducing the categories and in the result on the list of categories, wrong in his assertion of the need or the existence of synthetical propositions *a priori*, wrong in his doctrine of *a priori* regulative principles as of only subjective authority, wrong in his doctrine of a supersensible material world, wrong in his doctrine of incognizable noumena numerically different from phenomena; but he is not opposed on the point in question to the accepted method of science. He commences with experience and even with sensible experience, and then analyzes it and determines its contents and their relations to each other by what he supposes to be the most rigorous scientific method. Further, when rightly understood, the antithetic phrases, "conformity of cognition to objects" and "the conformity of objects to cognition," are not opposites, but equivalents. Phenomena are the same, whether we speak from the Ptolemaic or the Copernican stand-point; and they are the same, whether we speak from the subjective or objective stand-point. If cognition is in conformity with objects, objects are in conformity with cognition. Still, it is an unfortunate formula which was here adopted by Kant, though not more unfortunate than its older counterpart, whence by the law of antithesis he derived his. For objects do not wholly shape cognition, any more than cognition wholly shapes objects. They are inseparable, and together they form an active causal and cognized unity. There is always an interaction in which action and reaction are equal between the organism and its environment; and there is strictly no object before cognition, and no cognition before there is an object. They necessarily originate together. They invariably conform to each other, therefore; and the distinction between the antithetic phrases used by Kant should never have been made, except to observe their logical and experiential unity.

Hence, I accept as entirely true Mr. Abbot's description of the process and method of cognition according to the theory of scientific philosophy,—"that knowledge is a dynamic correlation of object and subject, and has two ultimate origins, the cosmos and the mind; that these origins unite, inseparably yet distinguishably in experience, *i.e.*, the perpetual action of the cosmos on the mind, plus the perpetual reaction of the mind on the cosmos and on itself as affected by it; ... that experience has both an objective and subjective side, and that these two sides are mutually dependent and equally necessary": only I add, by way of further analysis and explanation, that the kosmos, or the objective world, is the mind just as much as that which he so designates. The interaction here described is between the kosmos and the organism, and these are two great classes of the complex modes of "the mind." All motion, action, and interaction are changes in the modes of the mind.

This exposition discloses the false basis of most of the objections to idealism. They all assume that the *ego* is confined to the organism, within which therefore our knowledge is confined, if it is confined within the *ego*. Hence, they may speak with just but irrelevant contempt of the limitation of our "capacity to realize only what is contained within the narrow shell of our physical organism, and all the universe outside relegated to the realms of the unknown and uncognizable." All that universe is as much *ego* as the organism itself, and just as much known. While subject and object are equally necessary to consciousness and equally known in consciousness, the object is always as much *ego* as the subject, *two phases of the one reality*. It is entirely true that all cognition is relative, and involves two terms whose reciprocal action constitute the relation, and it is therefore irrational to confine cognition to one of these terms; and I do not do that. I extend it to all such terms, but I affirm that they are all and always *ego*. So neither do I affirm "a subject without an object." That is absurd, as it implies "a thinker without a thought"; but I affirm that the thought and the sensible object are both and equally *ego*. I do not deny extension to the *ego*. I give to it all knowable extension, and duration too. Such is one *ultimate logical result* of our modern psychological analysis, from which there is no longer any dissentient worth the name. Let not philosophers or scientists disparage their own record by starting back in alarm from a statement which is new only in its greater logical thoroughness and completeness.

Scope of Science and Philosophy.

Science seeks laws and lexical connections. Individual phenomena are sought only as exemplifying law. But, for this purpose, individuals are necessary. In them only, laws exist. Law has no separate entity; and it not only exists in individuals, but it is the individuals, and not a genus, except as it subjectively exists in us as an abstract or tropical conception. Hereupon, we are told that subjectivism, by limiting our knowledge to one individual *ego*, renders science impossible, because science implies a multiplicity of objects acting in conformity to general laws (p. 487). This is erroneous. It discloses an unfortunate incomprehension of subjectivism, which admits and includes just the same, and the same number of, objects and laws, as objectivism. It includes all the sensible and knowable universe (and much more), and objectivism never claimed more than that for the sphere of science. If there is but one individual known, that individual includes all the universe of the objectivist, with all its multitudinous phenomena and changes; and these, in all their relations, subjectivism is quite as competent to investigate as objectivism, for subjectivism includes all objects, all phenomena, all mutations, their causes and connections and logical implications. While it identifies relations with objects, it identifies objects with the *ego*, which is more than subject; and thus it absorbs relationism as a very little thing in its vast and measureless womb of a boundless universe.

Philosophy is scientific in its basis and procedure; but it is not science, and it is more than scientific in its comprehensiveness and in the results it seeks, whether it attains them or not. It is utterly erroneous to suppose that the great problem of the age is "how to identify science and philosophy." That is a problem only for those who have no proper conception of philosophy and who desire only that philosophy shall voluntarily abdicate existence, and bequeath to science its name. Philosophy seeks the ultimate analysis and resynthesis in a logical unity of all experiences and conceptions, all phenomena inner and outer, the ultimate actual and logical relation of substance and quality or attribute and cause,—cause as the intrinsic force of phenomena as well as lexical antecedents, and ultimately explanatory of such phenomena, and also of illexical phenomena, if any such are found. To this great object, all the sciences are ancillary; and all scientific methods and results are respected and utilized by philosophy. Philosophy stands at the supreme and ultimate centre of the universe, of which she is the light and glory; and, from every part, she seizes all scientific lights, and blends and combines them into one glowing orb of pure white illumination, which discloses the intellectual harmony of all worlds and all their parts, their high significance, their origin and destiny, and the necessary methods of working out that destiny. The humblest forces contribute to the greatest results; and, therefore, I labor for the promotion of this great end.

IV.

THE BLACK HOLE,—SOLIPSISM.

I have so far proceeded on the assumption that the reader would understand what I mean by objective evolution; but perhaps it would have been better, had I defined myself, and I will do it now. By objective evolution, I mean substantially that system of philosophy which has been concurrently expounded by Herbert Spencer, George Lewes, John Fiske, and others, and which has been called the cosmic philosophy, the synthetic philosophy, and simply evolution and agnosticism. It affirms that all the phenomena of mind and matter appear to be manifestations and symbols of one only ultimate and inscrutable power and reality; that the known world external to our organism is the immediate source whence have been evolved all the organic world of plants and animals and human consciousness, beginning with the lowest forms and advancing to the present time and to man as the most recent and the highest known form of the evolved force; that the organism and the individual, conscious *ego* have the same source and cause, and originate at the same time and appear to be ultimately one, furnishing two great classes of phenomena, the organic forms and processes, and the conscious processes or the feelings, including thought and volition,—which are feeling, but not wholly feeling, even as the sensations are not wholly feeling.

It is very remarkable that objective evolutionists

are exceedingly anxious to find *an external world as object and non-ego*, which they deem necessary to their theory; and they thus confound themselves on this point with the old dualists, whom they affect to despise. This introduces confliction and consequent obscurity into the theory. Its advocates are not aware that there is no real call for such an external world either in their theory of evolution or in anything established by modern science or philosophy. They are in reality animated only by an old prejudice, an idol or "phantom of the tribe," born of prescientific impressions. To accomplish this impossible task, they resort to the most flimsy special pleading, which, in any other connection, they would justly despise. They are also wrong in their objects as well as in their argumentation; for, as they aim to prove only an unknowable world, some inconceivable thing which is void of all sensible quality and of everything that can be presented either to thought or imagination, such a pursuit must be futile in its results relative to evolution. For, if such a world were proved, it could not be discriminated from the great Unknowable, the One ultimate Force manifest in all phenomena; and so nothing would be gained by it, and for it the theory of evolution has no distinctive place. The proof of such a world would also be futile relative to the popular feeling. The world in popular demand is a sensible world, and that world has never been brought in question by any school of philosophers whatever. One and all affirm its existence, and describe it in much the same way. Like the rest of mankind who are unwarped by speculative theories, I am not concerned about the existence and proof of a supersensible world of matter, as I hold it to be practically and speculatively useless, and conceptually *nil*, so that the assertion of its existence is a mere verbalism, as no meaning can possibly be attached to the words. It is to be expected that arguments for such a world will be as empty and obscure as the object sought. Some of these arguments we will now notice.

Involuntary Action.

The familiar argument that such a non-egoistic force is to be inferred as the cause of those organic experiences which are independent of our will and opposed to our will has always appeared to me quite puerile, though it is urged by some of the great minds of the world. It proves too much,—that the extra-volitional cause of every experience is *non-ego*; for this is its major premise, and it is utterly inadmissible. Within ourselves there is a variety of non-volitional causes, whose operation we long and vainly antagonize with all the energy of our will. There are natural organic appetites which operate with great force irrespective of our volition, and often against its sustained and strenuous endeavors, such as hunger, thirst, the sexual feeling, and certain acquired appetites for things which are confessedly injurious, as alcohol, opium, tobacco, and other narcotics. All bodily diseases exemplify the same principle. They are the effect of forces which begin their operation without our consent and continue in spite of our opposition, and are yet wholly subjective. All physiological functions operate irrespective of volition, and are pre-conditionally necessary to its action.

I do not forget that all organic appetites and all physiological functions would soon perish but for a force assimilated by the organism from without. But neither do we forget that all known extra-organic force and phenomena are egoistic; so that their causative relation to the organism is nothing against my position, no proof of a non-egoistic cause of our organic experiences. There is not in all the universe a single known example of a non-egoistic cause, though non-volitionary causes are innumerable, including all the sensible universe. The known *ego* is the known source of all known experiences on earth or in the heavens. To infer any other cause is equally unscientific and illogical, except on the theory that the *ego* is confined to the organism. If the *ego* is conceived as confined to the organism, the causes of its experiences are found in the external world; but these causes are not inferred and unknown, but they are experientially verified. This, however, is confessedly erroneous. The known external world, equally with the organism, is admitted to be a series of subjective states. If we infer a cause of all this, we reach either the Deity of theism or the "Great Unknown" of agnosticism, which is not the material world contended for. It is clear, therefore, that the *ego*, or subject, has the causes of its own non-volitionary experiences within itself; and, until we have the impossible proof that all non-volitional causes are *non-ego*, we shall have no ground for the inference that there is a non-egoistic material world. We know ourselves as the subject and source of an immense and infinitely various non-volitional causation, which dispenses with the need of any such world.

Alleged Necessary Belief.

To say that we cannot help thinking and believing that there is such a *non-ego* called matter, or the material world, is false as a universal proposition. Some men may feel so; but all do not, else this debate had never been. For one, I am unable to do other than disbelieve it, because it stultifies my intelligence. "The universal postulate" does not apply here for want of the universal conviction.

Spencer's Negative Proof of Transfigured Realism.

While I regard Mr. Spencer's *Principles of Psychology* as a very able production, yet I know nothing in the whole range of philosophical literature weaker than his nineteenth chapter, styled "General Analysis," in advocacy of his "Transfigured Realism."

After refuting the "assumptions of metaphysicians," the "words of metaphysicians," and the "reasonings of metaphysicians," he presents a "negative justification of realism," which consists in "an argument from priority," an "argument from simplicity," an "argument from distinctness," and two or three other arguments less definite and quotable. It is quite a startling novelty for a man to claim "priority" for the most recent invention or discovery, and it is surely richer in comic than in logical force. The "argument from priority" is futile, unless it covers his own peculiarity; and this peculiarity is set forth as an original conception. Equally striking, and for a similar reason, is the claim of superior distinctness in favor of a world which is void of every definite element and distinctive quality, so that it cannot be either known or conceived. The "simplicity" of such arguments, it must be allowed, is quite manifest.

Spencer's Positive Proof of Transfigured Realism.

Mr. Spencer next furnishes a positive justification of transfigured realism in five chapters. Here I agree to all he says (though not to all he means) on the subject under discussion. He says (*Principles of Psychology*, § 442), "If the states of consciousness are adequate to frame a disproof of the *non-ego*, they must be held adequate to frame a proof." This is true, but it is irrelevant. No one affirms a positive disproof of the *non-ego* from the phenomena of consciousness. That would indicate a blind temerity of which idealists are never guilty. They only say that consciousness furnishes no proof of a material *non-ego*, which is a very different statement. We say that all we know is *ego* or subjective states, and that from the existence of this known fact there is no logical or psychological warrant for the assumption of the *non-ego* in question. We thus virtually say that consciousness cannot furnish a positive disproof, still less a positive proof of a material *non-ego*.

But, when we advance from psychology as a study of the phenomena and conditions of consciousness to an analysis of the conception and logical implications of dualism of every form, then we become more positive. We see that the conception is unreal, because it has no logical unity, its self-contradictions being obvious and manifold. Mr. Spencer acknowledges this confliction, and consoles himself by saying that this is always inevitable whenever, from any point or in any direction, we attempt an ultimate analysis, whence he is called, with his own consent, an agnostic. But subjective evolution escapes these contradictions, carry analysis as far as you may; and on this account it is to be preferred. And it only is entitled to the name of philosophy, because of its ultimacy and completeness.

Mr. Spencer (*Principles of Psychology*, § 443) next argues as follows: "Realism, then, is positively justified, if it is shown to be a *dictum* of consciousness working after its proper laws. When normal acts of thought, like those which establish truths we hold most certain, are proved to be acts of thought which yield the antithesis of subject and object, no further demonstration need be asked." To all this, those whom he designates as anti-realists thoroughly assent. They hold rigidly that all the normal acts of thought yield the antithesis of subject and object. But they never forget (like Mr. Spencer) that object and subject are always equally egoistic or subjective states. We therefore need go no further with him in this discussion, because we agree to all he proposes to prove, the existence of the subjective states of subject and object in all the normal acts of thought. In all his discussion of this subject, Mr. Spencer strangely assumes that the sensible object in antithesis with the conscious subject is *non-ego*, and that, therefore, in proving the existence of such object (which no one ever questioned), he proves his transfigured realism.

In further proof that I have not misconceived him on

this point, I will adduce two other passages. He says (*Principles of Psychology*, § 404): "The postulate with which metaphysical reasoning sets out is that we are primarily conscious only of our sensations, that we certainly know that we have these, and that, if there be anything beyond these, serving as cause for them, it can be known only by inference from them. I shall give much surprise to the metaphysical reader, if I call in question this postulate; and the surprise will rise into astonishment, if I distinctly deny it. Yet I must do this. Limiting the proposition to those epiperipheral feelings produced in us by external objects (for these are alone in question), I see no alternative but to affirm that the thing primarily known is *not that a sensation has been experienced*, but that there *exists an outer object*." He occupies nearly six octavo pages in the illustration of this singular statement, that an outer object is not a sensation, and that, in affirming an outer object as the primary phenomenon in sensible action, he contradicts "the primary postulate of metaphysicians." How does it come to pass that his wonted penetration here so utterly fails him that "he is unable to discern that this outer object" is analyzed by all psychologists, himself included, into a sensation simply and solely? There is but one explanation. He pays the penalty which is exacted from all its votaries by dualism, which can be served only by the blind; and, hence, the ablest minds lose their usual perspicacity as soon as they become its advocates.

Elsewhere (*Principles of Psychology*, § 438), Mr. Spencer says: "Now let him contemplate an object, this book, for instance. Resolutely refraining from theorizing, let him say what he finds. He finds that he is *conscious of the book as existing apart from himself*. Does there exist in his consciousness any notion about sensations?" Here, it is obvious that the writer identifies the sensible object, the book, with the *non-ego*, contrary to the united utterance of modern psychology.

He confessedly makes an appeal from scientific analysis to spontaneous impression, and this crude impression he substitutes for his own better intelligence.

Perhaps it will be well here to remind the reader afresh that, in denying the right to affirm the existence of an unknowable material world, I raise no question concerning the existence of the known material world. A known and indubitable world as a fact of experience there is. It constitutes the visible heavens and earth and all tangible things. The existence and reality of this world I never doubt, nor does any other man; and no philosopher ever pretended to doubt it. It cannot be doubted, for the doubt implies it as a subjective state. Nor can it be intelligently mentioned except as the object, the "outer object," of sense, and as such existing constant and uniform, fixed and stable, so far as any experience testifies. But this is the extent of our experiential knowledge. What remains for us now to do is to analyze these sensible phenomena, and determine what they are and what are their psychological connections and their logical implications. This task has in the psychological aspect been well performed, and has resulted in the doctrine of the egoism of all phenomena as the general scientific verdict. Here, I take my stand, and refuse to obscure my position by throwing over it the dark pall of the unknowable and inconceivable. The logical implications of these phenomena have not been so fully explored as the psychological, and this is our task.

The Subjective World a Real World.

The subjective character of the world does not render it any less real than if it were *non-ego*. Surely, the *ego* is at least as real as the *non-ego*. We know the *ego* to be real. But we do not certainly as yet know anything beyond the *ego*. This is the point of debate. The egoistic theory of the material world is therefore a genuine realism quite as much as any theory which has appropriated the name; and it is not properly designated, because not defined by the term idealism. It is pre-eminently philosophical, because it is the simplest possible theory, and comprehends in purity all the facts of the case, and discards all needless conjectural and obscuring additions. Hence, Philosophical Realism is its proper designation. The term realism is in these days very popular. Everybody, even a metaphysician or an evolutionist, feels bound to be apparently real; and so his theory shall be called realism, however unreal it may be. And nothing that was ever in the brain of lunatic or philosopher or poet could be so thoroughly unreal as the material world of our metaphysical dualists, including the objective evolutionist. It has less reality than the purest phantasm, because it presents no form to the imagination, nor any concept to the intellect. Yet this supra-phantasmic world, with the help of obscure and inconsistent special pleadings, and buttressed by various supposed characteristic adjectives, has repeatedly and too successfully endeavored to get itself accepted as realism, pure, proper, and sole. With Sir Wm. Hamilton, the distinguishing epithet is "Natural," with George Lewes it is "Reasoned," and with Mr. Spencer it is "Transfigured." I therefore follow in the wake of illustrious predecessors in sticking to the word "Realism." I cannot call my theory natural realism, because, though infinitely more natural than that of Hamilton, it can appear natural only to philosophic minds; and I prefer not to call it reasoned realism, because it may be elaborately reasoned without being proved or provable, and least of all would I be willing to call it transfigured realism. We want a realism which is not transmuted either in figure or any other way, and a realism which is not only reasoned, but reasonably proved, and which will seem natural in the judgment of competent minds who have given to it due attention. Such a theory will be justly designated as philosophical realism; and philosophy will seek this till it is attained, however prolonged the search may have to be.

Nature and Evolution shut us up in the Ego.

By this time, it is surely growing quite clear that along no recognized route can we find any philosophical exit from the vast cavernous enclosure of the *ego*. And, if we could, it would bring no advantage to the main thesis of objective evolution, which affirms the ultimate unity of subject and object, of consequent and antecedent, of effect and cause, of all diversity in One ultimate Source. Hence, the method of reaching the *non-ego* by reasoning from subject to object, from effect to cause, would destroy evolution by destroying the unity of the universe in the persistence of force, or the identity and continuity of all force as that which is the same under all changes and in all forms. In short, a *non-ego* thus reached would not be the natural cause of known phenomena; and the process by which these are generated would not then be one of evolution, but of creation. A creative power is not one with the created. An evolving force is always one with all the forms evolved. Therefore, by the law of evolution, we can never transcend the *ego*. We stultify ourselves in the effort. Let the evolutionist heed the ancient oracle, "Know thyself," and he will labor no longer in this direction. Wherever evolution holds, there is unity and identity of essential being or force.

There is indeed a common method of transcending the *ego* by an arbitrary and artificial invention, the easy and not infrequent method of defining terms to meet the wishes of the definers. We easily transcend the *ego*, if we define it as limited in space (and time) to the organism, which is tacitly done very generally, though it contradicts the united testimony of modern psychology (at least in its implications, not in its articulate utterances); and that testimony I consider a sufficient refutation, and so leave it.

Objective evolution is the half-way house of scientific exposition and analysis. A more profound and thorough study shows that all that is included in that theory, combined with its forced confession of the subjective nature of all sensible phenomena, is justly described by the repulsive term, solipsism, since ultimately its universe is wholly subjective and egoistic, beyond which it knows nothing. In whatever direction we turn, we turn only toward ourselves; and never by any possible method can we directly know or experience anything but ourselves. Forever and ever, each man constitutes all the universe directly knowable to him. All the so-called men and animals, land and water, and all the celestial bodies are myself, affections and modes of my own all-pervading and perduring individuality. Hence, too, all that unknown and unknowable, whence the known is *evolved*, being one with the known, is one with the *ego;* and thus so far an absolute solipsism is the logical result of our investigations, whether as subjective or objective evolutionists. Since we directly and indisputably know ourselves as conscious subjects and agents, and thus know ourselves as a force and reality, it follows that wherever we go, by the law of evolution and persistence of force, we only go from some to other modes of the same one force, which is our own conscious being, and which we call *ego*. Evolution and solipsism are therefore terms of coincident meaning, and from opposite poles Fichte and Spencer meet in an immortal embrace : only, Fichte understood his logical position better than Spencer seems to understand his.

From this view of the *ego*, it will follow that I must speak of it very variously, because it is modally various and multifarious, and yet ever essentially the same. There is but One, and that One existing through all times and in all knowable spaces, under an infinity of different phenomenal forms and aspects, contemporaneous and successive ; and in reference to any class or to all classes of these phenomena or to the transphenomenal source and subject of them all, we may speak of the *ego*. To thus change the standpoint of observation and contemplation is not indicative of any vacillation of mind ; nor does it imply any obscurity or ambiguity of thought, nor can it becloud or befog any reader who has once grasped the conception of the universal *ego*.

This solipsism, it will be agreed, is theoretically unendurable and practically impossible as the final result. But let us be patient and consistent, which in the present situation, and in any situation, will best prove our philosophical spirit. Above all things, let us stand firmly and fairly by what we have clearly and unitedly determined,—that all the knowable is *ego*, and that within all that realm evolution reigns. Neither of these two cardinal discoveries of modern philosophy and science must be discarded or mutilated or overlooked. All further procedure must be in accord with these, if not based on these. It must, therefore, be henceforth an unquestioned, because proved, postulate that solipsism is true to this extent,— that every individuality includes the whole knowable universe, and universes are just as numerous as such beings ; that every being is hence absolutely alone ; that no being or universe can ever overlap or interact. Each is forever without any knowable boundary, just because the object and subject of consciousness are one, so that the knower can never transcend himself, though he travel forever swifter than the light. His latest stepping-stone and object of knowledge will always be himself. All other beings are removed from him by the diameter of his boundless universe, on the outer verge of which he can never even stand to hail a brother from afar.

A distinguished writer has kindly suggested (privately) that perhaps I might more fully utilize M. Comte in the prosecution of my task. I will therefore say that the essential spirit of Positivism (liberally constructed) presides over my work. I hold to the succession of the three methods of thinking and inquiry— the theological, the metaphysical, and the positive— in the development of the human mind. And it is the metaphysical method which now stands in our way, opposing the progress of psychological science in regard to the theory of sense-perception.

Positivism cannot limit its inquiries to external phenomena, nor even to sensible phenomena; for, then, it would not entertain its own expressed ultimate object in the region of sociology and morals, which involve supersensible feelings, thoughts, and volitions. And it would have to exclude all the pure mathematics, the first in the order of its hierarchy of the sciences, whence all science would be impossible; for this science deals only in conceptions, never in actual experiences, except so far as the conception is one form of experience,— thought-experience.

Positivism cannot justify mathematics, cannot therefore justify itself nor take its first step in the philosophy of sciences until it has vitally connected this pure abstract science of mathematics with sensible experience, its base of supplies. This it has not done, nor intelligently attempted, nor even recognized its obligation, so that here it discloses a fatal deficiency. This deficiency is supplied in the philosophy of mathematics given in my *Analytical Processes*. Pure mathematics is a science of pure and abstract conceptions; and, from beginning to end, its procedure is analytical, the conclusion being but the explicit affirmation of the implicit contents of the premises,— a part designated as contained in a larger whole. But the premise must have its base, not only in experience, but in sensible experience,— in the experience of extension, whether by touch or sight, because conceptual extension is the staple of geometry. The conception of extension is the intellectual light of the experience of sensation, and conception and experience are inseparable. And, in the conceptions involved in all sensible experience, all pure mathematics are contained, and thence analytically evolved.

It would be too much to expect that one man, in originating and expounding a great system, would be able to do it justice at all points, though Comte himself thought he did. There are several errors and deficiencies which the spirit of Positivism, in its further development, will correct or supply. The subjective study of psychology is one of these. This is a region of experience, and implied in all other experiences, and their ultimate light and guarantee. While, therefore, I attempt to work in this region a little, I claim to be strictly within the legitimate field of Positivism.

V.
REFLECTIONS ON THE SITUATION.

The conclusion to which we are driven by modern psychology will, to many minds, be very unwelcome. But, instead of wasting our strength in vain lamentation or in a passionate and credulous adherence to an old, exploded conceit, let us proceed to take a calm and thoughtful survey of the new situation, that we may discover how best to endure and judiciously improve the inevitable.

Individualism of all Evolution.

From the foregoing exposition, we see more clearly and correctly into the nature of evolution. We discover that, in making it co-extensive with the known universe, we only make it co-extensive with the changing modes of our own individuality. Hence, evolution is never the beginning and ending of successive individuals and races, each surpassing its predecessor in extent and variety and rank of faculty. It is always exclusively a change in the mode of the existence of the same one individual. The known evolving universe is the evolution of myself only. Its successive phases are myself in those forms and processes. Hence, the so-called known *past* is always the present. It is that which exists as known, and is known as thus existing ; and it is always a mode of myself. Even the fossil and pre-fossil world, back to the primordial chaos (to speak accommodatingly), is known as only a present phenomenon or subjective state. It has been said that the present has no existence, being always coming and going, but never here. We reverse this proposition. It is the present, and the present only, that does exist or can. This is true logically as well as psychologically, for its converse is self-contradictory. The very notion of past and future existence is that of non-existence now, and nothing can more perfectly contradict itself than to say these only exist. The past and future, then, we never reach, never directly know. When we have overtaken what was future, it is future no more. When we recede to what we call the past, we have only imposed upon ourselves, if we believe it to be the past. It can never be more than a symbol of the past. This is the avowed character of all monuments; but it is equally the character of all phenomena whatever, as all have their lexical antecedents, which, according to the proximate perfection of our knowledge of nature's laws, may be known from the known phenomena. This is the process of all branches of paleontology, and by this method we trace back the history of the universe to its most incipient condition ; and, as the known and knowable universe is *ego*, we thus in that process trace back its own history and show the route of its upward development and its successive stages where the *ego* has remained for a period comparatively stationary between the greater changes before and after. Thus, some modes of myself are vita-scripts of my successive states and experience and action. From them, I infer that I myself once existed in a state below that of man or monkey or any animal or vegetable, and that I have risen by successive changes through all the forms of existence up to my present condition, and that, hence, all inferior things are preliminary men. Thus, nothing is ever wasted. Everything is utilized forever, instead of being destroyed or dissolved to start again, as the common evolution assumes ; or instead of being created and then annihilated, as the common theism assumes concerning the lower animals. The very individuals of the lower orders of existence are always evolved into higher (with exceptional deterioration).

The pre-Animal World a Sentient World.

On the same principle, we are justified in inferring the sentient condition of the world, or *ego*, through all its changes and in all its forms and states of existence. The alleged pre-animal states of the cosmos are as really egoistic as any other of our experiences. As symbols of the past, therefore, none of them can represent the infra-conscious, or insentient, which is unimaginable and inconceivable, and hence cannot be represented at all by anything. Further, the inorganic cosmic forms of every order and class are admitted to be conscious forms or subjective states *now*; and they are also generally assumed to be just what they were before there was a human organism or any animal organism, and even before there was a vegetable organism. If, therefore, they are sentient states now, we must infer that they were sentient states then and always. They are not organic states now, and they never were; and they are supposed to have preceded and originated organic states. But, though not organic, they are egoistic; and thus the conscious *ego* existed in those states which constituted the inorganic universe before the origin of any of its fauna and flora. The nebulous gas which is an extra-organic subjective state of me now was a sensation or sentient mode of me then. And so, forward and upward, through all the cosmic changes till an animal organism is reached, and still forward through all the organic evolutions up to man, all the known are conscious modes of the *ego* and symbols of past sentient states. There was thus a pre-organic (and there will probably be a post-organic) consciousness. The *ego* is the universal power of which all cosmic phenomena are the conscious, or at least sentient, unfoldings. Thus, while protoplasm may be considered as the lowest and the symbol of the earliest or initial form of that action of the *ego* or energy which we call life, organic life, yet the *ego* and its sentient life were before the protoplasm, and were the source of it and of all that flows from it in all the subsequent successive stages of the evolutionary process. However ludicrous or absurd this may appear to some readers, it is but just that they should reflect that it is a logical necessity from the prevailing psychology, and direct their ridicule against the premise, and not against the legitimate conclusion from it.

It would not militate against my main thesis if any one, on the basis of inorganic phenomena, were disposed to infer an infra-conscious world, which for one while I held to; and, as such a world cannot be directly known, I could only suppose it to be symbolized by inorganic phenomena. But from this I was subsequently obliged to recede. There is no scientific ground on which to affirm this symbolism. Besides, if the assumption is made, it is a mental void, because the inconceivable cannot be symbolized; and such is the alleged infra-conscious world. Thus, the assertion of the existence of this world is arbitrary, baseless, and meaningless. It has no purpose to serve, no office to fill, no function to perform. Finally, if this infra-conscious world is admitted, it is insusceptible of discrimination from the alleged great unknown, the agnostic source of all the known. To this final conclusion, I do not here object, for reasons which will soon appear. But I object to such a method of proving anything, much more of proving the incogitable. Here, as everywhere, I prefer to steer along the coast and soundings of Positivism, as some would call it, but which, in its profounder conception and bearing, I call Philosophical Realism.

This gives me occasion to withdraw a previous blind statement to the effect that the organism and all its characteristic phenomena do not originate from the external world. This was consistently made in logical deference to the prevailing physiological psychology, which makes the organism a perceptive power, equivalent to the *ego*, instead of accounting it to be, as it is, only a plexus of sensations. If the known external phenomena are affections of the organic *ego*, they cannot exist before the organism. It is usually allowed, in general terms, that all phenomena are modes of the *ego*; and then the *ego* is tacitly assumed to be limited to the organism, whence all external phenomena prior to the organism are logically though unwittingly precluded. They cannot exist before that of which they are the modes or forms and manifestations. But, on the other hand, if we take the more common-sense view, which in this one case happens to be the more scientific, that the external inorganic world existed before our bodily organism, then it is clear that those external phenomena cannot be the creations or modes or affections of our organism ; and, conversely, if both these classes of phenomena, the organic and extra-organic, are egoistic, and if the inorganic existed long before the organic, then it follows that the *ego* is not confined to the organism, that it existed long before the organism, that it constitutes and is co-extensive with all the known worlds and agencies in the realms of space, and that thus and only thus the external and inorganic world can be the source whence the organism is by successive steps evolved. We thus see that the theory of objective evolution is here broken in two right in the middle, unless it be supplemented by our doctrine of subjective evolution; for the organic cannot be evolved from the extra-organic, unless the latter had a prior existence, which it could not have unless its subject, the conscious *ego*, had a prior existence in said extra-organic forms.

We cannot yet dismiss the question of the supposed infra-conscious condition of the pre-animal world. The shadow of pre-scientific notions here still stretches over us, as it always does with deepest density along the line where science and philosophy meet.

It will seem a needless truism to say that the infra-conscious condition is one which cannot be depicted or imagined, that this is possible only of the conscious. But just here all objective evolutionists have perpetually blundered, being blind to this very truism. They speak of what is affirmed to be an infra-conscious state, and describe it in detail as a familiar, sensible phenomenon, oblivious of the acknowledged truth that every phenomenon, external or internal, is always simply a fact of experience, a mode of the speaker's own consciousness. One writer, in words which have rung through the world, has spoken of the fire-mist or fiery cloud as the potent source of all the forms and powers of consciousness, as' the *u* .*sentient* fountain of all sentience, assuming that it is itself non-egoistic (*ego* not yet being generated). It is thus made the natural cause of the *ego*, and the womb and generator of all human souls and all their powers. On the same erroneous assumption that all the cosmic universe is unsentient, other writers elaborately trace back the evolutionary history of things to the nebulæ, and these to a probable single primordial gas, whence all consciousness has ultimately evolved. I do not quarrel with the philosophy which traces all later life and thought and cosmic forms and motions back to the earliest and lowest known forms of existence. On the contrary, I fully accept that method and doctrine. I only complain that the analysis here is imperfect and erroneous. Whatever be otherwise the rank of these gases in the scale of existence, they are modes of my present self: therefore, they are not unsentient; and, while their pre-organic existence is allowed, their pre-conscious existence cannot be allowed. Whence it follows that, while they could be the source of my organic forms, they could not be the source of my conscious existence. Before consciousness there was no cosmos nor nebulæ nor gas, because all these are modes of consciousness. A dubious view of this pervades some of the writings of Mr. Spencer. At times he loses sight of it, and then again it dimly recurs to him ; and he tries to explain it by saying that all phenomena are symbols of an unknown power or force. Whence it would seem that he thus relegates the effective agency and process of evolution to the region of the unknown, and leaves it to be supposed that the phenomenal forms and motions are only an ineffective play of unsubstantial images.

This Sentient Being or World is a Force.

Symbols of an unknown force these phenomena may be ; but they are surely themselves forces, else they could not be symbols. This explanation is, therefore, very erroneous and irrelevant, if it is designed to insinuate that all phenomena are forceless and that all force is unknown. While an objective evolutionist may thus escape from the false position that the lower cosmic phenomena are unconscious and the generator of consciousness, this escape is no better than its alternative. It contradicts the theory of objective evolution, and goes against the general index of all modern science, which surely declares or indicates that the known pre-organic world is a force which evolves the organic forms of life. It also confounds all speech and action in the practical world. If all phenomena are forceless, and so evolve nothing, then it is but to repeat the same in more concrete form to say that there is no force in all the known action of gravitating bodies, in all the motions of winds and waters, fire, hail and frost, thunder and lightning, or in what is called electric energy ; and all the science of modern dynamics is a nullity and misnomer. Surely there is no possible evasion of the fact that phenomena are themselves forces, and not merely symbols of forces unknown. "Whatever is, is force." It can prove its existence only by its action as force: so that not the forceful, but the forceless it is that must be forever unknown. To say in reply that the known is the powerless effect of the unknown is to say that all the heavens and earth and sense and inner consciousness do nothing and suffer nothing. In that case, they cannot symbolize and represent the action of the unknown; for to do that is a vast and varied exercise of power. Further, if the known universe is powerless, and so cannot do or suffer anything, what is it, and what is the use of it all? It is a wondrous panorama of nothing. Yet, being so wondrous, it certainly is a power to produce the feeling of wonder. But common sense and all science ascribe quality to all known things, and we classify and describe and designate them according to these alleged qualities; and the term "quality" is but another term for force.

This Sentient Being or World is One with the Alleged Great Unknown.

If we attempt a recession to a pre-sentient existence, we shall undertake a task which is much greater than we have imagined. That goal has heretofore been supposed to be reached as soon as we attain the pre-organic world. We have now seen that this was an error, that the said pre-organic world is only a complex mode of our conscious self, and that this must be so forever, however far back we go. The pre-sentient can never be known by experience. Whether it can be inferred from experience is the next question to be considered. This question must be answered in the negative. The world is known and conceivable only as phenomenal, and its lowest and supposed earliest known forms (as well as all later and higher forms) are sentient modes of the *ego*. Heretofore, no one has attempted the incogitable supposition that a world existed prior to all phenomena, before there was any gas or light or fire-mist. The proposition is without meaning, and only verbal because the term "world" is here empty of every thought or image. Were this supposition maintained, it would admit of no proof, because the proof must be phenomenal. In short, such a world is every way inconceivable, and there is neither logic nor common sense nor practical use to call for the assertion of its existence ; and the assertion, if made, would be only verbal, a mental nullity.

In considering the existence of a known force whose extent we may not yet know, a force which may in future exist in infinitely different and nobler forms than in the past, we have a very different question before us. We are not supposed to necessarily know everything that exists, or the capability of everything which is more or less known. We are conscious of perpetual changes. Forms come and go in countless multitudes and endless variety. These changes are not examples of annihilation and creation, but of evolution, and imply a continuity of substance and force as common to all phenomena. This great common substance or force is that which has been called the unknown. In one aspect it is unknown, but in its correlate aspect it is well known. It is that which appears in the phenomena ; and they are nothing else than it, and they are perfectly well known. But, then, perhaps no phenomena present it in its total capability. It has an unknown power of change. In this respect, and this only, is it unknown; but the unknown is identical in substance or force with the known or sentient.

And both the Known and Unknown of this Universe are One with the " Ego."

If, next, we inquire what these are in relation to the *ego*, the answer will be prompt and clear. All phenomena being one with the unknown and one with the *ego*, it follows that the *ego* is one with them. The *ego* and the unknown bear the same relation to phenomena. Their identity is therefore an obvious demonstration, an example of the axiom that things which are equal or identical with a third are equal or identical with each other. Hence, we need not go beyond the *ego* for any of the purposes of physical science. If there is an ether, it is *ego;* and all its vibrations are modes of the *ego*, conscious or unconscious. Egoistic are all the chemical forces, all the so-called correlated forces, as well as the uncorrelated force of gravitation, all forms, colors, and motions of chaos and cosmos, and also the great unknown whence they all are supposed to spring. Evolution is thus made complete and consistent by being made subjective. All phenomena and their intrinsic source are one; and, as the former are *ego*, so are the latter.

Sublime Representation of Man.

This exposition brings before us the nature of man in an aspect which is truly sublime. Man, in his essential being and quality, is not confined to a corner, like his organism; nor, like it, is he a thing of yesterday, but of all time and all space. Every man may say of himself: "I am not only descended from the worm, in the common meaning of descent, but once I was a worm. Yet I was never all worm. So, with less emphasis, I am a worm yet (known worms being modes of me); but I am also immeasurably more. Just as each of my modes is me, but not all of me, so my organism is me, but not all of me. I am all that my senses can know, and all that the instruments and researches of science can reveal. Oceans, worlds, suns, and stars are rays and flashes of my individual force and fire. The pealing thunder and the vivid lightning are exhibitions of an energy of unknown extent stored up in the magazine of my being. All knowable space and time are of me, and are marks of my presence and action."

Relation of "Ego" to Organism and Environment.

We shall hence be led to modify certain prevalent notions concerning the relation of the *ego* to the organism and its environment. We allow that the organic world is evolved from the inorganic. But our organism is not all of the *ego*, not the sum total of man. It is only one complex form in a countless host, a very small fraction of the known *ego;* and what remains unknown we cannot, of course, define.

It should also be observed that every man who is in the possession of all the recognized human senses has at least two organisms and two brains and nervous systems, the visible and tangible. These are utterly unlike each other, and have no identity or connection except as they are both modes of a common subject A blind man has only one organism and brain, the visual brain being extinct or undeveloped.

Now, all objective evolutionists uniformly expound the relations of the organism to the environment on the assumption that they are thereby expounding the relations of the *ego* to the *non-ego*, strangely overlooking the fact that all the environment, whatever its place, form, or influence, is itself wholly *ego*, though not the whole of *ego*,—a great, grand combination of its conscious modes, a portion of the surface and crust of the egoistic world. The relations of the brain and the organism and environment to thought and to each other are but relations of some modes of the *ego* to other modes of the *ego*.

Hence, another obvious conclusion is that the *ego* is not evolved from the environment (though we allow that the organism is thus evolved), since the environment itself is *ego*. It is the evolution of one mode of the *ego* from other modes of the *ego*, not from the *non-ego*.

We are now prepared to see that we have no proof nor any reasonable ground for a conjecture that the *ego*, as such, is the product of evolution. As it includes all the knowable universe, there is nothing conceivable from which it could be evolved. If the *ego* had a beginning, that could not be by evolution. It must be created. Evolution is only the beginning of new modes in that which has existed previously in other modes. The *ego*, or universe, cannot, therefore, be evolved from anything whatever. It is eternal, indestructible, and self-sufficing, or it is the product and created pendant of a Higher Power.

All knowable evolution, then, is within the *ego*, a change in the modes thereof by the interaction of part on part; and it is the great office of science, in all its various departments, to observe the laws and conditions in accordance with which this evolution occurs, whether as between the organism and its environment or between the different parts and forms of either of them. The *ego*, as the individual man, is the great abiding and universal fact and factor, and the seat of all immediately known authority and power; and we have nothing but its modal changes to observe and chronicle, to deduce their laws and thence to learn how to make use of them. And, while doing this, an imitator of Pascal may find more evidence than even Pascal could ever before see of "the greatness and littleness of man."

Relation between Thought and Brain.

A little further reflection will hence teach us that we must modify some of our notions of the relation between thought and brain, and that we should learn to be less profuse and confident in our comparisons between thinking things and what we call unthinking things, which, so far as we know, are modes of our conscious selves. To say that we know of no thought or consciousness without a brain has now become unmeaning or false. Thought is everywhere, and everything is thought. Thought is the substance and force, the essence and form, of all the universe. We know nothing else, and nothing else can we conceive; because everything is mind in action, a mode of consciousness. Whenever known, brain is itself simply a mode of the conscious *ego* equally with every tree, rock, or star, or other sensible object. There was thought before there was brain, because there was a pre-organic world, or conscious *ego*. Brain, so far as we know, is always associated with an *organic* form of consciousness, but with no other; and that form is infinitesimal compared with all the rest. This annihilates the modern *a priori* argument against the existence of intelligence without a brain and nervous system. The contrary fact meets us everywhere in the inorganic world. To deny the existence of a personal Deity because he cannot be supposed to have any brains is an apparition of the old defunct mediæval apriorism in antagonism with the acknowledged *dicta* of modern psychology. This, of course, is no proof of Deity; but it is a rebuttal of an opposing and false assumption.

Relation between Organic and Extra-organic Phenomena.

The most difficult task which sensism has ever been called upon to perform is to explain the connection between organic and extra-organic phenomena. Here the old dualists enjoyed the comfort of a supposed obvious advantage over the old atomists. For years, it is said, Hobbs labored unsatisfactorily to answer the question, "What kind of motion can it be that produces the sensation and imagination of living things?" Modern evolutionists are here in little better condition, according to their own confession. Several of them, Spencer, Huxley, Tyndall, and John Fiske, have given utterance to the feeling of despair on the subject. They have said that no satisfactory explanation has been given, or seems as yet possible.

I hope I shall not be hastily and inconsiderately pronounced superficial if I say that, if the old atomism is abandoned, the case is altered so that even on their own theory they make this gulf artificially wide and raise an unscientific difficulty. I deserve the credit of candor for saying this, because I could easily make capital for my own theory out of their admission, if I thought it anything more than a misapprehension; for, on my theory, I can easily show the scientific unity of inner and outer phenomena, which they despair of showing on their objective theory. The subject should be contemplated simply and solely in the light of the great scientific law of phenomenal uniformities. Science does not recognize the legitimacy of any inquiry or answer concerning the mode or the "how" of the results of nature's operations, except so far as they refer for explanation or justification to the uniform connection of phenomenal antecedents and subsequents. When these are not traceable there is no scientific explanation. When they are traceable, then the explanation is scientific. I hold that such a connection is traceable between the extra-organic world of phenomena and the organic consciousness. We have no right to say that no molar or molecular motions in the external world in any condition can produce the forms of organic consciousness; and we have no evidence of the power of aught for the production of aught else, except from their uniform relation as antecedent and consequent or subsequent. Hence, we need not in any case to do more than show this connection (and in no case can we do more) in time and place as proof that the connection is one of cause and effect. On this ground, I see no more gulf between these two classes of phenomena, on the objective theory of evolution, than I see between different classes of external phenomena regularly connected. There can be no question that the organic and inorganic are as regularly connected with each other as are the phenomena of the external world with each other. So much in aid of a theory which I supersede or rather absorb, and which will be my most vigorous opponent.

This question, however, assumes quite a new aspect under the light of philosophical realism, which annihilates the gulf between things and feelings or thoughts, by making all things to be modes of consciousness, different species of feelings under one genus, as egoistic modes or subjective states; and so the change of chyle into muscle and nerve and brain and thought and volition is only the evolution of one set of experiences or subjective states into others. The transition is, therefore, not so great on this theory as on the other. There is no transmutation from unconscious thing to feeling, for all things are feelings. The change is only of inorganic and extra-organic feeling into organic feeling and super-organic feeling or thought and volition. The whole known universe being but one individual, which we call the subject or *ego*, there is throughout it very manifestly a perfect unity of efficient causation. The origination of organic life from pre-organic forces presents on this theory no *a priori* improbability, as it is only the progress of one individual from a lower to a higher condition, a process which in various forms and degrees is allowed by all, without any question.

VI.

Superficial Expositions of Objective Reality.

Mr. J. H. Fowler's essay on "Mind Expression in Evolution" (in *The Index* of Aug. 9, 1883) is so able as to entitle its errors to elaborate correction; and a direct debate on questionable points is the short cut to a general attainment of the truth. I will therefore stop to take some of his statements and subject them to criticism, because they affect the whole world of thought, and exhibit the vague and erroneous and inconsistent mental habit which in these days has a wide prevalence, even in the high places of science and philosophy.

Mr. Fowler's prime error is very common and twofold, and consists in the assumption that whatever is external to our organism is *non-ego*, and that this doctrine is necessary to evolution and to the main principle which he wishes to expound. These errors he shares in common with Spencer and all his followers. I have already given them considerable refutation, but a little more in this connection may be of service.

In the first place, it is wrong to suppose that evolution, or mind expression in evolution, depends on any theory of sense perception or psychology. That may be true; and I doubt not it is, whether we explain evolution subjectively or objectively: only, I think that the most thorough analysis makes a demand for a subjective treatment, in order to secure entire consistency in the process and results. At all events, when we have for our declared object simply to show that evolution is mainly or wholly an expression of mind, it would be every way better for us not to entangle ourselves with any theory of opposing philosophies or psychologies which are or may be held different by evolutionists. If Mr. Herbert Spencer had not pronounced himself here, he would have been less vulnerable; and so would Mr. Fowler. If it should eventually turn out that there is a philosophical realism in what they assail as idealism, their labor is so far in vain, and all their work has a false coloring on it. I yield to no man on the score of the extent of evolution; but I claim that this can be consistently maintained only on the basis of a realism which is generally stigmatized as idealism, and that the opposers of this doctrine overlook admitted facts and contradict themselves. In further justification of this statement, let us look at Mr. Fowler's preliminary attempt to prove objective evolution.

He asks: "Can I go out of myself to a limiting cause of my own sensations? Common sense answers, Yes. Practically, this affirmation holds good against all negations of philosophy. Instantly and irresistibly, my eyelids close at the approach of a stick. So close the shells of a living oyster. Sensing pressure, the unhatched chick pecks and bursts the binding shell; then, in sense of want, guided by sight and smell, gathers nourishment, and fails not to interpret rightly sounds of friendly call or warning. Thus is reality environed and recognized by reality."

This performs the self-contradictory feat of making sensation transcend sensation; for every thing here adduced as being a reality beyond sensation, and affecting or causing or limiting sensation, is itself nothing else than sensation in every case. The stick and its motion, as well as the action of the eyelids, are simply sensations; and the two classes of sensations are related to each as causes and effects. All we know of the oyster and its shells and actions are nothing but another set of sensations lexically related to each other. The same is true of the egg and its hatching chick and all its action and experience, and the mother hen with its friendly call or warning. If there is anywhere a living thing answering to the sensations we call oysters, the stick which it fears is a mode of its own consciousness or subjective state. If there is anywhere a living thing which answers to our sensations which we call the chick, that shell which it pecks and the mother's call and the mother herself, so far as known to it, are only its own subjective states; and the same is true of the food it eats. "Thus is reality environed and recognized by reality," not as *non-ego* and *ego*, but as two great classes of the modes of the *ego*,—our subjective states, which are all we know. Beyond these experiential phenomena, we know nothing, and all comparisons made by us must be made between the forms and changes of these, the only known or definitely conceivable realities. And all these are *ego*.

I understand all this to be expressed by Helmholtz in the following passage from his *Psychologische Optik* (p. 443), and quoted, I believe, within a year in the *Princeton Review:* "I hold that to speak of our ideas of things as having any other than a practical validity is absolutely meaningless. They can be nothing but symbols, natural signs [relative to each other], which we learn to use for the regulation of our movements and actions. Only when we have learned to read these symbols aright are we able with their aid to direct our actions so that they shall have the desired result; that is, that the expected *new sensation shall arise*" (new sensations or other experiences being all we can find and all we should seek, each guiding to others by their sematic force, which grows out of their uniformity). Mr. Helmholtz adds: "That no comparison between ideas of things and things in themselves is in point of fact possible, all schools agree. But we insist that any other comparison is unthinkable and meaningless [unless between phenomena or subjective states]. This latter is the vital point which one must see, in order to escape from the labyrinth of conflicting opinions." I have read between the lines, because of the general indisposition to stop and take it all in.

I assent to the affirmation that "a sense of objective reality is clearly implied by the behavior of every organic being." But objective reality is not, therefore, non-egoistic reality. Whether it is so in fact should be determined by scientific analysis, and the science of modern psychology has determined that it is not; and its opposers are only those who appeal to "*common sense*," which is mere assumption, and generally an ignorant and false prejudgment. "Whether vegetable or animal, every individual responds to heat and light. Each senses environment as objective reality, and therefrom selects material with which to build up its own structure and secure internal economy and external harmony." But, so far as known to us or to any subject, all this is only so many changes in the forms and relations of subjective phenomena or egoistic states. It is a change of the inorganic into the organic, which is balanced by the opposite change of the organic into the inorganic, but no more. Both the organic and inorganic are egoistic or subjective states. Hence, "the recognition of a primitive, simple sense of objective reality, common to all organic beings," would here be of no avail. No matter how it originates, it is egoistic. We gain nothing by ingenious inventions concerning the *modus operandi*. If the material used in building up the organic structure were, for instance, known and admitted to be *non-ego*, and if it became *ego* by being organically assimilated and transformed, that were a theory sufficiently clear and simple. But the universe is not so simple a thing as that, or else it is ultimately much simpler; for psychology steps in, and says that this theory contradicts fundamental facts, and that all known plurality is an ultimate egoistic unity, whether organic or inorganic.

We have a fine distinction drawn for us in the following sentence: "*In* states of consciousness, not *as* states of consciousness, I trace my being back, step by step, through successive stages of evolution, to the time when there could have been no state of consciousness." This is important, if true; and true it will appear to all objective evolutionists. But we ought to be informed when that time is reached when there could be no state of consciousness. That information cannot be had. No such time or place or condition can be proved. The possible states of consciousness we cannot *a priori* know. That is the prerogative of Omniscience. For aught we can tell there are unknown and unimaginable states of consciousness of some beings which are related to the moon or to Jupiter or the sun analogous to our relations to the earth. We know nothing about that one way or another. The pre-conditions and possibilities of consciousness are not questions either of science or philosophy. We can, however, trace the development of *organic* consciousness back to a pre-organic world, which is not a pre-conscious state, because it is only a complexus of sensations or states of consciousness. An unconscious state we can never know. The supposition contradicts itself: because, if unconscious, it is unknown; and, if known, it is conscious. Directly, we can never get beyond ourselves. This is surely positive and final. Our experience can never transcend ourselves, else it were not experience, which is a state of consciousness. We cannot therefore transcend the present directly, since all experience is present; and the past is only an extinct experience, which may be symbolized by a present experience. While it is true that we know nothing except *in* states of consciousness, it is equally true that we know nothing except *as* states of consciousness, when we "know ourselves" well.

The distinction is plausible, but superficial. The prescientific mind does not recognize the phenomena of sight and touch beyond the organism "as states of consciousness," but the psychologically scientific man does; and the one class will, and the other class will not, trace the historic development of phenomena "*as states of consciousness.*" And it is the latter class which can trace their own being back the farthest and most consecutively and thoroughly, because that being is commensurate and coeval with the universe.

On the other hand, with those who make the extra organic to be non-egoistic, the case is entirely altered. With them there is a constantly recurring break in the historic continuity; and all individualities are being continually annihilated, and new ones formed out of a common substance into which the old individualities are reduced or dissolved. On that theory, *my* being cannot be traced back beyond my birth or the pre-natal organic condition in the fœtus; for that was the beginning of my being as an individual. My parents were not I, and their parents were not they, and so on back to the primordial cell and protoplasm. On this theory, it is, therefore, not true, as asserted, that in the psychical element of the primordial cell "I find my identity, which has never been lost, and which to-day constitutes my personality." That element is either common to the world or it belongs only to that individual cell, and not to me as a whole and specialized individual. That primal cell has been comminuted into utter destruction and fashioned into other forms a countless number of times before any cell became a part of my organism, and only those cells which are or were parts of my organism are or were parts of my being as an individual, unless this individual extends beyond the organism and existed before the organism, as philosophical realism affirms. These cells also being in a continual flux of generation and extinction, there is no fixity to my individuality, if it is only composed of these cells.

Now, consider all these cells and all the world to be—as they are—sensations, as I do, then we have at once the absolute unity of my individuality and personality with all the past, and all its forms and cells, of all of which I am the constant and abiding substance and force; and it is I that has undergone all the changes which are indicated as the successive changes of the world. And there are as many such world-changes as there are individuals like me.

We are also informed that "we cannot conceive of mind in space as matter, nor can we conceive of mind under the guise of dynamics. Mind is not a force, but a force cognizer and director. It is not matter or form, but a cognizer and director of these. Mind is the organizing reality, the architect of nature.... It is that which becomes intelligible in nature and intelligent in man." When men speak of inability, it would sometimes be well if they spoke only for themselves instead of speaking for all the race. For one, I can never acknowledge the inability here confessed by this writer. To me, it is perfectly easy to conceive of mind under the guise of dynamics; and this small feat I am constantly performing, because I always conceive all dynamics as modes of mind. If mind were not a force, how could it be a cognizer and director of force, or the organizer of reality and architect of nature? Further, if it is "that which becomes intelligible in nature," it must be extended in nature as if identified with matter. The discrimination of mind and matter, except as modes of the same one reality, is impossible, because, so far as known or knowable, they are both subjective states or modes of the mind, the intelligible and intelligent in man.

"*Matter, force, space, and time,*" says Mr. Fowler, "are cognized as external. Feeling and thought are in the mind as states or actions. Matter and force cannot be conceived as in the mind as states of consciousness or as phenomenal or real mind elements. The identity may be asserted, but cannot be conceived.

We cannot think matter, force, space, and time, being in the mind. . . . Space cannot be abolished or conceived as absent. Time is necessary succession: we cannot conceive of it stopping; but my consciousness, every and all consciousness, may cease. Matter, force, space, time, continue. They may be symbolized in thought and feeling, but not identified with them." If matter, force, space, and time are known, known directly in experience, they are not external to the mind, are nothing else than modes of the mind or states of consciousness. Their identity with mind, so far from being inconceivable, is a logical necessity, because the denial is self-contradictory, affirming that experience is something other than experience or a subjective state. If they are not thus directly known or knowable, they are not phenomena at all, and they do not come within the range of scientific discussion. The unphenomenal is a mental void, and all special assertions concerning it are void. Positivism only is scientific, and positivism only can be the *basis* of philosophy.

The *known* matter, force, space, and time—and it is only the *known* we can discuss—cannot be abolished so long as consciousness exists, since they are modes of consciousness; but, for the same reason, they would perish with the extinction of consciousness; and if, therefore, the extinction of the latter can be conceived, the extinction of the former is conceivable.

To say of these four terms or things that "they may be symbolized in thought and feeling, but not identified with them," implies that they are not directly known. But, if they transcend all phenomena and are unconscious, how are they to be symbolized? How shall we know that any alleged symbol is a real one and not an unmeaning invention? How shall the phenomenal and conscious symbolize the unconscious and unphenomenal? To these questions there is no answer. Legitimate and scientific symbolism is only of the possible phenomenal. One phenomenon may be a symbol for others, and indicate the law of their occurence and recurrence.

If matter, force, space, and time are only symbolized and not known, they are surely unknowable. If we do not know them now, we never shall. It is surely very evident that we have never made any progress here, and that there is no law by which we can. Their relation to our consciousness is a fixed fact. It does not come within the law of evolution, which is good only for phenomena. If, therefore, they are unknown, they are unknowable; and the unknowable is rightly, by Mr. Fowler himself, ruled out of the sphere of science and philosophy, in the following language: "The unknowable,—a name of power to conjure by, of strength to support a weak position, but, as an ally in philosophy, cowardly and treacherous. What cannot be known or conceived should not be relied upon."

If there are other beings besides me, real beings, conscious or phenomenal, they are conceivable; and they may be symbolized so far as they are conceived to resemble anything known or conceived by me, and no further. Experience and the analogies of experience and the logical consequences which these involve are all that science or philosophy can ever justly admit. Let us learn to be more sparing in our assertions. Let a genuine but broad positism rule science and lay the basis of philosophy.

The doctrine of Relation is always admitted to be of primal importance, but the correctness of our doctrine on the subject is equally important. On this point, Mr. Fowler delivers himself as follows: "Nothing is sufficient unto itself. Subjective reality implies objective reality: the two are related by phenomena and knowing. Everything is conditioned by all things. Sensation must have object as well as subject, and we deny our perception of the outward realities at our peril. The distrust of our senses is mental insanity, and leads to physical destruction."

It is a striking fact in the history of thought (in all departments), and often quite discouraging, that errors, and even blunders which have been often corrected, continue to be repeated, and that with all the assumption and aspect of an important truth well said or argued.

Now, while it is obvious that no individual phenomenon is sufficient to itself and must be conceived as one of two counterparts, as subject or object, neither of which can be alone, this is not true of the knowable or conceivable universe taken as a whole. This may be sufficient unto itself and, as a whole, absolute, unrelated. This is the theory of the world held by all non-theistic evolutionists. Relation is only between parts of a whole. The relation between all the phenomena of sense has never been doubted. The only question is as to whether all the related phenomena are all *ego* or not. Now, as they all belong to one universe, they all belong to one individual, if the individual constitutes the universe; and that he does is the unformulated doctrine of modern psychological science, which affirms that all phenomena are egoistic. Here, there is no distrust of the senses, but only an explanation of them; and all phenomena, subjective and objective (so called), are fully admitted in their mutual relations and the relations of all to the *ego* as their grand central source and cause and conscious subject. This is ultimate and all-comprehensive. Nothing more remains to be said; and no possible peril can its abettors incur, except the frown of "common sense" and the laugh of fools.

VII.

THE ABSOLUTE AND RELATIVE.

Our further progress is here obstructed by some prevalent and subtle errors on the nature of absolute and relative and the relativity of knowledge. All nature, all existence which is a living substantial reality, metaphysicians have anatomized and sublimated into a ghost called the "absolute," and to this ghost they have given a shadow called the "relative"; and, then, they are unable to tell which is which or what is either. They follow closely the directions of Mephistopheles to the student: "See that you conceive profoundly what is not meant for human brains. A fine word will stand you in stead for what enters and what does not enter there. . . . Generally speaking, stick to words: you will then pass through the safe gate into the temple of certainty. . . . It is precisely where meaning fails that words come in most opportunely." A system may be built with words, the devil truly adds. And systems have been built with the terms "absolute" and "relative," and kindred terms, used without real and definite meaning, such as substance and noumena as opposed to quality and phenomena.

This false [method of philosophizing was first in modern times made conspicuous by Locke by the emphasis which he put upon the old distinction between substance and attribute and between essence and quality. Substance and essence, being discriminated from attribute and quality, are void of them; and they are, therefore, a nihility alike to knowledge and conception, empty words. So that substance and essence are really ruled out of existence, though nominally retained. Berkeley battled earnestly, but with inadequate light, and therefore ineffectively, against this distinction. Hume took it up, and properly affirmed that all our knowledge is hence comprised in impressions and ideas, which Locke himself had explicitly affirmed in saying that essence and substance are unknown. So that nothing but impressions and ideas remained to be known; and these two Locke includes under the one term, "ideas," and he expressly and frequently affirms that these are all we know.

Kant adopts the distinction under the terms "phenomena" and "noumena"; and he is therefore obliged to confess that he cannot furnish in logical unity an ultimate speculative system. Fichte and Schelling substitute the term "absolute" for the term "noumenon," and vainly attempt what Kant held to be beyond human power,—the reduction of the absolute and relative to a logical unity. Here, Hegel burst in and boldly took the bull by the horns, declaring that the impossible logical unity is not necessary, and that to seek it is fundamentally wrong; that contradictories may both be true, and are true, since being and nothing are one, because the universally accepted definitions of being—essence, substance—are defined as qualityless, which, to conception, is just the same as nothing. Thus, the great primal logical law of non-contradiction is discarded; and a new logic is invented, which consists only in showing the orderly concatenation of phenomena or phenomenology.

Sir William Hamilton reimports the ill-starred distinction under the terms conditioned and unconditioned. But, as he does not follow Hegel, he alternates back to Kant and ultimate mystery, or Agnosticism; and he is followed, with a slight modification in the dogmatic direction, by Mr. Spencer in his *First Principles,* only he uses the terms absolute and relative, instead of unconditioned and conditioned.

The absolute should be considered as numerically different from the relative, else the two terms are merely synonymes; and much of what all these philosophers say of them implies their duality. On the other hand, they all really—and, except Hamilton, all expressly—make all things an ultimate unity. On this theory, the difference between absolute and relative is only modal, and yet to the absolute there are, it is alleged, no modes; and, if they are ultimately one, the unknown absolute is very closely and vitally related to the known relative, though incapable of relation. This kind of writing in the name of philosophy makes its way and maintains its authority, because it is too incomprehensible to be refuted like the mummeries of witches and gypsy fortune-tellers; for, as Goethe's Mephistopheles says again, "A downright contradiction remains equally mysterious to wise folks and fools." I allow that his utterances are not always immaculate, but on some spirits they are not without power; and, of their pertinence and probable influence here, the reader must judge.

The paralogism in this lofty conceit of the absolute is more conspicuously flagrant in sensist or objective evolution than in connection with preceding theories, because this professes to be simpler, and even at times affects to despise metaphysics. Mr. Spencer affirms that the absolute is unknown and incogitable; that yet it exists and is proved by the known existence of the relative; that, if we suppose the absolute annihilated, the relative itself becomes the absolute, in which case the phenomenal becomes unphenomenal, since this is the character of the absolute. But since he makes the absolute and relative together to constitute the universe, the one grand totality of force and action, the vast and labored distinction between the two is without a difference. They are both forces and causes, and as such they are mutually related in an endless series of changes; and so the absolute is as much a relative as the relative itself; and it *is* the relative, for the two are intrinsically one and the same. In short, this high dialectic absolute is not only an intrinsic absurdity, but it is especially foreign to the theory of evolution.

This style of pseudo-thinking has generated a false theory of cognition concerning the relative as the known. Our positive experience and thought have made it necessary for us to speak often of subject and object, of *ego* and *non-ego*, of outer and sensible forms and inner and supersensible experiences; and, now, this class of philosophers assail us with a perpetual clatter about our knowledge of these things not being absolute, but only relative; and, with an empty verbal ingenuity, they bewilder equally themselves and others, and erect a fabric miscalled philosophy, less substantial as well as less charming than the palace of Kubla Khan of Coleridge's dream. Our first task, therefore, now is to sweep the air clear of these phantasms; but it is their unsubstantial character which makes the difficulty of the task, for they do not obey the laws and forces of the real world, and the motion or stroke of solid things has no power to drive or crush and destroy them. Go through them, and trample them and roll over them, and they rise again or reappear as large as before, like a parted fog.

Vast is the flood of words which has been poured out on the high metaphysical conceit of the Absolute, pure and simple, as the alleged unrelated; and the utmost degree of misled subtlety, in wandering mazes lost, has been exercised only to render a dark and formless topic still more obscure and perplexed. The main proposition is intrinsically self-contradictory, and should thence be considered as self-nullified. But logic has no rights which this *a priori* metaphysics is bound to respect. A little reflection will make it apparent to any one that nothing that we know or can conceive is perfectly simple. Every atom contains or constitutes a plurality of qualities. It has locality, extension, weight, and chemical force, and what else I know not. But of all these, or all but one, we cannot conceive it to be divested. A more profound analysis will show that everything, whether considered as object or subject, must include in the conception of it a set of logical categories. For instance, it must be of some quality, some quantity, some duration; must be either cause or effect, or both; must be of some number, one or more; must be whole or part, and have some degree of worth; and there must be a degree of relation and community between all these.

If there were only one being, it would have no external relations. But, as such a being would include all things, its internal relations would be infinitely or indefinitely multifarious. But, if there is a plurality of beings, these have various relations to one another. In any case, therefore, the unrelative absolute is an impossibility. Relativity belongs to all real existence, by whatever name we call it.

The absolute as related is a reality and a genuine concept, because it is a thing of positive qualities which have various relations to each other; while each complex reality is related to all others, so that it is relative as well as absolute. It is absolute only in the sense of having a real existence as a thing of such or such a quality or intrinsic force or nature, and would be such though it were the only existence. Relations spring from the existence of things, not their existence from their relations. Something there must be as an *a priori* condition of relation. In this sense, the relative not only presupposes the absolute, but also that the absolute is the very thing which is related, and is therefore also the relative. Any other absolute than this is an illusion, a void form of thought, which has imposed on many.

An Erroneous Notion of Relativity.

In a region less aerial, we are also presented with a false metaphysical doctrine of relativity concerning the senses and supersensible matter. This doctrine is that, as all subjective phenomena vary with organic condition and constitution, though outward things are the same, our experience is never a direct cognition of outward things or extra-organic realities, and no just expression of truth, except as relative to the conscious subject and the connection of its various experiences with each other. Flavors and odors of various viands are imperceptible to some, while very powerful to others. Savages receive impressions through eye and ear which are impossible to Europeans. Abnormal conditions as to health beget sensations of smell, taste, sight, and sound, and even of the muscles, which in the same circumstances in health are impossible. In normal conditions, we all have different sensations from the same object, if it is only changed in its position relative to the different parts of the organism; as, for instance, snuff, pepper, and ammonia have very different effects, according as they are applied to the hand, tongue, eyes, or nostrils. The hand is sensitive to heat, but not to light; while the eye is sensitive to light, but not to heat. In the language of Spencer, "We are thus driven to the conclusion that what we conceive as space-relations cannot be either in their nature or degrees like those connections among external things to which they are due." In plainer terms, sensations are not like their external causes, because they vary not only according to the variations of external phenomena, but also according to organic subjective variations; and that, hence, known sensible objects are not ultimate realities, but symbols of such which are beyond our reach. Thus, it turns out that we know only subjective states in experience, and that these states or phenomena represent transcendental realities, which answer to the noumena of Kant, at least in a good degree; and Mr. Spencer is a transcendentalist as well as an agnostic, which was true also of Kant.

Source of this Error,—Fossil Metaphysics on Matter and Mind.

This is a relict of scholasticism, which was excusable in the earlier times, when they knew not the scientific compass, which should teach us how to escape these dark and vacuous regions, where empty words are the only stars. All this barren show of reasoning and profound ulterior conclusion is based on the assumption of a supersensible world, whence a comparison is drawn between the sensible and the supersensible connections; the latter being described as "those connections among external things to which they [sensations] are due." The confusion is augmented by an oblivion of the oft admitted fact that all phenomena are subjective, and the consequent institution of a blind comparison between sensations and external realities, so called, extra-organic phenomena being thus assumed to be *non-ego*. Herbert Spencer (*Principles of Psychology*, § 77) says, "Having contemplated feelings in their relations to one another as components of our consciousness, we have now to contemplate them in relation to things by which they are produced." He then proceeds through the chapter to carry this out, on the assumption that whatever is beyond the organism is beyond consciousness, and thence to explain the variations of sensation relative to extra-organic objects as *non-ego*.

The whole truth in the expression of facts of the relativity of sensations is as follows: Sensations vary uniformly, according to a simple law of forces in mutual relation. So that, if all the related terms are the same, the sensation is the same; and, if any of the related terms are changed or their relations changed, the sensation is changed. This law, instead of being a mystery and pointing to a spectral world, whether called noumenon or the unknown,—and these are one,—is, when the facts are duly apprehended, seen to be the simplest possible expression of the necessary facts,—a logical truism, in fact,—because the variation of the related terms is itself a variation of sensations as well as of the forces of the related group, since all the known terms are nothing else than sensations (with their implicated forces). Some of the terms may be sometimes more or less unknown (but never unknowable entirely); and yet, relatively to the changes of these, sensations will change, because we are always the subject of the action of forces which are only partially disclosed in consciousness. But it is only for phenomena or the forms of consciousness that we seek a law. This shows our knowledge to be real, direct, and perfect. These phenomena or sensible objects being sensations only,—or conscious forces in said form,—to know them is to know everything involved in the case, and that so thoroughly that nothing more remains to be known. Sensations are always known as they are, precisely and absolutely.

The term "relative," so far as it has any real meaning, *does not refer to the nature or forms* of sensible objects, but only to their temporal and spatial order and connection. They are variously related to each other in space and time and as cause and effect. As objects of sense, they are always perfectly and absolutely known, else they are so far not sensible objects; and this knowledge is not vitiated in the slightest degree by the fact that we have another knowledge,—the knowledge of their relation to each other in space and time, and their relation to the *ego* as their common subject, which may be wholly conscious or partly unconscious. One knowledge does not nullify another. And it is entirely certain, that we have indubitable knowledge of certain sensible objects, and that these are lexically related to each other, and that they are all the modes of a common, conscious subject, which we call 'I, or *ego*. This is all there is to be known or surmised. There is no logical necessity or possibility of going any further, and there is no room for the introduction of the old relativity. The relativity which I have admitted as the only possible one does not in the least detract from the knowledge or the value and verity of the facts as known. Facts are facts; and sensible objects are what they are, notwithstanding their relations, which do not annihilate or obscure or alter the nature of the facts or objects. It is only a false ontology and psychology which have led to the adoption of any doctrine of relativity which implies that we are shut off from a real and direct knowledge of things as they are. It is preposterous to suppose that things can be known otherwise than as they are, for else they are not so far known at all. So far as we know or can conceive, nothing exists but experiences and their subjects; and these are one, and directly known. Here, therefore, there is no possible room for any unknowable background, no fathomless and vacuous gulf of the absolute discontinuous from the known, nor an unknown, bewildering something—nothing called the material world beyond the senses.

As a further exemplification of dementation caused by the dualism of a sensible and supersensible material world, I will quote a passage from a representative author of France and then of Germany,—one from M. Janet's much-praised work on *Final Causes,* the other from an article of Lotze in *Contemporary Review*, January, 1880. Janet says: "Despite the warnings of the greatest minds and of all great minds, are we not ceaselessly tempted to yield to the automatic instinct which makes us believe things *to be as we see them*, makes us suppose the existence of a *matter, sonorous, cold, or hot, such as the senses acquaint us with?* No doubt, nothing external to ourselves can be known internally by us; but, if the exterior be the expression of the interior, is not the one equivalent to the other? And to ask more would amount to asking to be more than men. Science teaches us that all appearances have a fixed and precise relation to reality. *The visible, apparent sky is strictly what it ought to be to express the real sky.* The deeper our knowledge goes, the more we see the perfect conformity of the apparent to the real, the more do phenomena translate noumena." A strange scientific sin it is to "believe things to be as we see them." Surely, there *is* "a matter, sonorous, cold, or hot, such as the senses acquaint us with," else the senses do not acquaint us with it. It is a matter for deep regret that the distinguished academician has not described to us more fully the two skies, which he designates respectively as the apparent and real skies, or tell us where we may find them, in order that we may be able to verify or test his assertion that they are equivalent to each other and conform to each other, so that one is an expression of the other. We have never known but one sky, which is apparent to our senses, and which we have confounded with the real sky in spite of all warnings from great minds; and because we have no proof of any other sky, and because the assertion involves many logical difficulties, besides being unscientific, we are content with this one sky,— the sky which daily floods our world with light and at the same time constitutes for it a variegated, fleecy canopy, the sky which by night looks down upon us in deeper colors and with myriads of eyes more brilliant than diamonds.

The promised passage from Lotze is as follows: "Whencesoever our knowledge of the world, of its contents as well as of its great fundamental principles, may come, it remains always our representation of its object, and not that object itself." To the initiated, this means that the world itself is unknown, but represented by certain sensible experiences. This passage does not shed a brilliant light on its own darkness, like stars on a dark sky. In this only it differs from Janet, and it is the general difference between an erring Frenchman and German. How Lotze knows that sensible phenomena represent a thing he does not know and never can know, as he confesses, or how there is anything representable, he does not inform us.

These extracts exhibit the Kantian notion of relativity (which here is Spencerian) and its paralysis of ultimate speculative power. It affirms that what everywhere uniformly appears as real is not real, but only a representation of an unknowable real; and that what appears to our intelligence as an ultimate necessary truth, and which we are obliged to act upon in that light, is not such, but may be a reflection from such a truth. It proclaims philosophy proper (ultimate) an impossibility, and stultifies all intelligence, and by consequence its own statement. These are dark clouds which are yet exhaling from the primeval metaphysical world, and they will gradually roll away before the light of a true analysis. We do not, with Janet, hold to any instinct which makes us believe a lie. We not only *believe* that we see things as they are, but we *know* it, else we do not see them at all, since these things exist only as they are seen or are sensibly manifest. For them, *esse* is *percipi* and *percipi* is *esse*. It is no false faith nor even a faith at all, but a knowledge that the solid and sensible material world exists. All the darkness and mystery here, all the philosophical difficulty, limitation, and confusion, arise from the baseless and persistent assumption of dualism that there is a non-egoistic world, non-egoistic to me and all men and common to all, which world, it is reluctantly allowed, is unknown, since the known is *ego*.

It were to be expected that they who affirm that a false and misleading instinct dominates our sensible judgments will exhibit a similar principle concerning supersensible judgments. Whoever affirms that "there is never any sensible object, but only a representation of an object," may with equal reason say that there is never any mental object, but only a representation of such object, so that we have no logical protection against utter philosophical scepticism. This is the present and ultimate result of all existing forms of relativism, intellectual as well as sensible.

Confusion of Identity and Similarity.

Our attention is now claimed for another oversight in the common analysis of sensible phenomena concerning relativism. It is that the word "same" is constantly and unwittingly used in a false connection and with a meaning which implies identity, where in truth we should have a word which denotes *similarity of relations*. Thus, Mr. Spencer says that a fox, a man, and a snail, *going over the same ground*, will have very different experiences. The fact is that no two living things ever do go over the *same ground*. Each of them as known to me is a mode of myself, as is the ground over which they pass. These cannot have any sensations or experiences at all, being themselves only sensations. If these moving phenomena are taken as symbols of living beings, thus correspondingly like or unlike each other, then we must carry out the symbolism to all their environment. Thus, no two beings can see or feel the same thing nor be in the same world or the same space. Each is a universe to itself and of itself, said universe, organic and inorganic, being its various modes, a grand complexus of sensations. Whence, again, it follows that all experiences are true absolutely and not merely relatively, and are conformable always to facts and relations, because they constitute all the facts and all the relations. The only sources of error consist in a false analysis or a false inference beyond experience, and these present no logical or philosophical difficulty. The possibility of such errors is a consequence of our finite limitations, and the possibility of progress till we are able to correct our error has the same root. All the dense shadows and cavernous obscurities and philosophical nullifications of relativism thus pass away, and "there is found no place for them."

Cause of Relative Sensitive Variation.

Our analysis and exposition must now take another step. Psychologically, we have already reached the ultimatum; but a logical procedure is still possible and called for. We have seen what is the ultimate psychological law governing the facts, which are couched in the general statement that there is a variation of experience corresponding with organic constitution and condition, though there are no extra-organic changes. We will now state the ultimate reason and cause for this law. *It is found in the intrinsic nature of all being as a force.* These phenomena are necessary facts as the expression of the various existing and therefore operating forces. Things cannot be different without operating differently in producing different effects, which are the causes of other effects correspondingly different. So the effects will vary according to the connection of the forces in mutual operation. A spark dropped on water and a spark dropped on powder is expected to be followed by different effects. These are absolute facts and absolute perceptions. So, if the spark drops on my organism, the effect will be again different, and in different parts of the body the effect will still be different; and, so far as my knowledge extends of either the causes or effects and their relations in the case, it is absolute,—that is, it is direct and real and ultimate. Antecedents will be followed, and must be followed, by different consequents, whenever the relations are varied, and only then, whether any of these related terms include an animal organism or not. Hence, it is an absolute necessity, according to the known general law and the essential conception of force, that, if in any respect my organism is different from another, my experience must be different in the same connections, and the experience must vary in different parts of the body.

It may be thought that this leaves us just where we began, with the knowledge of things in their relations to each other only, so that we have only relativity at the last as before. This is a misconception. It is true that we know only things in their relations to each other. But the point I make is that that is just the way to know them, because that is the way they are. Since they are related to each other, our knowledge cannot be real and correct, if it does not embrace these relations in all their forms and variations and effects. We know things in themselves *and* in their relations, and these are different and the knowledge of them is different; and these include everything. Before 'it falls, I know that spark in itself irrespective of all its antecedents and consequences as an object of sight or a visual sensation, which is all it is, brilliant, transient, mobile; and this knowledge is real, absolute, and ultimate. And I also know that spark in its origin and cause, or its preassociation with other sensations, which is another real and absolute (though not unrelative) knowledge or set of knowledges; and, then, I afterward know it in its subsequent relations or effects or its post-associations with other sensations, which is another knowledge or set of knowledges, real, direct, and as absolute as anything can be. Nothing more remains to be known, because everything is known as such or such, and as in such and such relations, and always as sensations or modes of the conscious *ego*, which is just what they are and all they are; and here our ultimate, logical, as well as psychological goal is attained, so far as it affects the doctrine of sense perception; and, as concerns the ontology of the *ego*, that must be left to be treated in its proper connections.

No Unknowable Absolute.

Relativists next unite all phenomena into a grand totality, and say that, when we have traced them up to their highest unity, there is implied beyond them all an unknown, if not unknowable and even inconceivable, something as their explanation by way of substantive base or cause or we know not what. All schools and parties (except positivists) have agreed on this in general; but they have differed in the attempted determination in detail as to what constitutes that implicated transphenomenal reality and the amount of our knowledge and proof of it. Phenomena, it is said, are known only in relation to this, and this is only conceivable in relation to phenomena; and the conception and knowledge of both are relative only, relative to each other as well as relative to the conscious subject. So that all our alleged knowledges and conceptions are indirect, a mere alternate reflection of things unknown, like double or treble echoes responsive to each other, only the echoes are in kind like the original, while these are not. A very little labor now in the line of our previous expositions will here winnow the chaff from the wheat. The phenomena, because phenomena, are perfectly and absolutely known in themselves, and they are also known as being related to a self-conscious egoistic reality as modes thereof; *and this reality or ego is definitely conceived simply as a force causative of these phenomena*, in which phrase the nature of the force is described with accuracy, though not necessarily with perfect fulness. We have thus an absolute knowledge of phenomena, and of their ultimate relation as modes and effects of the conscious subject or *ego*, the force which is their cause. Thus, again, the mystery of relativism disappears; and, to the utmost of our inquiry, our knowledge is real and direct or absolute.

VIII.

THE EGO.

What is Ego, and its Proof?

Questions concerning the ego, or self-conscious subject of phenomena, have for some time been pressing upon us for attention. What is the ego we have defined as subject and cause of phenomena? But another point we must now endeavor to ascertain. The question here to be considered is, Can we scientifically justify the affirmation of the ego as a known reality and as substance and cause relative to phenomena?

I answer that *we know the ego, and know it as substance and cause, in knowing egoistic phenomena.* It is universally agreed that phenomena presuppose a subject, whatever this may be or imply. On this ground it is that a transphenomenal reality is generally affirmed, a few extreme positivists being the only dissenters from this. But this is to go at a bound further than I wish to go. I do not here affirm a transphenomenal subject. I cannot affirm the existence of anything entirely unphenomenal, because such an affirmation were an empty verbalism. Neither can I, on the other hand, affirm the existence of pure, unsubstantial, and forceless phenomena, because phenomena cannot be conceived and explicated except as relative causes and effects, and as having a common and pervasive unity, and as being subjective states with a perduring conscious subject or ego. Thus, the subject or ego is the fundamental force felt in all changes, the essential unity manifested in all diversity of forms and motions; and it is one with these forms, as it is these very forms so and so existing and acting, though I do not say that it is wholly. Thus exhibited. Yet it is there and thus (for these are itself) directly known, really, absolutely, and ultimately.

The conception of the ego, therefore, is not with us a mere cris-cross, interlaced chain of phenomenal network, as it is with Mill. The ego is all that, but also much more. I define the ego as that which feels, thinks, wills; and this is also my definition of mind. Nothing can be broader or simpler or ulterior. It is thus distinguishable, but not separable from its modes, from sensations which are matter or material, and sensible modes from emotions, thoughts, volitions, which are immaterial modes; but all phenomena are modes of mind. Yet all of mind or the ego may not be phenomenal. The ego is perhaps and probably more than its phenomena, as the total force of any thing is more than its separate transient exertions. Substance and quality, action and force, are one, and one with all phenomena, whose unit is ego, which at once causes and constitutes the phenomenal network, and will endlessly modify it. Without this there is no possible continuity, and all apparent community is illusive. Without this there is separateness and juxtaposition, coexistence and succession of different phenomena, and nothing more. There is nothing answering to our consciousness of unity and of the One being or force which speaks in all and through all as identical with all. We have many without the One, whereas consciousness speaks of the One as modally many and the many as the One. In reference to every phenomenal form and change, we say, "I,"—I experience that, or That is a mode of me. So that ego and all phenomena are one, and they are known together as a unity of force in various and ceaseless operation; and the knowledge is absolutely ultimate, the knowledge of substance and quality or force as one and phenomenal, one force or substance in all these many forms or phenomena, which are therefore forceful.

We are now enabled to form a perfect and ultimate conception of personality. With the Romans, a person was an actor, the visible organic automaton on the stage. With the Greeks, it was similar,—a prosops, a visible, organic phenomenon. It is both of these yet. But it is not these only. Nor is it limited to the organism, nor to any one known thing or object. It includes all the known universe. Neither can we say that this is all. The only person I know is the power which is the subject of all the phenomena of the known universe, and these are put forth and endlessly modified by this power or person. This is the individual that I am, an omnipresent reality of unknown extent and variety of power, which, while manifested, is not wholly manifested in its capability in any or all of the existing forms, motions, and self-conscious actions of the universe, since the future is not yet manifested.

Personality and Individuality.

I would distinguish individuality from personality. Every individual is not a person, but every person is an individual. A person is an individual which is self-conscious,—not merely sentient, but self-conscious. There may be sentience without the power of self-conscious reflection; and this I suppose is exemplified in most, if not all, of the lower animals, in which condition human persons once existed, and from which they have evolved into their present nobler rank. (But, if animals are ever pleased or displeased with their own action, as they surely are, are they not self-conscious?)

Personality and individuality are alike in this,—that they are not constituted into any particular permanent shape or form exclusively; and neither has any knowable, physical bounds. All physical forms, masses, motions, and changes are nothing else than the sensitive modes, relatively permanent or transient, of each individual. The individual itself is formless, except as it exists in these forms, itself the simple subject of these phenomena. It is purely a power to experience these, partly irrespective of volition and partly by the aid of volition. The subject ego is the soul of the world, which is its feeling and action. So that this soul of the world is the world.

Personality does not necessarily imply limitation, and an infinite personality is just as conceivable as a finite personality. Finite personality is a self-conscious individual of limited power. An infinite personality is an almighty self-conscious individual, *able to do whatever does not involve a self-contradiction.*

Alleged Obscurity of this Doctrine.

Sticklers for common sense in a region where uncommon intelligence is called for object to this, merely because it is not to them easy of comprehension. They say you can never secure credence for such a doctrine as that, that it is all too vague and abstract, that it refines away the individual until he becomes an airy nothing without a local habitation,—nothing but a name, without form or shape, without spacial or temporal limitation and circumscription, so that it is entirely shut out from the sphere of imagination and definite conception. How can we believe what we cannot imagine or conceive? Our individuality as connected with the organism presents something real and proximately precise for the understanding, but as timeless and spaceless as something back of all phenomena, and which appropriates to itself all the known universe as a series of modes of itself. It is then worse than the genie of the Eastern fable, which, being let out of the teapot, becomes diffused and dissipated till it is lost in universal space. An objection of this kind will long and widely prevail and with pernicious effect, because of the vastness and subtlety of the new thought, which not only extends beyond the wonted range, but also opposes dominant tastes.

Whence comes the Apparent Clearness of the Vulgar Notion?

The prevailing notion is at bottom merely sensism, or, at best, organicism. It limits the ego to the organism. Whether it identifies the two or not, it gives to the soul a sort of spacial outline, and thence a form or image which appeals to the imagination, if not to the senses. In this way, the ego is proximately defined. This is the crudest and most primeval notion, but it prevails practically or theoretically over the most advanced thinkers as well as over the vulgar mind. A distinguished academic president recently said to the author that he considered all beyond the organism as non-ego, and the rest as ego, expressing the same idea also at the same time by gesticulating the difference. I replied that that is the essential theory of sensism and objective evolution which makes the ego to be the organism and never the same at two successive moments, the ego and non-ego being continually transmuted into each other; and that, besides being self-contradictory, it is contrary to the most familiar principles of optics and psychological science. All this my learned friend could see at once, but could not conceive any other notion of the ego than that which is one with the organism or confined to the organism.

Two Exclusive Conceptions of the Ego.

There are only two main conceptions of the ego possible,—that which transcends the organism and that which is confined to the organism. The latter is of two forms,—that which identifies the organism and ego, and that which pluralizes them. The latter is the orthodox religious view, for religion has always insisted on some psychology and philosophy. Both these have an advantage over the first relative to the senses and imaging faculty or imagination, which are the faculties most in exercise even by many educated men; and even reasoning is distrusted or repudiated where its successive steps cannot be presented as a series of images, and intellect is thus considered as a "faint" impression of sense, as Hume affirmed and Spencer has repeated. To this class of minds there is a great advantage in being able to screw and circumscribe the ego within the confines of a limited time and space like the organism, and its convenience has a dementing influence of great and insidious power.

Now let us pass beyond this, and we are obliged to traverse the utmost extent of the sensible universe, and include it all as modes of the ego. If we affirm anything beyond the organism to be ego, we have no stopping-place anywhere. The sphere is boundless, commensurate with all phenomena of every possible form and quarter. Now, we are out on a shoreless ocean as to sense; while thought rises to the imageless, which is beyond and above all sense, just as the lark rises above embrasured turret and gilded spire to sing viewless in the viewless air. But it is not strictly spaceless and timeless, because its modes constitute space and time.

This is the logical outcome of modern science, which makes all phenomena to be subjective states, so that all the known universe is ego, and ego is at least commensurate with that universe, and the power which evolves it, which is sensible or organic only so far as it evolves itself in sensible and organic forms; and, beyond this, we can only conceive and describe it as a power of so and so thinking and acting.

This will appear appalling to all but minds of the strongest fibre. Even brave old seamen have often shook with fear in unknown seas. But shall philosophy surrender itself to cowardice, and shall we fight against our own intelligence, because it calls us to a brave conquest of new lands, or because it disturbs our old prejudice and mental comfort and ignorant and delusive sense of power, and yet calls us to the possession of a grander dignity and larger power?

Mutual Destruction of the Organicists.

The two parties into which the advocates of organicism are divided are in deadly hostility; and, in their frequent tournaments, each is always able to unhorse the other by using different weapons, and each party has again and again confessed its relative weakness. Each proves the other to be inconsistent and irrational somewhere; and the battle always ends by the affirmation of each that it is less irrational than the other, which is the utmost that either can claim. Their relative merits is not our concern. We care not which of the two is the greater fool. Enough that we cannot accept either of them without shutting our eyes; and that for those who prefer to keep their eyes open there is no logical alternative but to accept the theory of extra-organicism in the simplest possible form, as we have expounded it.

Superior Clearness of Extra-organicism.

This theory, so far from being specially obscure, is perfectly clear, and the only theory that can be clear, because it only is self-consistent and rational. It has no mental *lacunae*. It does not require us to ignore our intelligence anywhere. It is self-justified and luminous in every part. And it is the least possible assertion that can be made self-consistent and in harmony with experience.

The supposition that a peculiar vagueness is characteristic of this theory is erroneous. It is ultimately quite as definite and precise as its rivals. It gives us consciousness in all its forms, all phenomena,— organic, extra-organic, and super-organic, if there is any of the last,—and all these it presents in a consistent formula; and no theory can do more. It says that the ego is the power of being and of knowing all these, and this is perfectly definite. We could have no other ultimate definition, if we should limit the ego to the organism; for it would still be nothing more nor less than the power of so being and acting,—that is, as the subject of these phenomena. The only difference between them is in their implications. The limitation of these phenomena to the organism involves various contradictions, from which the other is exempt.

Unrecognized Prevalence of Extra-organicism.

While organicism, monistic or dualistic, is a very common habit of thought, yet on the other hand, side by side with this in the same minds, the opposite notion to organicism is generally entertained, so that it is extensively ingrained in modern literature. We give one striking example from a brilliant French writer (Taine), who cannot easily be referred to any recognized class of dogmatic theorizers. It is from his *English Literature* (Intro. II.), and is as follows: "When you consider with your eyes the visible man, what do you look for? The man invisible. The words which enter your ears, the gestures, the motions of his head, the clothes he wears, visible acts and deeds of every kind are expressions merely. Somewhat is revealed beneath them, and that is a soul. An inner man is concealed beneath the outer man: the second does but disclose the first. You look at his house, furniture, dress, in order to discover in them the marks of his habits and tastes, the degree of his refinement or rusticity, his extravagance or his economy, his stupidity or his acuteness. You listen to his conversation, and you note the inflections of his voice, the changes in his attitudes, in order to judge of his vivacity, his self-forgetfulness or his gayety, his energy or his constraint. You consider his writings, his artistic productions, his business transactions, or political ventures, in order to measure the scope and limits of his intelligence, his inventiveness, his coolness, to find out the order, the character, the general force of his ideas, the modes in which he thinks and resolves. All these externals are but avenues toward a centre, and that centre is the genuine man. I mean that mass of faculties and feelings which are the inner man. We have reached a new world, which is infinite, because every action which we see involves infinite association of reasonings, emotions, sensations new and old, which have served to bring it to light, and which, like great rocks deep-seated in the ground, find in it their end and their level. This underworld is a new subject-matter proper to the historian. If his critical education is sufficient, everything is a symbol to him, whence 'he works out its psychology.'" Though this author's object here is not metaphysical, and shows no steady philosophical vision, yet it is quite evident that he makes the ego to be something other and vastly greater and more subtle and persistent than organic forms or any other forms,—a wondrous and incomprehensible unit, which is partially manifest in all phenomena. And, in this, he has nothing peculiar.

Ultimacy of our Doctrine.

Our exposition gives us not only a combination, but a perfect unity of the permanent and transient, the substantial and phenomenal, and makes them equally known, each in the other. Phenomena are always changing. The ego is always the same through all the changes; and it changes while it remains the same, changing in its modes and remaining the same substantive subject and source of such changing modes. It therefore comprises at least all the phenomena of both sense and inner consciousness, and is the womb of other possible phenomena which we cannot yet even imagine. These phenomena are organic and extra-organic and super-organic. The ego is at least commensurate with all of these; and, in all these, it is known, though not fully known. It cannot in any sense be less than all these taken together, nor less enduring, so that it covers all known and knowable space and time. It does not exist in space and time for these, so far as phenomenal or knowable exist in it with all their contents. Nor is there any more mystery about its existence than about anything else. All else, if there is anything else supposed to be known, simply exist and operate as so and so related; and it is just as simple and clear to say that the ego exists in relation to them as conscious subject. It is only as phenomena of the conscious subject that they are known, and the subject or ego is known only as knowing them, as the thing which knows them; and then analysis shows us that to know them is to be them, to be their subject and source, so that they are but so many modes of the ego, the ego itself so and so existing and acting. To ask anything beyond this betrays obtuseness instead of acuteness and thoroughness of mental power, because it is meaningless.

Environment of Organism not Environment of Ego.

Evolution, so far as it has yet evolved, is a form of organicism. Hence, it has considered its chief task to be to show the interaction between the organism and its environment; and laboriously has it wrought at this on the assumption that in so doing it has been showing the interaction between the ego and the non-ego. It finds that an environment of constant action, yet always lexically changing, is necessary to the evolution of the organism, and determines its forms and duration, whence it is inferred that this environment effects the same for the ego; and, as the chief quality of human personality is intelligence, this is said to have the same origin and end. From their objective stand-point, they are right. If the external world is non-ego, there is no other legitimate conclusion. But we now see that this is a great error; and that, compared with the greatness and grandeur of the facts disclosed to us, it is very narrow and superficial. Relative to the organism, an environment is a fact and a necessity, physically and logically. But, to the ego, any environment of space or time is impossible, a self-contradiction, because the ego is and must be commensurate with all the knowable forever, all space and time,.and all their contents. Whatever is known is a mode of intelligence, is the knowing subject in said knowing mode. An environment is therefore neither necessary nor possible to any intelligence except an organic intelligence. But we know no intelligence which is purely organic. Even our sensible intelligence is mostly extra-organic, and spreads over the whole universe, with which our personal intelligence is identified, which excludes the possibility of an environment. This is important as we go along. I will add that it annihilates the argument against an infinite Personality, which it is said requires an impossible environment, an argument which further on will receive due consideration.

Argument of Comicality.

"Common-sense people," no doubt, will readily, if not necessarily, conceive this in a light which is sufficiently comical, apparently ridiculous, and a good refutation of it, or at least a good reason for holding it in small esteem. Nearly every new truth in science and philosophy, and elsewhere there is nothing new under the sun, is comical, if not ridiculous, to old error and prejudice. How absurdly ludicrous it appeared to the pre-Copernicans to affirm the existence of people and things at antipodes to each other, which was supposed to make those opposite to us to be upside down, as how could it be otherwise, since we are upside up? We all now easily see that no other kosmic conception than the Copernican is really possible, that all are equally antipodes to some others, and yet all are equally right side up, and that all people and all mundane things cling to the earth in every situation by the same one law of gravitation. Organicists may laugh at the idea of a man always seeing and handling, embracing or fighting, or eating and drinking only himself, and of his being burned or crushed to death by himself or drowned by himself or devoured by himself, whether in the form of sharks or wolves or worms. But there is at least one mind to whom it appears that we must either return to the prescientific condition or advance to the clear perception, that this is the only way of conceiving the present or past forms of our existence, and that this is the course and nature of all existence under organic and sensible forms. The organism is engendered or destroyed by other physical forms which are egoistic; but the ego itself never is, so far as we know, because through all known and knowable mutations the ego persists, else we could not know the mutations.

IX.
Permanence and Simplicity of the Ego.

By the simplicity of the *ego*, I mean that it is not an aggregation of parts and particles, but one and the same homogeneous thing throughout,—simply a force which is able to be and to do and suffer so and so.

This doctrine stands opposed to the theory of organic atomism, whether the atoms be the monads of Leibnitz or the material particles of Epicurus and Lucretius or of modern chemistry and evolution. It is opposed to the dualism of mind and matter of all ages. Still more is it opposed to the theory of a few in different ages and recent times who have held to a trichotomy of substances in the human individual. From all these, the doctrine of the simplicity of the *ego* needs to be well discriminated and defended.

The Constant and Perduring Ego.

There is a sense in which the *ego* is rightly considered as various, complex, and multiplex. This is the organic *ego*, which is inconstant, variable, local. But this is not a full account of the *ego*, and it becomes false when taken for the whole and proper *ego*. All along our history, through all the changes of our experience, both organic and inorganic, the *ego* asserts itself as abiding the same simple, indivisible, and unchanged (yet changed) and continuous *ego*, as a perfect unity without parts or organs. The stars of childhood are the stars of maturity and old age, and I who saw them then am the very one who sees them now. If they have changed, I have not. With all my modal changes since childhood, I am the very same person I was then,—the very same substance and reality, nothing removed, nothing added. All the changes I have undergone in the long interval are only modal, while I remain the same individual force in which all the changes occur, and which evolves them all from and in itself, because such is its abiding nature. Thus, through all the successions of the memory, and far beyond, the *ego* is the same. It is not memory, nor the continuity of consciousness, which makes it the same, though these may help a certain class of verifications. The *ego* exists, and exists through all these changes, which are only and always its modal mutations.

We must here refer again to the commonplace in philosophy, and signalized by Kant, that change is only possible in the permanent. Without a perduring permanent, there is no possible change, but only successive annihilations and creations; and, as the latter horn of the alternative is inadmissible, the first is inevitable. Not creation, but evolution, is the nature of all known change in the varying and successive phenomena of the world. In accordance with this, all the atomists admit and contend that there is a great perduring world whose total force remains the same through all kosmic changes. The same principle surely holds good for the *ego*, especially when we consider that the great world is the *ego*. All its forms are known only as sensations, and hence its source and subject is the *ego*, which is the substantive force and generator of all phenomena. Thus there is certainly an unchanging *ego*, which remains the same through all atomistic mutations and combinations.

Its Immortality.

What remains the same through all the mutations of the human organization and of the kosmic world may be reasonably presumed to remain or continue to exist through the mutations of the dissolving organism. Its annihilation is declared to be inconceivable when it is contemplated as the kosmic force, which is the *ego*, though unrecognized as such by the kosmicists. In short, the *ego* full and proper is the unchanging subject of all phenomena, the abiding force which is the cause of all change, and which must forever change because it is a force, and yet must remain the same force.

The great law of change in the past, so far as known to us, is one of progress. Man is the evolved product of all the innumerable past changes. And man, as an individual substance and force, did not begin his existence with his organic birth. Innumerable were his successive births and lives and deaths before that; for he had previously existed in every type and form from chaos up to mammal, yet remaining ever the same in all the great features of life constituting the world (which yet was always changing), and at the same time undergoing specific changes in organic evolution. What has lived in and through and constituted all these forms and changes is not likely to perish with the dissolution of the present organism.

In the next place, our survival of the organic *ego* is supported by our doctrine of the simplicity of the nature of the *ego*. As it is not organic, it cannot be disorganized nor dismembered nor in any wise fundamentally affected by any possible changes.

It is supported by our doctrine of the *ego* as a force, which is the source of all its own changes,—that is, of all the changes of the universe whose soul it is; and so there is no known or conceivable force to operate on it from without and hurt it.

The organic *ego* is mortal; and, if this were all there is of us, the notion of immortality would be baseless. But this is the doctrine of materialism, not ours. Let materialists perish, if they wish, as they will, and their doctrine, too; and the sooner, the better. Doubtless, they will die hard, and will endeavor to prolong their existence by feeding on our argument, as moth and mice often feed on fine garments when they can get at them in a dark place.

They will plead that the external world is only known through the senses of the organism, so that, if these are all destroyed, the whole universe is to us blotted out, and conscious existence and individuality are destroyed. This is a combination of truth and error, both as to fact and inference.

In the first place, we do not see the external world through the senses, as we see things outside the house through a window, as is often supposed. We are not inside the organism as the organism is inside the house. The organism and all the universe are in us; and we see the extra-organic world directly as a spirit-power, super-organic. The eye is blind, the ear is deaf, and the tongue is dumb, the palate knows nothing of taste nor the hand of touch. It is only I who know and do all these things; and all the senses, total and several,—that is, the whole organism and all its forms and motions,—are only so many sensations, as are all the forms and motions of the world beyond; and these senses of our body have no more power of discernment or experience than those rocks or clouds or stars which are equally sensations. *There is a law of connection between organic experience and extra-organic experience.* This is the statement of the truth and of all the truth on this subject. The soul sees both, and all things directly, but only in accordance with certain subjective laws (and there are no other laws). There is, therefore, no logical difficulty in conceiving that the soul may develop a power of knowing what answers to sensible phenomena, though the present organism be dissolved. In what we call the normal state of the present order, the two classes of perceptions, the organic and extra-organic, are lexically connected; but this, so to speak, is only an accident. It may at any time be changed by the ever-active forces of evolution within the soul. Still, the possible proved is no proof of the fact; yet since the soul, and not the senses, and that directly, discerns extra-organic objects, we have here a ground on which, in connection with other material, we may build up a probable argument for conscious activity after the dissolution of the body, and plenty of other material is at hand.

This material, in addition to the arguments furnished above, is found in the set of facts which has given rise to the doctrine of sensible relativity that experiences change with the changing conditions and circumstances and forms of the organism. How different the world of the ant, the fly and elephant and man! Now, all evolution of the past has been a change of the modes of the subject, which has thus attained new organic forms and sensible experiences. That is, in brief, the history of all organic evolution in the past, and the only index we have of the future. So that, presumably, our death, so-called, or organic dissolution, is simply a change of organic experiences; and so the world will be different and yet connected with this, perhaps as the lower animals are with the higher, and the animals of the water, air, and land with each other.

Then there are evolutions within the present life which exhibit a transition from one state to another, which is equivalent to a transition from one world to another. It is seen in all fœtal existence compared with the after life. It is still more fully seen in the larval condition compared with the insect condition, especially where the larvæ lived in the water. It is seen with equal clearness in some batrachians, especially the frog, which first lives the life and wears the fish form chiefly, and then takes a singularly human form and breathes the air.

In men, also, there are some wonderful experiences indicative of a latent supra-organic power struggling for freedom and development. Among these indications, we may mention trances, clairvoyance, and action which cannot be attributed to any known organic agency; as, for instance, writing between two slates pressed close together, separated only by the rim of their frames, and so held together by many strong hands and even by an iron clamp,—a phenomenon which, with others equally wonderful, has been often witnessed and testified to by many of the ablest men of our times. Whether these are considered as the effect of human agency or ex-human agency is all one relative to our argument. They prove that the human spirit has a super-organic power of perception and action.

Numerous testimonies of the highest authority also certify the existence of sensible knowledges without the action of any of the recognized senses. Things are seen at a distance and through stone walls and through various coverings. For example, nine men of ability and culture have each rolled into a pellet a sentence on a separate slip of paper, and then mixed them all together, so that no one knew his own paper or could tell the contents of any one of them by specification. Yet a tenth man in the company, who has had no sensible knowledge of any one of them, direct or indirect, has told the contents of each one in succession with entire accuracy, as verified by all the nine men. Whatever was the agent or faculty or operation which achieved this result, it was not organic vision or tactual impression or hearing; and yet it was accurate and unerring perception of visual forms and their meaning.

These phenomena are not adduced as supernatural, but as the natural evolution of human power, whether its action be considered as originated in the men of our world or with those who have left and who return to operate upon it. As they demonstrate a super-organic power already existing and operating in and through man now, they utterly disprove the materialist's notion that our individuality with all its power is the product or the action of the material organism with which, it is alleged, it began its existence and will end its existence. The proof is surely very strong that the *ego* is essentially super-organic, and will survive and probably evolve into a higher condition on the dissolution of the organism.

Finally, for this topic here, who will believe, who can believe, that the dissolution of my organism is the utter annihilation of the entire universe? No one. Yet that is the event which constitutes my extinction ; for I am the universe, which is only a congeries of my subjective states, modes of the *ego*, which is the only conceivable substance of the universe, the one great force everywhere and always working and generating and destroying the myriads of forms and motions which constitute the sensible kosmos, as well as all the supersensible experience and action of feeling, thought, and volition. All are known only as the modes of the one *ego*; and, if they live, I live also, and only because I am are they possible.

The Aggregated Monadism of Leibnitz.

The monadistic, not monistic, theory of Leibnitz is so thoroughly and purely an invention, so completely unbased on observed facts, that it is a wonder how it should ever have received so much attention, though it is probably quite as much founded on fact as some other noted systems,—as, for instance, those of Schelling and Hegel. But, when such systems are at many points inconsistent with themselves, the wonder grows that they could ever have been developed to such fulness in the author's mind as well as in the interest of the philosophic public. The theory of Leibnitz is irreconcilable with any rational or scientific doctrine of individual unity. According to it, the individual, so called, cannot even admit of a collective unity, such as belongs to an army or a nation, still less of the unity of a vital organism like an animal body. For these are supposed to be the effect of perpetual interaction of part on part and on environment, so that every part and the total result are thus continuously modified, exemplifying a law of cause and effect all through. All otherwise is it with the theory of Leibnitz; for his monads are all self-sufficient, so that no one can be affected by anything beyond itself, and each is a force only for its own conservation and development, never for operation on one another or others or on aught else. Hence, it is impossible for their aggregation to be ever anything more than so many contiguous unities, like grains of sand in a heap.

Then these monads are entirely unknown; and their infinitely multitudinous and minute existence and separate action are opposed to our conviction of individual unity, and equally opposed to the known action of our modalities in causal relation to each other. Again, Leibnitz makes time, space, matter, and motion to be, not any realities, but merely phenomena; but, if these are all nothing, what is there that is real? Our thoughts and volitions are no more real than matter and motion, which in the last analysis are subjective states; and these two classes of phenomena, the sensible and supersensible, are all we know or ever can know, and so the monads are nowhere found within the range of science or philosophy or common sense or imagination.

Still further, these monads are said to be without extension, and yet are perceived only under the relation of extension because of their aggregation; but how the inextended can be aggregated, collocated, and thence seem to be extended, he does not explain.

The difference between body and mind in this theory is quite pretty,—the difference between sleeping monads and waking monads, which, in the proper place, would be as good as some poetry; and to learn how these sleeping monads may be waked into life, and to see them rising, would be very interesting.

This theory has been much noticed because of the great name of its author, because of its appeal to a certain order of religious feeling, because of its alliance with a certain kind of atomistic rigid necessity in the world, and because of its inconsistent capability of being interpreted either in accord with dualism or modern materialism by judicious selections from its incoherent materials. Besides, it has the real merit of affirming that all things are intrinsic force, though they can affect only themselves.

Organic Atomism.

Far more simple as well as more familiar is the atomistic theory of material organicism, according to Epicurus, Lucretius, and modern evolution. This makes the *ego* to be an organic evolution from the world, changing as changes the action of the evolutionary forces, and perishing with the dissolution of the organism. The human *ego* is thus only an organic mode of the world-force. It is constituted by the building up of the material atoms in certain relations to each other into the living structure of the human body; and it continues to be the same only while they continue the same forms and relations, which is never a measurable moment at once, and it ends entirely when their organic existence and relations end. Emphatically is it true, according to this theory, as Dr. Maudsley unblushingly, and without any spasm of the larynx, observes, man "never continueth in one stay." This is thorough-paced atomism. Many who reject dualism and every form of spiritual monism are unwilling to avow this; and they prefer to obscure their position and mental action, and wrap themselves in the *nimbus* of agnosticism. This may be to their credit in some aspects, but not in any philosophical aspect. From the lofty position and faculty of immortal duration and ever-rising power and felicity as a supermaterial being down to the rank and condition of a mere congeries of animated material particles, an *ego* ever changing and speedily dissolving away, the descent is awful and horrid. Those who have cherished the loftier view, whose entire moral and spiritual life has wrought in accordance with it, who have found in it an elevating and ennobling enjoyment, cannot abandon it for this low-born theory without the very strongest of reasons. That man so far above himself should erect himself through all the ages, and with growing facility, delight, and grandeur as the human race makes progress, is immensely improbable. Beanstalks do not grow up into the clouds. Heaven-invading agencies must be of stronger and more enduring quality than material atoms organized into animal consciousness, which is constantly perishing as soon as it begins its existence. Such a thing as that could not survive the night for Jack to see it in the morning, much less climb up on it to the land of the giants. "The superior man" will demand something stronger as an argument against his best thought and life than the base and impotent negative that matter cannot prove spirit and immortal life. (Whoever thought it could?) And what else is our science of objective evolution than an utterance like this? It is the evolution of sensible phenomena and of all else from sensible phenomena; but it cannot prove to us that the power which underlies all these phenomena, and gives to them all their significance and importance,—that is, the subject which experiences them,—is not itself immortal. It has no right to speak on the question at all; and, but for its infinite impudence, it would be like the man at the wedding feast without a wedding garment on, speechless, and speechless it deserves to gnash its empty teeth forever.

Again, this ex-animal thinker of low development needs to be reminded of the principle that transient phenomena imply a perduring *ego* as their common subject, so that there is no such constant mutation and dissolution and generation of *egos* as atomism implies; and there is nothing in the world which philosophically implies any limit to the duration of the *ego*. If the principle of subjective continuity through all known and knowable phenomenal or modal changes fail, then intellectually (and morally, too)

> "The pillared firmament is rottenness,
> And earth's base built on stubble."

Our opponents may retort that this may be so for aught they know, and they may be willing to believe it. But we are not, and deem we have good reason for believing better things.

It is but right to add that the doctrine we oppose is contrary to a series of facts which are attested as directly and experientially known by a vast number of witnesses in all lands and all ranks of society and all grades of intelligence and culture. Passing by the ghost stories of the olden time, which have helped to keep alive the belief of immortality in the world, the phenomena of modern Spiritualism demand at the very least a suspension of judgment concerning personal extinction by organic dissolution. That there is much fraud and folly connected with this movement there can be no doubt; but let who says there is nothing else beware, lest he be found belying the oracles of the superior gods. It is not according to the spirit of science to say that all men are knaves or fools, because some are such at times. It is not the spirit of science which refuses to analyze, discriminate, and classify, or which draws final conclusions from a few experiments which do not exhaust all the methods and conditions of testing and determining the question under consideration, as Dr. Tyndall does in his singular paper on this subject. While I have given small attention to the phenomena in question, and have had little experience of them, I think there can be no reasonable doubt of the well-proved existence of very many facts which material atomists have not assimilated nor scarce attempted to explain in accordance with their philosophy ; and, till they have done this satisfactorily, they have no right to *affirm* that these phenomena *are not*, as is claimed, indicative of supra-mundane presence and agency. Let these dogmatic scientists remember that their own utterances will be short-lived in proportion as they overlook or ignore any class of facts, and the honors of a broader as well as a profounder philosophy will be won and worn by others.

Dichotomy.

On the other hand, if evolution is required to disprove or assimilate the phenomena of Spiritualism in order to be complete, so there is a reciprocal duty binding on the philosophical advocates of Spiritualism to square themselves with evolution, which cannot well be disputed, though its special bearing on the final philosophy may be questioned. Therefore, evolution must be recognized ; and all exposition must be in accordance with it. The external world is the source of our bodily organism. Of this there can be no doubt. And with this organism are vitally connected and identified an organic life and *ego*. Is this to be explained consistently with the supra-mundane theory of the existence of the individual as a self-conscious personality after the dissolution of the body ?

The advocates of the theory may invent an answer which satisfies themselves. They may suppose or conjecture that, along with the grosser world of the commoner senses, there is also a finer world which the grosser senses cannot discern (except in very rare and exceptional conditions which change their nature and action), and that, out of this finer world, a finer form of the *ego* is developed, which is the real and superior *ego;* that the two *egos* and worlds coincide, so far as the inferior extends, and until what is called death ; that the finer world and *ego* survive the dissolution of the grosser, and form then a more exclusively spiritual economy, with laws of action and enjoyment and expression peculiar to itself, so that it and its action can be made known to us in the gross body and world only partially under the limitations of certain poorly comprehended conditions.

Now let it be remembered that this finer *ego* and world, as co-existing along with the common world of our recognized senses, is only a conjecture. No such world is certainly known by us nor any such *ego* or evolving process. It may possibly be true, but that proves nothing. Yet, if the alleged phenomena of Spiritualism are true, and if this theory is necessary and sufficient for their explanation, it is worthy of respect. But, even in that case, it would be far better if Spiritualism could abut on a foundation of *known* fact, instead of resting on an ingenious theoretic invention, as it would thus become thoroughly philosophical. Here is indicated a defect which probably it can never supply.

This theory also involves a personal dualism which is irreconcilable with the unity of consciousness. It is analogous to the old dualistic doctrine of soul and body. But consciousness and science, physiological or psychological, know of no such a duality. These identify the body and the soul. As before observed, the soul identifies with itself all the motions, actions, pains, and pleasures of the body. Here, the unity is equally constant and perfect.

Further, if a part of what has ever been really *ego*, and especially so great and important a part as the body, can be separated from the *ego* and cease to be such, we may say the same of any other part and of all the parts : so that, after all, this *ego* is only an agglomeration of parts, whether organized or crystallized or merely juxtaposed. All definite conception of the *ego* thus vanishes, except as a varying aggregate of material atoms, of which we can never say it is so and so, because, before our sentence is uttered, it is, or may be, something else. We must steadily hold to an *ego* which is always one and the same through all changes, because this is demanded by experience, by logical consistency and definite conception.

Trichotomy.

All these difficulties are augmented and intensified in the theory of trichotomy. This makes the sensible organism the outer rind and husk of the *ego*. Within this is its animating force, the soul; and then within this is the reason or spirit,—the principle of pure intelligence, which gives to body and soul the light and authority of general laws and imperative principles. Such a triple *ego* is utterly fanciful. At least, we know nothing of it in this life. We know these three great lines of phenomena, but we know them as modes of the one, indivisible, only known *ego*. This conception is clear, consistent, and ultimate and all-sufficing and the simplest possible, so that nothing more is admissible,—a simple *ego* of many modes, among which are body, soul, and spirit.

Perhaps, however, it ought to be observed that this trichotomy is incomplete. It omits the regnant element of our nature,—the will. Will is the executive faculty, and hence it is often considered as the prime element of personality. These four great classes of faculty are integral parts of our nature as now existing and known. But they are inseparable, and have not merely an organic unity, but a substantive unity, which may possibly change in form, but not in substance. Will implies intelligence and feeling, else it would have neither guide nor motive of its action; and it implies a body of some form and kind as a fasciculus of personal power. So intelligence implies feeling, else there could be no preference of one thought to another, and no comparison of better and best; and feeling may be of various forms, sensible or supersensible. These are one in many, simplicity of substance or force with modal variety.

Logical Difficulties of all Forms and Pluralism.

All the four theories of pluralism which we have criticised involve in common certain logical falsities which through all the ages have been the vampires of the philosophy of pluralistic egoism. Sir William Hamilton, in support of his philosophy of the Conditioned,—a species of agnosticism, which with the Kantians was pure criticism,—reduced these illogical dicta to fifteen, and gave them utterance; and they are all involved in all theories of philosophy except those which explain matter, time, space, motion, and all sensible phenomena as spiritual,—the modes or subjective states of a simple unitary being; and these paralogisms are adduced and adopted by Spencer in his *First Principles* in justification of agnosticism, which is a denial or doubt of the possibility of philosophy. Certainly, no theory can be perfect which does not dissipate these contradictions. As truth is always self-consistent, every theory which involves self-contradictions is somewhere false.

One of these contradictions, as given by Hamilton, is as follows: "A quantity, say a foot, has an infinity of parts. Any part of this quantity, say an inch, has also an infinity (of parts). But one infinity is not larger than another. Therefore, an inch is equal to a foot." In these days there are some who imagine that the doctrine of ultimate atoms removes this logical difficulty as far as it concerns matter, because these atoms are indivisible. But who knows that they are indivisible? No one. The assertion is merely an unverified and unverifiable theory. But, if it were a known fact, it would not remove the difficulty as a conception. It is not an actual and sensible but a theoretical divisibility about which philosophy is concerned. It is a logical necessity that no atom of matter, no quantity of space or time, considered as objective realities, can be so small but it can be conceived as divisible, so that the smallest possible may yet be smaller, and the smallest may have as many parts as the largest. By no physical or dynamic theory of atoms as ultimate actual units can we escape these contradictions. All objective non-egoism is therefore slain by these hair-fine cimeters.

The Ego of Philosophical Realism a Pure and Simple Unity.

Philosophical realism, which is absolute egoistical idealism, is invulnerable to all such weapons. This theory is the most simple and modest, because it affirms nothing but the phenomena of consciousness (including sense), and their necessary logical implications. It is therefore entirely self-consistent, as well as conformable to facts, necessary to the explanation of facts, sufficient for that purpose.

It exemplifies, first, the unity of consciousness as of a personal individual perduring through all the many forms and conditions of experience, sensible or supersensible, organic or extra-organic or super-organic; so that, all known things being the conscious modes of one subject, we demonstrate the unity of all at once as egoistic. As this has been previously expounded, it needs no further elucidation here.

There is a class of very striking and extraordinary phenomena which have commanded much attention in recent times, and which in such a connection cannot be wisely overlooked. They constitute what is supposed by some to indicate a change of personality. Persons have been known to forget all at once everything in their past life, so that they have had to begin their education afresh from the very bottom or thereabouts. Then, again, after a while they have suddenly changed back to their first state, and their old knowledge and feelings and habits and dispositions return. While these phenomena are very striking, they present no special logical or psychological problem any more than any other changes of feeling and disposition and lapses of memory. The individual person is the same, whatever be his modal variations, and whatever be the extent or limit of his knowledge or memory of them. That he does not know that he has done so or so alters not the fact. He is, notwithstanding everything, the very one who did it; and he has been the one, the very same, through all the changes which have intervened, however numerous or various or long continued they may have been. We often forget what we did but a very few moments ago, and these minor but ever-recurring lapses of memory differ from the other only in degree; and as these involve the same principles, and give us no trouble on the score of identity, so neither should those. If in the morning I remember not the circumstances of my going to bed the night previous, which is quite too common with some men, that does not destroy the fact that I my very self did go to bed one way or another, and that I who thus lay down am the one who now gets up. The cases in question are simply unusual examples of modal changes in a perduring subject. For the identification of such persons we have to resort, in some degree, to the connection of circumstances. But, then, that is what we are all doing to some extent most of the time. That I am the one who did a certain act yesterday or last year, I prove to myself and others by the aid of circumstances, without which my memory would not serve me with due certainty.

But observe that I do not in any such case doubt that I am the same person I was yesterday or last year. I am only ignorant, or in doubt, concerning my own history. So, in all other cases, the only rational question is not whether any individual remains the same through successive modal changes, but only what are those changes, and how to determine that an individual now in a certain state or condition is the same individual as the one whom we knew in a very different state or condition, and this may be variously determined at different times; and whether determined or not, or how determined, does not affect the continuity of the individual himself. Every individual is a simple unity of force, a subject undergoing modal changes, the forms and extent of which we cannot anticipate. The plurality is in the modes or activities only ; and, because everything is a force ever active, it is always necessarily changing its own modes.

If our personal and conscious existence continues after our bodily dissolution, which I doubt not, and if it is made known by many infallible proofs, as a large number of respectable people affirm, we have still only the same individual under different psychological or subjective states. The sloughing off of the body is only a change in the modes of the soul. It loses nothing, parts with nothing. The body is ever only a mode of mind ; and, at death, the mind simply undergoes a change, so that the old bodily modes give place to other modes, just as daily one thought or experience gives place to another. We often say that at death the soul enters on another *state* of existence. That is a literal truth, the whole truth,—all that has occurred : only, the change is wholly subjective, not chiefly non-egoistic, as the vulgar suppose.

X.

THE ABSOLUTE AND LOCAL EGO.

LONG we dwell on the *ego*, and it is necessary ; for, in more senses than one, this is the pivot on which everything turns. Till the *ego* is well determined and defined, no further progress can be made or intelligently attempted. We can never know when we leave the *ego* till we know what the *ego* is ; and only after such knowledge is attained can we begin to understand the conditions on which a philosophical transit from the *ego* is possible.

The Absolute Ego.

It was the absolute *ego* which was expounded in the last chapter ; and this *ego* will be understood by very few for a long time, I fear, fit subject deemed by most for amusement instead of philosophical investigation.

The absolute *ego* readily emerges from an analysis of phenomena, all of which are found to be only subjective states, whatever their form or action or relations ; and the *ego* is simply their common subject, that of which they are the conscious modes. The *ego* must at least be commensurate with its own states or modes ; and, therefore, it cannot be less than co-extensive with the known universe forever. All time, all space, and all their contents and changes are one with their subject ; and their subject is the one absolute *ego*. Thus, I and all that ever has been known, is known, or ever can be known by me, are one, the only difference being that between the subject and its modes; and these are the same substance or force, for the modes are the subject or substance or force itself existing in said modes. This we will consider as having been sufficiently expounded and supported; that is, for all whom any amount of exposition and evidence could benefit. This is what we call spiritual monism. On this theory there is no possible discrimination of the *ego* from the *non-ego* within the bounds of the universe, because the *ego* includes all that universe. The absolute *ego* is all the knowable, and the *non-ego* is all the unknowable. This is precise and final.

This *ego* includes the whole deity of pantheism, which identifies God and the universe, from which I exclude God and all else except myself. Spinoza's deity is extension and thought, a duality which constitutes the universe in all its forces, forms, and activities; and all this I expound as constituting my own exclusive individuality.

One of the most notable of recent thinkers is Lotze, and he also identifies the world with God; though he does not say but that God transcends the world, and (however inconsistent) he sometimes seems to think of man as different from the world. On the other hand, our exposition allows of no such line of discrimination between God and man or between the world and man. The universal substance of the world which he pronounces to be God I call man and my own sole individuality, because it is certain that the known *ego* and the known world are one. If there is a God and any other being besides myself, they are purely extra-mundane. As says Emerson (Essays, First Series, p. 245), "The art of seeing and the thing seen, the seer and the spectacle, the subject and object, are one." But that does not include God and all beings, as he imagines, but only one man, the observing *ego*.

Against this absolute *ego*, sole individuality of the universe and constituting the universe, the empty shells and dried skins of effete metaphysics will be freely thrown ; and we must brush them aside. One of these is the assertion that the *ego* can become conscious only through interaction with the *non-ego*. Not a particle of proof has ever been offered of this dogma, which is worth as much as the poorest of dogmas in other departments of human invention ; and I take it for what it is worth. It has arisen from a confusion (very obvious in Fichte) of the absolute with the local or organic *ego*. The latter is evolved from the external world, and changes by interaction with it, which is *ego*, to the organic *ego*.

But the absolute *ego* includes the world and the organism, and its diversity of modes operate on each other or relative to each other. It is objectively conscious of itself in its consciousness of these diversified modes, which are itself ; and it needs nothing else as a condition of its conscious action. We may, if we will, call these diversities parts, and sometimes that will be convenient in practice ; and they are parts proper only in the sense that they are not *wholes*, but necessary constituents of One, the Grand Totality, which some call the Unknowable, some call God, and which I call *Ego*, which some think is unconscious, but which I know to be conscious, if it is I. All agree, however, in making this great Being a simple unitary force, with a possible infinity of modal diversity. Even those who attempt to deny it, and who, therefore, use the vaguest possible term to describe it, are obliged to come to this at last, allowing an ultimate "*potential* substratum, out of which issued the divisions and separations, the heterogeneity which constituted the properties and qualities on which all conscious experience depends." This I grant ; and, on the other hand, it must be also granted that this "heterogeneity" is the same potency and essential reality as the "potential substratum."

So that here, also, we have diversity as the modal unfoldings of the Abiding Unity, which is my doctrine; and this opposition to it is a mere logomachy. Fichte himself affirmed this kind of a simple unitary force, working and manifesting itself in infinite diversity, only he strangely mistook it for the *non-ego*, contrary to his idealism.

The Local Ego.

There is a special and elliptic form of the *ego* which we will designate as the local *ego*. This is limited, because local, in distinction from being everywhere. The absolute *ego* is virtually omnipresent: this is limited and localized, though it may not be agreed as to what are its exact boundaries. This local *ego* is variously conceived, and all the disputes among psychologists concerning the *ego* have been about the local *ego*. It was necessary to discriminate such an *ego* from the *non-ego*, because the *non-ego* is supposed to be known, and indefinitely vaster than the *ego*. But this necessary task has not been satisfactorily performed; and the local *ego* has assumed different aspects to the mind, according to the method of performing this task.

The Local Ego defined as Transphenomenal, and all Phenomena as Non-ego.

Some philosophers have pronounced all phenomena to be non-egoistic; and the *ego* they have considered to be a transphenomenal subject and agent, lexically connected with organic phenomena. This is the method of the pre-scientific mind, and of the initial stages of scientific inquiry; and this method often shoots far onward, into the era of cultivated thought. It is the source of Plato's doctrine of superhuman ideas as the regnant principles of the human mind; for those ideas are not described as modes of the human mind, but as external to the mind, though intimately connected with it, as divine glories at which it gazes with a charmed reverence. The doctrine of the non-egoistic nature of all phenomena finds distinct utterance even in so recent a writer as Bishop Berkeley, who was Platonic in his spirit and style, though he was an ardent nominalist. In the first paragraph of his *Principles of Human Knowledge*, Berkeley describes ideas as follows : "It is evident to any one who takes a survey of the objects of human knowledge that they are either ideas actually imprinted on the senses or else such as are perceived by attending to the passions and operations of the mind, or lastly ideas formed by the help of memory and imagination." It is clear that he uses the term idea with the same breadth of meaning as Descartes and Locke, to denote all phenomena, whether sensible or supersensible. In the next paragraph, contrary to the theory of Descartes and Locke, perhaps unconsciously, he says the *ego* is something besides these, as a different thing from them. "But, *besides* all that endless variety of ideas or objects of knowledge, there is likewise something which knows or perceives, and exercises divers operations, as willing, imagining, or remembering about them. This perceiving, active being is what I call mind, *spirit, soul, or myself. By which words I do not denote any one of my ideas, but a thing entirely distinct from them.*" This is clear and distinct verbally. The *non-ego*, according to this, is immediately known, and that with indubitable certainty, because it constitutes the phenomena of sense and consciousness. Whenever the mind acts or is conscious, the *non-ego* is then present as a known object. This is the most simple and easy method that could be invented of transcending the *ego*. The *non-ego* is of two kinds, sensation and reflection ; and the former, according to Berkeley, is created by God, and the latter by the human mind, or *ego*.

This theory, in the first place, is antiquated by modern psychology, which makes all phenomena to be modes of the *ego*, and one with it. In the second place, the distinction between *ego* and *non-ego* is merely verbal, an intellectual void. The *ego* rendered absolutely unphenomenal is therefore unknowable and inconceivable, so that it cannot be discriminated from or identified with anything whatsoever. On the other hand, if all phenomena are *non-ego*, most or all of our mental processes, so called, lose their significance. All pronouns, personal and possessive, are nullified. Thought, feeling, volition, are neither states nor qualities nor acts of the mind or spirit; and we have no means of knowing that they represent our mind or spirit, or sustain any relation to it. All principles are destroyed, and all intellectual guides and indicators are obliterated; and it is utterly gratuitous to talk of the mind, or *ego*, forming and compounding ideas of reflection by the help of memory and imagination, or any other way. Every assertion whatsoever concerning its nature and action and relations is utterly unwarrantable. In the third place, its explanation of the origin and existence of sensible phenomena by referring them to the creative will of God is a vast and needless leap, however pious. A philosopher will spare himself such an effort, if he can find an easier explanation; and this explanation is found in the subjectivity of all phenomena. But it may be also found in Berkeley's own doctrine of the *ego*. If it is unphenomenal and the author of the ideas of reflection, it may be the author of the ideas of sensation. The only objection he brings against the subjective origin of the sensible work is that it is involuntary. He assumes that it is different from us, because against or irrespective of our volition, forgetting that he has already defined volition as non-egoistic: so that to be different from it is not to be different from the *ego*.

The Local Ego conceived as Supersensible and Sensible Phenomena as Non-ego.

The next method to be noticed is that which defines the sensible phenomena only as *non-ego*, and affirms that all the phenomena of interior consciousness are egoistic. This is the old dualism of matter and spirit in its purity. On this theory, the *non-ego* is composed of our organism and all sensible objects beyond it; and, then, all that is identified with the remaining forms of experience is *ego*, spirit. We are conscious of various experiences which have in them no element of extension or motion or any recognized form of matter or sense. These are all egoistic and spiritual and modes of the *ego*, which pronounces itself a spirit in distinction from matter; and it is also conscious of perceiving sensible phenomena as external to itself and non-egoistic.

This sensible *non-ego* has been considered by many others as only a series of images flashed upon us by God, a series of divine acts, a multifarious form of the divine energy. But that involves vast theistic assumptions, and such a creed should wait on proof or some reasonable evidence. It is more simple and ulterior to say with common dualists that matter is a solid, forceful reality of many varying forms or modes, which, according to its nature and internal relations and its various external relations, operates upon itself and upon us.

As the personal *ego* is thus contradistinguished from matter, it is free from all the elements of mutability which are characteristic of all the organic forms of matter; and its immortal capability and independence are thus disclosed as possible and highly probable. We hence see also that it cannot be evolved from any previous condition of matter.

This is a fair picture; but, like all pictures, it shows only one side. It is dualism in its most unsophisticated form of philosophic creation. A lunatic said he had two sides to his head, a potato side and a brain side; and that he was sane or insane according as he spoke from one side or the other of his unfortunate cephalic dualism. We have seen one side: now let us see the other. This other shows all human action, utterance, and history a mere dead force. The soul of things is fled. Man has left the stage, and mere puppets play in his place and name. All men, so called, and all their motion and action and speech, as known to each other and to history, are only the motions of organic matter, never of real men and human beings. All the play of domestic and social or public life and interest, all the inventions and discoveries of physical science, all physical work, pleasures, pains, battles, sieges, wounds, healing, nursing, are nothing essentially human, only the various plays of material elements. War, murder, death, birth, marriage, kisses, tears, laughter, groans, and songs have all lost their chief, their human significance and importance. Where before we had seen the flow and eddyings of a vast and varied tide of human beings, now wallowing in vice or reeking with blood and crime, now flashing with the coruscations of bright genius, now gleaming in the loveliness of beauty, or shining in the loftier power and charm of pure goodness, we now see nothing but so many automatic motions of matter as distinguished from spirit, non-human, unconscious. It may be said that these phenomena are symbols of human realities. But, as a system of symbolism, it is not less ghastly than the Ancient Mariner's company of dead shipmates working at the ropes, without the associated relief or explanation of angelic agency.

The further and popular allegation that these bodies are really alive, conscious, and purposeful, being animated by spirits which use them as their several instruments, is good, if admitted; but it furnishes a reason for its own rejection. For, if a finite spirit can give life and conscious energy and purpose, much more may the Infinite Spirit do the same for all these forms ; and, for aught we can see to the contrary, the evolution of this result may be, under certain conditions, a necessity from nature's intrinsic force. And, as this is the more simple and scientific hypothesis, it is to be preferred, so that we are bound to dispense with the hypothesis of finite spirits distinct from matter, and step at once on to the more solid and sensible foundation of materialism, pure and simple.

This theory is utterly without proof or evidence at any point; and it is everywhere inconceivable, because it is either a mental void or a self-contradiction. As we know of no mental phenomena dissociated from matter, so we have no evidence that they are not at the bottom the same. There are different classes of phenomena, but this is no proof that they have not the same subject and substance. It is also too late in the day to pronounce all sensible phenomena to be *non-ego*. So far as the *ego* is connected with the organism, it is identified with the organism. We always say "me" and "my" concerning bodily forms, feelings, and motions, and that they are egoistic is as well proved as that any of our mental states are.

The Local Ego defined as Organic and the Non-ego as Extra-organic, which gives us the Physiological Ego.

This brings us to the physiological *ego* of the material monists, who hold that mind and matter are one, and differ only in their aspects or phases ; that the organism is the *ego*, which changes as changes the organism, and which therefore begins and ends its existence with the animated organism. This theory is burdened with the contradiction of consciousness affirming personal unity and sameness all through life, while its individual substance is not the same. The me of yesterday is not the me of to-day, while consciousness affirms that it is. No one ever attempted in a criminal court to prove an alibi on the ground that the crime imputed to him was committed a long time ago, though on this theory he has abundant right to do so. The spontaneous as well as the reflective action of consciousness repudiates the theory; and all human institutions are based on that repudiation, for they all assume the continued personal sameness through all organic changes. Without this, society could not exist, and life itself would be impossible. To say that the *ego*, or conscious unity, is the organic unity, which at any moment prevails, is only to say that this *ego* is forever changing, never the same; because this is the case, not only with the material particles of the organization, but also with the form and action of the organic structure in many of its functions and faculties. On this theory, it is true that we may say "I"; but it must always be of as well as in the present only. It is I who write this word, but it is not the same "I" who wrote some of the earlier pages. Yet my consciousness affirms that it was the same "I" who wrote at the far distant times, thus contradicting the theory. In all this, it is like the antiquated French sensism.

On the other hand, it is very clear that there is a relation of responsibility between successive periods of the same community. A nation may be saddled with a duty to-day, because of an act of the nation generations or centuries ago. This is constantly seen in the action of its internal economy. It is exemplified very constantly in the application of common and statute law; and we all easily see how certain actions of parents may devolve obligations on their heirs for generations, and one administration of government devolves obligations on another, though the latter may be of very different political views. But it is only by mental confusion that any one can imagine, as some have done, that these facts favor the doctrine of physiological egoism. The communication of responsibility is not limited either to the same individuality or organic connection, but only by power and circumstance. The story of the "Good Samaritan" suffices to show that responsibility is derived from opportunity and power in given circumstances, no matter who is responsible for the situation. An action of one generation devolves duties on another generation, not because the latter generation is morally responsible for the first, but because each and all are under obligation always to do the best they can with their powers and opportunities. Our relations to each other, whether individual or corporate, affect our obligations, not because we are parts of a common and organic individuality, but because of our personal individuality in relation to others. Each is responsible for his own action in all connections, and that collectively constitutes the action of the whole.

On the physical side, there is found in the modern discoveries, by the microscope, of germ-cells a strong argument in favor of a bold utterance to the effect that personality is but the abiding expression of an organic combination whose constituents are always changing. The organism is made up of an indefinite number of microscopic cells, each of which is alive, an organism in itself, and gifted, like the general organism into which it enters, with the power of procreation or self-multiplication, and that by three (or four) different methods. According to this, there is a combination of a vast number of individualities in each organism, and our personal individuality is their combined and organized expression and representative ; and thus its continuity and responsibility are analogous to that of a municipality or a nation, which in its corporate capacity is represented by its legislature, its executive, and its judiciary. Communities are held responsible, though always changing, and in this they are like our organic individuality ; and they, too, are organic individuals, only they are more complex organisms than that of our body. To escape this result, a result which was claimed before these cells were discovered, dualism was invented, according to which the organism is not the *ego* or a constituent of it, that the *ego* is a spirit in contradistinction from matter, spirit being alleged to be one and simple and continuous, and that the individuality of communities is only figurative.

Sensism can defend itself against dualism by showing the radical, logical inconsistencies of the latter. Yet the latter possesses a vast and manifest advantage in its appeal alike to reason and consciousness in support of its fundamental position that the *ego* is substantively one and the same through all organic or other changes. This is infinitely more sublime than its opposite, and it is in perfect accord with all mental and moral phenomena ; while its opposite is not. However much we may explain and evade, it still remains clear that responsibility belongs only to agents ; and these are responsible only for their own action, not for any action which is attributed to them hypothetically merely because of certain organic associations. Two animals of different species have been organically spliced together, so that they shared the same blood and organic life ; and what fed or poisoned either fed or poisoned both. Men might be treated in the same way ; and nature did this for the Siamese twins. A good man and a bad man might thus be conjoined, retaining their separate and opposite moral consciousness and character, which are always wholly and absolutely individualistic. In the community, each is responsible only for himself ; and, if he suffers from others, that is not a moral consequence relative to himself, is not a moral punishment to him. On the assumption of this perduring, substantive individualism, all thought and all action proceed ; and no analogies or arguments can change or obscure it. Here, sensism of every form is baffled and beaten into hopeless defeat.

But, though dualism is irrefutable in its affirmation

of an *ego* which remains absolutely the same unit all the way through the progression of the hours and years with their multifarious metamorphoses, yet it has a weak point which it cannot protect,—its denial of the unity of body and mind. Here, the physiological psychologists occupy an impregnable position. Their arguments against dualism are conclusive, and they ought to be repeated till they become universally effective. There is a law of invariable relations between certain conditions of brain and certain forms of consciousness, and these connections are historic and evolutionary. This *ego*, therefore, is not strictly constant, but variable. It constitutes the aggregate of conscious states existing at any given time. Hence, also, it has all the extension which belongs to organic phenomena. This individuality is an inconstant field of life, of special form and development, a definable portion of the larger life of universal nature, a portion which is transient, as all the various forms of this universal nature are transient. This *ego* is therefore susceptible of disintegration in various forms and degrees, and to the utmost; and with the signs of such operations we are painfully familiar in bodily diseases, in mental derangement, and in some forms of vice and crime. Since this *ego* is composed of all organic forms and forces and motions, with the brain as the central organ of bodily synthesis, sympathy, and synergy, it follows that the disorganization of the cerebral centre is the dissolution of this *ego*, so far as the dissolution of the physiological unity extends.

On physiological grounds (which are also ultimately psychological grounds), Dr. Maudsley is rigidly just and scientific in using the following language: "The consciousness of self, the unity of the *ego*, is a consequence, not a cause; the expression of a full harmonious function of the aggregate of differentiated mind centres, not a mysterious metaphysical entity lying behind function and inspiring and guiding it; a subjective synthesis or unity, based on the objective synthesis or unity of the organism. As such, it may be obscure, deranged, divided, apparently transformed. For each breach of the unity of the united centres is a breach of it: subtract any one centre from the intimate physiological co-operation, the self is *pro tanto* weakened or mutilated ; obstruct or derange the conducting function of the associating bonds between the various centres, so that they are dissociated or disunited, the self loses in corresponding degree its sense of continuity and unity ; stimulate one or two centres or groups of centres to a morbid hypertrophy, so that they absorb to them most of the mental nourishment and keep up a predominant and almost exclusive function, the personality appears to be transformed ; strip off a whole layer of the highest centres, ... you reduce man to the condition of one of the higher animals ; take away all the supreme centres, you bring him simply to the state of a sentient creature ; remove the centres of sense, you reduce him to a bare vegetative existence, when, like a cabbage, he has an objective, but no subjective *ego*." (*Body and Will*, Part Third, Sec. 6.)

To this theory considered as "the conclusion of the whole matter," a fatal objection is presented by one of our modern sciences, the science of optics, whose long and undisputed deliverances on this subject Mr. Maudsley and all physiological egoists here overlook. Optics teaches that the objects of sight are never the same as those of touch : so that the tangible and visible organisms are not only dissimilar, but numerically different. It follows that there are at least two physiological *egos;* and there is no unity or community between them, unless we go back to an extra-physiological and extra or supra organic reality and agent, which is common to both of these organisms, and to all phenomena ; and this agent is our absolute *Ego*. Thus, this physiological egoism is broken utterly asunder ; and it can find no rational or logical and scientific bond until it abut on our basis and adopt our doctrine of an absolute and universal *Ego* as well as the sub-doctrine of a local and physiological *ego* as one of the generic classes of the modes of the great and absolute *Ego*.

This narrow conclusion of pure organicism is the prevailing view of modern science working on the physiological side of our nature. It is modern sensism; and it coincides with a very early, if not primitive, notion of man. Indeed, it shows the still common and popular line of demarkation between the *ego* and *non-ego;* and, in spite of themselves, it invades all isms and theories. But a faithful and progressive conformity to this method leads us to far loftier heights and broader and grander vistas than material monism can ever attain. It leads us to the discovery of an *Ego* which is infinitely more glorious than the organic or physiological *ego*. The same style of investigation and argument which identifies the organic soul and body, or proves the organism to be *ego*, compels us to identify both these and all extra-organic phenomena with a super-organic *ego*, commensurate with them all in duration, in spatial extension, power and variability,—a modal variability,—while itself remains the same, the same substance or force. While the organism is *ego*, it is not the whole of *ego*. All the known, *including* the organism as a very small fraction, is *ego;* and the physiological *ego* is not discriminated, as is supposed, from the *non-ego*, but only from certain other forms of the general or absolute *Ego*, and so the degeneration and dissolution of the physiological *ego* are only a small modal change in the absolute or total *Ego*.

The Panheisenist Ego.

Here creeps in panheisenism. If there is an *ego* general and an *ego* local, and *as many local egos as animated organisms*, and if these constitute all the knowable universe, what is this but to say, with

Spinoza, that the universe is one being and substance, with many special forms of conscious, personal beings of limited power and duration perpetually evolving from it and then again relapsing into it? It will be very natural and easy for some to state my doctrine in this way, and draw the inference contained in this interrogation. For we are seldom duly careful or competent to understand an unwelcome system or theory and its logical issues. Therefore, I so state it now by anticipation, to prevent such perversion. *The terms above italicized are incorrect.* I have affirmed only one known *ego*, local or general. The many local personalities are only apparent. I, who affirm my personality in connection with my organism, affirm that other organic forms are not persons, but only symbols of persons and modes of myself : so that I recognize but one being in all the universe, myself, who am the conscious subject of all the knowable. So that the absolute and universal being of this theory is an entirely different conception from the unconscious and impersonal universal absolute existence of those philosophies which have been considered pantheistic or panheisenistic. This existence as expounded thus far in Philosophical Realism is simply and solely my own conscious individual self, multifarious and ever-changing in its conscious states. It is always and forever absolutely alone, knowing itself only, and evolving only into new forms of its conscious self without end, but never more than one consciousness or conscious subject.

Now, the question arises whether I am the only reality. On this question there will be no serious debate, so that we may consider it settled as soon as raised. We all believe in the existence of other beings. On what grounds? In experiential knowledge, I am shut up to myself, which includes the whole universe. How can this be scientifically transcended? This is the great question for us to answer, now that we have thoroughly defined the *ego*.

XI.
Inductive Method of Transcending the Ego.

WHEN we speak of transcending or of being shut up in the *ego*, we must hold clear in mind what *ego* we mean, whether the absolute or the local *ego*. We are always transcending the local *ego*, are, indeed, always beyond it as well as in part within it. Sight and touch directly acquaint us with objects which are external to the organism; but those objects external to the organism, or local *ego*, are modes of the absolute *ego*. What we need now is a method of transcending the absolute *ego*, which is our total individuality, in distinction from the local *ego*, which is a part of the absolute *ego*.

Fichte's Efforts at Transcending the Ego.

The failure to notice this important distinction is one of the causes of the failure to find a logical egress from the true and total *ego*. It makes the whole effort confused and inconsistent. There is a frequent unconscious sliding between the local and absolute *ego*, and, because the local *ego* is transcended, a halt is made as if that were all that is called for; while the dimly perceived inconsistency of this with the doctrine that all phenomena, whether beyond the organism or not, are egoistic, reveals a hopeless bewilderment. This describes a phasis of nearly all modern philosophies of perception from the time of Descartes, but especially of German philosophy since the time of Kant.

Here, the failure of Fichte is not more real, though it is more striking than the rest of Kant's followers. Like his master Kant, he was critical rather than constructive; and his failure was just what the critical philosophy necessitated. His failure was also made the more complete, because of his defective knowledge of induction and his erroneous notion of substance and quality. He held the old superannuated doctrine which, in different nations and ages, has been variously designated or indicated as the doctrine that we do not know things in themselves, but only certain phenomena with which they are in some inconceivable way connected; that, especially, while quality or attribute is known, substance is unknown, except as an unphenomenal, inconceivable something which is supposed to be necessary to the action and existence of phenomena, or attribute or quality. This doctrine generates nescience and contradiction everywhere. It throws an equal shadow over *ego* and *non-ego*. Both are shut away from us in perfect darkness. We have nothing to start from and nowhere to go to. We must at least have the *ego* known, in order to begin an inquiry for the *non-ego*. If the prime substance or essence of the *ego* is not known in consciousness, and is of that non-distinguishable and inconceivable character (without *character*) as the so-called substance or thing in itself, then, of course, it is utterly impossible for any distinctive individuality ever to be proved, whether *ego* or *non-ego ;* and even the conceptual distinction between them and between all things fades away, for all characteristics have perished. Pure and universal phenomenalism is the necessary result, and here it is agreed on all hands Fichte was held in logical confinement.

But Fichte differed from other philosophers on this subject only in his superior boldness and thoroughness. He only carried their doctrine to its logical issue. They laugh at him, and know not that they are pouring a double ridicule on their own heads. In this, they are all alike.

Very different is the logical position of Philosophical Realism. It holds that substance and quality and phenomena are one, so that, in knowing phenomena, we know substance or the thing in itself, which is always and only quality or force. Hence, the *ego* is the conscious subject, whose very essence or substance we know in knowing phenomena as subjective states; because these are the *ego*, its very substance and essence existing in these modes. Therefore, one substance we absolutely know in its very essence; and our conception of it is definite, clear, and precise,—a force active, and manifested as the modes of consciousness.

But another and chief cause of Fichte's failure was his *superficial and unsteady view of his own logical position.* His doctrine of idealism absolutely isolates each individual, and makes him commensurate and identical with the whole universe knowable to him. This, I believe, he never saw, though he saw what so clearly implies it, the egoism of all phenomena. Indeed, no idealist has ever clearly seen this. It is one of the most astonishing of historic phenomena, as an illustration of the fragmentary working of the human mind, that one of these should be so generally seen, and the other never seen, though the two are one. Hence, Fichte generally speaks as if all men belonged to the same world and were partial exemplifications of its one mighty force, which at first evolves them and then reabsorbs them into its mighty unity. He is thus really an objective evolutionist of a vague and indefinite rank. I will give a free translation of an eloquent passage from his *Vocation* or *Destiny of Man* (*Die Bestimmung des Menschen*), which shows his prevailing thought on this subject. It is as follows:—

"We behold ourselves in the midst of a vast concatenation of forces, in which no one can work for himself without working for another, in which the prosperity of one is the prosperity of all,—a spectacle whose beauty and harmony and intrinsic beneficence, which we behold in infinite manifoldness, make our spirit mighty. The interest rises when a man begins to consider himself as an integral member of this great intrinsic unity. The sense of our dignity and power still rises when a man says, as every man may: My life is not vain and fruitless! I am a necessary member of the great connection which moves ever onward from the evolution of the first man to its full manifestation in eternity." Such radical and unrecognized contrariety of thought is proof of partial and inadequate comprehension of both sets of thought, so that no philosophic issue is possible. He flies from one system of thought to the other with more speed and agility than Ariel, and so easily that he is all unconscious of the infinite gulf he has crossed. Still, his great achievement is not unparalleled. Indeed, it has from his day to this been a common and every-day performance by advanced psychologists; for all these have resolved all phenomena into modes of the *ego*, and then they have straightway proceeded to speak as if the great organic connectional unity called the world (Fichte's *Verbindung*) were a non-egoistic thing, on whose common surface all men subsist. Concurrently admitting that all phenomena are egoistic, they fail to see the truth of the same thought put in its converse form, that the *ego* comprises always all the known universe, all its forms, motions, forces on the earth or in the heavens, organic or inorganic ; and, while the former is admitted by the competent, the latter is universally denied, and scouted as lunacy. It is the lunacy of this effete metaphysical method which here stubbornly stands in the way of the positive method which seeks a consistent generalization and ordination of what we know by experience.

This universal blunder arises, as we have said, from the failure to discern the distinction between the absolute and the local *ego*. The local *ego* is related to the world, as they describe that relation. It is evolved from the world, and returns to the world. It is one of the parts and forms of the great world's force and action, and it originates, develops, and decays by lexical regularity and necessity, just as Fichte describes in the passage above quoted, where he also assumes that he is thus describing the course of the whole man, man as man ; whereas, he is really describing only one of the innumerable complex modes of man's existence and action,— a description of the relation of the organic *ego* to the inorganic and preorganic *ego* which constitute the kosmos, which, again, is a mode of the absolute *ego*, which is the true and complete or total *ego*, and that which philosophers have never recognized, though all affirm that all the known universe is *ego*, or a series of subjective states.

Here, all theories are equally faulty. They never pretend to transcend the universe ; and, therefore, they never transcend the *ego*, though they know it not, and see not their inconsistency. Phenomenal fulness and completeness and logical unity demand that we find a scientific egress from the *ego*. How shall this be accomplished ? Past failures to answer the question enjoin, not silence or despair, but fresh effort, guided by lights which those failures supply. Let us also be reminded that no failures of theoretic construction can alter facts. The inscription of truth on the granite walls of the universe is not erased by our unsuccessful effort to decipher it. Part of this inscription we know, that all we immediately know is *ego*, and this is neither to be ignored nor perverted merely because we cannot yet read the rest of the inscription.

But, while only the *ego* is known, an altruistic faith is universal ; and on this faith all thought and action proceed. It is the scientific justification of this faith which is the task now on the hands of philosophy.

Sematism the Basis of Induction.

An immediate knowledge of the *non-ego* is forever impossible. It is only possible, at the utmost, to reach an indirect proof of its existence and character by inference from the known. But it is also possible for this proof to be so clear and strong and scientific as to satisfy all the demands of the most rigorous investigation, and I am quite confident of being able to give as good an *inductive* proof as science usually requires in concrete investigations. Deductive or demonstrative proof I do not promise. This is a necessary inference from accepted premises; and no other inference is admissible in the abstract sciences, as in pure mathematics. This argument, and no other, always forms a perfect syllogism, if formulated. It is not always, nor even generally, available in the concrete sciences, whether physical or psychical. Here, induction must suffice; and induction is a probable or reasonable, but not necessary, inference from accepted premises. In deduction, the premises always contain the conclusion. In induction, they never do.

We may adduce the modern proof of the derivation of the horse from the Eocene Eohippus and Orohippus as an example of a good induction, which is yet not the very clearest and strongest. The induction is based on resemblances of structure, on known laws of structural mutation and evolution, which are indirectly observed to obtain and operate in a line between these two extremes or terms, the Eocene animal and the modern horse; and, though all the connections cannot be traced in the geological record, yet what we do know of this record is taken by nearly all physical scientists as a sufficient ground for the inference that the later animal is evolved from the earlier. What we know, the actual phenomena of geological science, are taken as *signs* of what we do not know. As a different and far stronger example of induction, we may adduce the law of gravitation, which always and everywhere, as far as we can go, admits of being tested, and which has been verified wherever tested, and which yet may possibly fail to answer to the test in some future experiment, though that is utterly improbable; but all that we know is considered as an *index or sign* of the extension of the law beyond the region of our experience.

This leads us back to a presupposed law or doctrine of Sematology, implied in all induction. Sematology is based on the knowledge of nature as a force.

All force is necessarily active and effective, according to its nature and quantity or degree. Its action and effect must, therefore, be absolutely uniform in the same connections, so long as its nature is the same. This is a logical necessity from the conception of being as a force, and it is supported by our experience of nature's uniformity. This principle of nature's uniformity is the basis of all induction and all that is necessary for its exposition. It is useless and futile to enter into a long and elaborate and obscure inquiry for the support of a questionable hypothesis of causation, like that of John Stuart Mill. It is enough for every purpose of science and every inductive argument to know that nature always operates in the same way. From this, we can proximately anticipate its action where we cannot sensibly trace it, and draw reasonably probable conclusions where we cannot verify them. Hence it is that, to a skilled anatomist and physiologist, a fossil bone is a good, though not a perfect, index to the whole skeleton to which it belonged, and to the habits of the living animal; and the conclusion which we thus reach from these phenomena as signs is an induction. Hence it is that, by induction in every department of human research, we are enabled to widen indefinitely the area of mediate knowledge; and, in every department of practical life, we are also, hence, enabled to regulate our action, so as to secure good, and escape evil to a degree.

Many writers are (sometimes at least) under an erroneous impression (fostered by one portion of Mr. Mill's inconsistent work on Logic) that nothing can properly be called science till it is verified by experience. This makes the reasoning power to be always only a servitor to experience, instead of a grand and superior complement of experience. This is not sustained by the course of any of the acknowledged sciences. They do, indeed, indefinitely extend the area and particularity of our experiential knowledge; and this is their primal object and the foundation of their progress, but it is not their largest, their grandest and most ulterior result. These are all inferences beyond experience or the physical possibility of experience. Such are the law of gravitation, the paths of some of the comets, all the past conditions of the kosmic universe, all the past history of the flora and fauna of our own world, and very many of the relations of existing phenomena, of which examples can be given in every recognized science. Verified experiential knowledge is, therefore, but a very minute fraction of what are included in the legitimate conquests and treasures of modern science. Experience is the fulcrum on which we rest our inductive lever, which is a compound of the principle of lexical sequences and of the sematic significance of all phenomena, as lexically related to each other or to something beyond our experience.

We are thus led to see that all inductive reasoning is a process of lexical sematism, and the word Sematology describes the ultimate philosophical character of induction. By the uniformity of nature, certain events necessarily become signs of other events which are as yet beyond our experience. The most striking exemplification of the certainty and uncertainty which attend the application of this principle in practical life is seen in the phenomena of "circumstantial evidence" in criminal cases. We combine and concatenate the phenomena which are considered as signs of certain events into a strong inductive argument. Yet it may not be true, and an opposing argument of equal or greater strength may be constructed from these phenomena in different combinations. The whole argument on both sides is a process of sematism; and, though the result is less certain here than in many departments of acknowledged science, yet sematism is no less essential to induction in one department than in another. In some concrete sciences there is more certainty in sematic or inductive reasonings than in others, as in astronomy compared with sociology; yet it is equally necessary in all. In all, it is the great light of modern thought, the electric illuminator of the modern scientific world, which without it would speedily perish in utter darkness.

Now let us apply this principle in prosecuting the most important of the sciences, Psychology, especially in relation to the senses. We will begin with the relations of the senses to each other. Here, we are in a path not wholly untrodden. Indeed, practical sematology in some form or other, and in some degree of comparative purity, is as old as human thought, though the reflective exposition of it must necessarily come in at a late epoch, and a scientific justification of it has, I believe, never before been attempted. Berkeley's theory of vision made it necessary for him to utilize it more conspicuously than any preceding thinker. Following in the wake of Berkeley, though deviously, blindly, and protestingly, Dr. Reid also makes some use of the principle. But neither of them could explain its grounds and reasons, because neither had any adequate philosophical or scientific conception of nature and force.

Sematism between the Several Senses.

To begin, then, where Berkeley used it, in the comparison of one sense with another. All the phenomena of one sense have a lexical connection with those of all other senses, and on this account each can stand as a sign in relation to all the others. While the objects of each sense are different from all the rest, they are practically connected and made of mutual service only by the law of Sematology. What I see I cannot hear, because I see only color and hear only sound. But because of the uniformity of the action of the senses, what I see is a sign of what I may hear or touch or smell or taste; and, on the other hand, the action of any of these other senses may become a sign for the action of sight. In short, the prior action of any sense is a sign of what may be the experience of any other sense; and so each allures to pleasure or warns of pain, and acts as sentinel and signal for all the senses, and also for internal consciousness.

On this basis, we are able to prosecute extended, systematic researches, the results of which will by classification and generalization form distinct sciences as well as scientific conclusions, because the uniformity and fixedness of nature afford a sematology for all science as well as for all practical life.

Sematism between all the Senses and their Common Subject.

So far, its action is all subjective. All the senses and all their objects are egoistic, and we have considered their action only relative to each other. A step further, and we consider all the senses relative to their subject. On our principle of sematism it is that my organism is especially and pre-eminently the sign and symbol of my sensitive and cognitive and absolute individuality. It is not itself that individuality, proper and total; for that individuality

spreads over all the universe, all of whose lights and
shadows, forms and motions, are its various modes
and inadequate manifestations of its all-pervading
presence. Of this wondrous individual, the organism,
as the local *ego*, is the special symbol. The organism
fills a peculiar and extraordinary office. While all
known things are equally modes of myself, nothing
else sustains to my experience and action and responsibility the same office and relation as those which
belong to my own organism. Through it, and usually
through it only, by laws which are more or less familiar, I become the *organically* related subject of
certain external or extra-organic experiences, and by
means of it I change or modify these external experiences in various ways and degrees. Thus, in certain conditions and relations of the organism, I have
certain experiences of sensible phenomena which are
external to the organism. In the light, for instance,
with my eyes open, I discern certain visible objects,
and, by varying my organic position and direction of
vision, I change the visible objects. Likewise, external, tangible objects are discerned and varied by
varied organic connections. These objects are truly
external to our organism, and not a part of that organism, as the clouds, the church-spire, the hand of
my friend, or my cane or pen; and so these objects
are not themselves my *organic* changes or phenomena or experiences. Their subject is therefore extra-
organic, the total or absolute *ego*, which is the
common subject of both organic and sub-organic and
super-organic phenomena.

Sematism between the Ego and its Organism.

I also treat my own organism as my representative
relative to all other organisms, and in special and
distinctive contrast with all other modes of myself;
and, in that light, I treat it with pre-eminent distinction and respect. It may be indifferent to me how
stars and sky and earth and certain animated forms

are treated. It is far otherwise when action or speech is directed toward my organism. That is addressed to me, and treated accordingly. Through this, also, I have feelings which come to me through no other medium ; and my pains and pleasures are so peculiarly identified with it that with it I peculiarly identify myself, and say of it I or me.

My organism is also treated by other organisms precisely in the same way as the symbol or embodiment of a distinct personal agency, and as such it is courted, favored, shunned, feared, opposed ; and, thence, speech as well as action takes shape and direction.

Sematism between our Organism and Other Organisms.

There is, in the next place, an evident and peculiar causal connection between our action and that of other human forms (as well as animal forms). We know that their action often varies regularly relatively to ours, proving clearly that the antecedent and consequent are somehow related to each other as cause and effect. But the peculiarity here is that all the forms seem to be animated by passion and will, while they are certainly not animated by the passion and will of our local *ego*. We know our own feelings and volitions, and their connection with our own organism. But those other forms and motions have no such connection with our consciousness; and, sometimes and not unfrequently, they are in decided and forceful opposition to all our desires and most earnest endeavors. How, then, can we escape the inference that they are the symbols of other spirits who thus express and exert their passion and will and power? This is the universal and spontaneous inference of the human mind, an inference which the latest science justifies and necessitates and explains. The pre-scientific inference is only too large and indiscriminate, as it generally is. It considers that the external sensible form is *non-ego*, because it is not sensitive in the same way as is the form which we call our own organism. Science corrects this, and at the same time confirms the inference that these forms and motions are signs and effects of a spirit corresponding to our own as their cause. In passing thus beyond the universe to beings who exert their power upon us, we do not pass from the relative to the unrelative absolute; for those inferred beings are causally related to us in various ways, which relations are the grounds of our inference, and furnish scope for the action of the principle of Sematology.

As these egoistic forms are Symbols of spiritual individualities, so the activities of these forms and all their passivities are also for the same reason symbolic of the phenomena of the unknown but symbolized or represented spirits. And as all our phenomena vary relative to each other according to law, including all the phenomena of the universe, and the action and passion of all phenomenal men and animals, they are all symbolic of the lexical variations in the action and experience of the beings represented, that thus there are laws of inter-communication between these various beings and their universes, that there is a lexical correspondence between them, though they have no direct connection or communication with each other.

The principle through which this mediate knowledge is attained, the law of Sematology, through known likeness and uniformity, is not a mere instinct, but the operation of intelligence, spontaneous and reflective. That the burnt child dreads the fire is a maxim which shows the early operations of the understanding learning wisdom by experience, one experience leading it to fear that another of like kind will be equally painful,—a fear which has abundant cause in due time to ripen into perfect assurance. The child and untutored barbarians are strongly disposed to think that all bodies have feeling, just because their body has. But, as their knowledge advances and becomes rectified, they learn to distinguish between animated and inanimate bodies. But how is this done? It is impossible except by comparison on the principle of analogy. Even men of science sometimes find it difficult to determine whether a body is animated or not; and they settle this point by a careful investigation for some phenomena which from consciousness and observation they know to be peculiar to animate organisms.

This is precisely the way in which, as a Philosophical Realist, I attain the knowledge of other beings subject to the same laws with myself. I observe how my consciousness is uniformly connected with my own organism; and I then observe that there are other organisms than my own which present all the varied phenomena that my own does, and this knowledge of the resemblance is so full and minute, and so continually repeated, that the conclusion is irresistible that these organisms represent other spirits essentially like my own.

In the same way, from the organic phenomena which comprise the bodies of animals, by comparing and contrasting their differences and resemblances in reference to my own, I discover that these also are symbols of sentient beings correspondingly like and unlike myself.

While the principle of Sematology everywhere operates spontaneously, it is for that reason susceptible of scientific exposition. From the conception of natural force whose action is uniform, we have a very great probability, if not certainty, that the same phenomena will have the same antecedents and consequents. The color sensation called fire, being followed by the touch sensation called burning, we infer that it will be so always. This is the method of physical science in all departments and all cases. It is on the same method and the same principle that we say that the organism which we call our body, being peculiarly associated with our personal *ego* in its conscious activity, we infer that other bodies like ours are associated with and emblematical of other spirits or self-conscious beings like our own, and that animal bodies prove the same of animal spirits of corresponding likenesses and differences. Deny this, and we confound all philosophy, we deny a primary principle and procedure of all science, and we transmute all the phenomena of supposed animated existences into mere chimeras without a meaning or an object. If any one elects to take this position, it is not our fault. Our doctrine is scientific in its proofs and philosophic in its results. While in common with other philosophies it makes all animated phenomena, as well as others, egoistic, they are not meaningless and confusing to all intelligence. Being made significant of transcendent realities corresponding with the phenomenal forms, then philosophy, science, and practical intelligence are illuminated.

XII.
PSYCHE-MORPHISM.

We are now logically driven to a conclusion which has often been conjectured and widely accepted among Oriental minds, but which has never been rationally conceived, much less scientifically supported, and which has generally been contemplated with repulsion or disdain by the intellect of the West. We are now prepared to understand that there is a demand in the known natural law of cause and effect for a theory of metempsychosis, or, more strictly, metamorphosis of the soul, or, still better, psyche-morphism.

Problem of Permanence and Change in Causation.

One of the chief and fundamental problems of the ages concerns the possibility of natural causation, or the rational conception of it. The cause is described as an antecedent phenomenon, uniformly connected with a subsequent,—its effect. In these days, with the law of correlation before us, we often define the effect as its transmuted antecedent. But, in either form, the problem concerning the nature and possibility of the change is inevitable. The difficulty arises from its implication that the cause must cease to be before the effect exists, else the relation is not one of antecedent and subsequent. But, in that case, how can it operate as a cause? How can the non-existent do anything? That is self-contradictory. On the other hand, if it has not ceased to be, how can it exist as a transmuted form in its lexical subsequent? To explain this, philosophers have always assumed a transphenomenal substance. But this is ineffective and illogical, unless the substance is conceived as ultimately one and the same for all phenomena, as Spinoza did; and then, further, we must identify the substance with the phenomena, so that the latter are the lexical modes and working of the former, which is thus made a force, and the only cause. Then and not till then have we a rational expression of permanence in causal changes. Mr. Spencer resorts to the same assumption of transphenomenal substance, which, in order to be of use, it must also be assumed that this substance is cause. But neither he nor any of his predecessors gives any reason for this assumption, and to explain the relation of the substance to the phenomena has always been treated as an insoluble problem; and so, to evade one problem, others are invented. Mr. Spencer only says that phenomenal changes cannot be supposed to be absolute beginnings and cessations of existence, and that, therefore, there must be a permanent somewhat back of them, which they represent.

All these problems find an ultimate and perfect solution in our previous exposition of the Absolute and Relative as one, and both as one with substance and phenomena, and these, so far as known or knowable, as one with *ego*, as conscious spirit. It is not phenomena as phenomena merely that are causes and effects. But it is phenomena as modes of a substantive force or spirit which perdures through all phenomenal changes, and operates them all; and the phenomena are not the trajected and disconnected creations of the spirit or substantive force, but the very thing itself, so and so existing, as its transient modes, because whatever is is force, which must exist in some mode and in various modes, since force must act, and so undergo modal changes. Then, as these phenomena are known as egoistic, and, therefore, as conscious spirit, as substantive and perduring force, that which operates everywhere, and perdures through all changes, is known as such *ego*. We thus attain a perfect unity amid all diversity, and permanence combined with causal changes; the law of natural cause and effect is preserved real and intact, and philosophically expounded; and our ultimate abutment is not a mere postulate or assumption, much less a somewhat, which is confessedly unknowable and inconceivable, but that which is directly and indubitably known, egoistic phenomena, which are equally spirit and substance and force, all these being one. And these phenomena are the *ego* existing in these modes, and acting because it is a force, and acting according to its nature, or the kind and degree of its force or being, and therefore acting with regularity, and, in so doing, lexically changing its modes, ending some and beginning others forevermore.

With this light, and on this basis, we can discuss even such a subject as metempsychosis philosophically and with scientific rigor, by showing it as a succession of different forms or modes of the same soul,—psyche-morphic changes.

Pre-existence in Other Forms.

Objective evolution makes individuality to be very superficial and factitious, merely apparent or phenomenal, but not substantial. It makes all individualities of every grade and kind to be but the modes or mutable forms of the one great, only, and eternal force or power, and all generation and births are merely changes in these forms; so that progeny in all cases, whether in the seed, egg, or living animal, is a transmutation of what was once a vital part of its parent source. It forgets that all these individualities, as well as all other phenomena, so far as they are known or knowable to any one, are states of the knowing subject, and that all births, deaths, progress, or decay, and all possible known forms and mutations of the universe, are modes of the perceptive *ego*, and that the real generation, birth, death, or extinction of any other individual, or of its mode of life, is never known to us ; and that we know only certain present changes in ourselves, which are taken as signs of corresponding changes in others and in our past conditions. When my organism was generated, that which was or is known and designated as such by others (each knowing a different organism) was to them the sign that I had passed over from some other state into this, which ranks me so and so with men. Now, the question arises, "What was that other state?"

We must reply that it was some mode of my own individual self. Here is a fact of vital importance, of which only subjective evolution can take cognizance. Objective evolution makes one being or individual to become extinct, and its disorganized forces to become transmuted into another by fresh organization, the utter ending of one and the absolute beginning of another, as individualized forms of the one eternal force. But that is irrational and does not agree with known facts. The known facts are only modal changes of the same one subject or individual, which, in every case, includes the whole universe, all its force and all its forms. No evolution can transcend the universe to which it belongs. The course of evolution is, therefore, always confined to the modal changes of the same one individual, which undergoes a succession of changes, answering to, or rather constituting, those of the known universe. As this egoistic universe contains other forms like ours, it symbolizes that there are other men who have undergone the same line of successive evolutions as we have, from the lower stages of existence up to organic man.

Pre-existence in the Human Form

The human stage being reached, it were unreasonable to suppose that the process of evolution here ends. Such a view finds no support in the analogies of experience. As a rule, evolutionary changes are not great and sudden, but by successive small degrees. Yet very vast is the difference between the highest and the lowest intellect of man, between the most advanced and the least advanced of our race. This advance cannot be supposed to have taken place all at once. There has been gradual progress, though with steps of varying extent. Hence, to the question as to what was our immediately preceding state, we may answer, with considerable confidence, that it was some other and lower human form and condition, on the ground that all scientific indexes seem to point to this conclusion. Phenomenally, all human forms and states follow in birth upon others, as the effects or transformed force of those others. This is also the utterance of objective evolution, and accords with all serious popular thought and expression. But, as all phenomena are modes of one individual subject, and as my organism especially represents me, and as its generation represents the beginning of my present organic mode of existence, so it apparently represents that my previous state, as symbolized in its phenomenal parents, was proximately like my present state. The phenomenal difference between phenomenal parents and offspring being generally not very great, and of lexical regularity, we may or must infer that such is the same concerning the real individualistic changes which these phenomena sematize. These changes carry us back successively to lower human conditions, till we reach the dark border-land of Moss-trooper contests as to which side of the line a thing belongs, and then back to the pre-human, then the pre-faunal, and even to the pre-floral condition.

Some phenomena may be considered as symbols of what is below organic consciousness. All the inorganic world may belong to this class. It is the form of my infra-organic and human consciousness, and it shows what was once wholly my life and consciousness. That I or anything is or was wholly unconscious I know not. It cannot be proved nor conceived. It is the supposition of a state which is wholly devoid of all intelligible marks. There may be egoistic force which is not yet or always in full conscious action. But even of this we can never have any direct proof. We know that different states of consciousness frequently fail to connect in memory, and all apparent unconsciousness may be of this kind. At all events, the spirit has evolved itself (not *from* itself), first, as chaos, then as kosmos, and then as the forms of organic life, vegetable and animal, and the process of evolution is still advancing; and what further capabilities are within the vast and awful womb of this spirit, the absolute *ego*, only everlasting experience can disclose.

Number and Duration of Psyche-morphisms.

This conclusion, it must be confessed, is very sweeping and very far removed from prevailing modern thought; and, on that account, it will be held to be very objectionable. It implies a doctrine of universal psyche-morphisms of vast and incalculable multiplicity and duration. It implies that every advanced human being has probably undergone a psyche-morphic change many times between his present state and the state in which he first emerged or evolved into man, if we may suppose such a point, on the location of which we are not likely to agree. It implies that this same creature or individual in that supposed immediately pre-human state probably underwent many such transformations between the first and last generation of the whole monkey family previous to the evolution into the human state. It implies further, perhaps, as many more psyche-mor phisms as there were generations from that time back to the beginning of its organic life.

But we should not assume that life had only one point of beginning and only one time for all. There were just as many as there are living beings, or individuals, which are never derived from any other or others, each form being evolved from its previous state, and all from the first state, which in each case was a separate creation, if not eternal; and each one, let us remember, is itself always a universe. There can be no natural symbol for creation, because it can have no lexical antecedent and no natural process. Abiogenesis, were it well established, would only show another example of evolution; and in that light it has been investigated, and the failure to establish it is of small account, by the methods used, because it is not necessary. Subjective evolution shows it to be a logical necessity which gives a theoretical completeness to the order of things: first, creation, which is unimaginable, but not inconceivable; second, the first and lowest created condition, which is, perhaps, infra-conscious and therefore pre-kosmic; third, evolution into the lowest conscious condition, a pre-organic kosmic experience; then, fourth, abiogenetic evolution from the kosmic form; and, then, successive biogenetic evolution as before indicated, and every such change or evolution simply a psyche-morphic change.

In this long course of psyche-morphic changes, the change, as indicated by the symbols, is sometimes a deterioration; but the main trend, the vast and overwhelming force and sweep of movement, is in the direction of progress.

I have spoken of a possible unconscious pre-kosmic condition (though I do not believe it), because the kosmos is a mode of our consciousness, and, therefore, whatever is in that state is conscious; but, as many think we have reason for believing there is occasionally even now an unconscious state, I name that the pre-kosmic or infra-kosmic state, and suppose that it is the lowest and preceded the kosmic.

This appears to me consistent, thorough, and complete; and, so far as I can see, it is a legitimate induction from facts and principles which are known and acknowledged by all. We ought not to be utterly repelled from the consideration of it because of its novelty in part; for, if it were nothing new, why should I write? Nor should its apparent proximate resemblance to any theory supposed to be obsolete condemn it without investigation. It is not improbable that some hoary errors are partial anticipations of truth. Many will identify the last few pages with one portion of Buddhism, and with that, too, which is deemed the most unfounded and fanciful. But the metempsychosis of Buddhism is without a scientific basis. It is a dualism all through, the body being always other than the soul. Its final goal is indifferentism absolute, if not entire unconsciousness and personal annihilation. In all these points of great and vital importance, our psyche-morphism differs from the metempsychosis of Buddhism. Yet, notwithstanding this difference, the one point of coincidence with Buddhism will extensively stand in the way of its reception, and in some minds excite a stubborn prejudice and opposition. Some interesting inquiries will grow out of this exposition, which we cannot entertain, much less conclusively develop.

A Method of evading Psyche-morphism.

There is, some may think, another course open to us, and leading to different conclusions, arising from the reasonable possibility of making a different inference from one class or series of facts which we have been obliged to use as symbols of transcendent realities. As our organism is the sensitive expression of the *ego*, and as other human organisms, though egoistic, are symbols of other men, so what we call our parents represent other human beings, who sustain to us very peculiar and important relations. Now, since phenomenally the progeny is from the progenitors, a part of their force transformed, it may be asked whether the law of symbolism does not require or justify the proposition that all real successive generations are not merely changes in the same person or individual, but the generation of new individualities from the parent sources, the progeny being a transformed part of the former energy of the progenitors, and now specialized into new individuals. It will appear, at first sight, very reasonable to answer this question in the affirmative. This would afford us a subjective theory, quite analogous to the popular objective evolution. This, like that, implies that all forms of existence are but modes of one all-embracing and all-perduring Force, which evolves itself into all these forms according to laws of its own generation. This Force may be appropriated by Theists as the Supreme Being, though some may oppose it because of its implicated pantheism.

Objections to this Method.

I object to this because of its superficial individualism. I cannot believe that we are all simply modes of One. All the logical implications of experience compel me to think that each one of us is an individual, distinct and separate, at once, always, and forever. I am not a mode of God, or of the great and only One, call it by whatever name you will. It makes all men one, just as all the members are one body, which my consciousness and reason repudiate.

I object, again, because, like objective evolution, it logically excludes personal immortality. The whole existence of each is included within the period between birth and death. Our existence as specialized individuals consists in this form and its functions; and, when these are ended, our existence has passed away as individuals. This mortalism is distasteful to my higher aspirations, and cannot be admitted without the strongest evidence. Of course, I shall be reminded that all do not feel like this, and that, if they did, a mere feeling proves nothing. It may be right or it may be wrong, and the feeling of to-day may not be the feeling of to-morrow, which is very true ; and so much the worse for him, I say, who ever feels satisfied with mortalism.

I object to this mortalism, because I believe it is inconsistent with a regnant moral economy. It may be that there is no such moral economy as that which is conceived by me. But I am glad to be able to despise an economy which can seldom live more than three or four score years, and usually not so long, and which, after that, is only an imaginary shade, hovering in impotent menace or approval around imaginary shades, which are equally impotent to be either cursed or blessed. I cannot conceive the moral life to be an insignificant ephemeral or a hothouse annual, but a tree (like the Igdrasil) which perdures through all the ages and ages, whose roots grasp all the nether universe, and whose top extends and spreads through all the heavens. Perhaps there is no such thing. Perhaps this conceit is only a relict of the old fuliginous pre-scientific brain. So think some of our modern scientific ephemerals and animalculæ. But, if time and occasion offered, it were easy to show that morality is this or nothing.

I object, again, because, apart from any moral scheme, evolution has thus in it no element of distributive rational propriety and honest verity. Forms come and go, and set themselves up for something distinct, as if they were ultimate individualities, when they are only automatic members of one Individuality. This is an intolerable falsity, ever and forever repeated. The theory here conflicts with all psychological assumptions and convictions and the practical judgment of mankind, and makes all nature a series of hollow, deceptive, and deceived simulacra. That falsity cannot be the truth. We treat these simulacra as verities; and, therefore, our theories should accord with this, or they will justly and speedily be relegated to shades themselves.

I object to this theory, in the next place, because it divests the order of events, always and everywhere, of all rational significance and moral propriety. No reason whatever can ultimately be assigned why any of the innumerable figures of the universe should be what it is, or why it appears and disappears where and when it does. Very true, indeed, it is that this system can admit of no final causes. It is unintelligent and non-moral. "It knoweth not whence it cometh nor whither it goeth." Gradually, we see it sloughing off every distinctive intellectual as well as moral quality; and there is left to us a mere black hulk, rolling on waters ever dark and restless. Live there who can. It is the primeval world of falling, simmering waters, of vapors, clouds, and gases, with all the lights of heaven obscured. It cannot long be accepted as the ultimate evolution of the intellectual world, especially with those who, as subjective evolutionists, have already proved the agency of a mighty personal and supernatural Power.

I object to this theory, in the next place, because it conflicts with the fundamental notion of being, which is deduced from subjective evolution. Subjective evolution directly knows no being but the subject, *ego*, which is personal spirit. All being is force, and all is spirit and individualistic, though often of a very low order; and, as each includes all of an entire universe, there is nothing in common to any two, though there may be much of resemblance between many. Therefore, the notion of one great, underlying root, from which all phenomena are temporary outshoots (not offshoots), like the extemporized feet, hands, or mouth, or stomach of the monera or amœbæ, is inadmissible. The universe — every universe — is

one, one individual; but all universes together are
not one individual, but many. And these are absolutely isolated from each other. Infinite vacuum is
between them, and they can reach each other no
more than the swinging of bells in airless space will
generate sound.

I object to it, in the next place, because it involves
a notion of the *ego* indefinitely inferior to that which
is logically necessitated by subjective evolution,
which identifies all the power and glory and duration
of the knowable universe with the *ego*, so that no
natural bridging of the gulf which separates one from
another is possible; and all limitation to their power
and duration, except as somewhere within the finite,
is precluded. After attaining this conception of the
ego, there is no room left in the mind for the beggarly
notion of a transient wafe, which is well compared
to a vapor or breath or a meteor, or to burning
stubble. The organism is but an infinitesimal portion of the *ego*, and each organic life is but such
a fraction of the total life of the *ego*. So the absolute
isolation of individuals precludes the possibility of
one being the natural issue of another, as one subjective organism is from another. Such a notion
makes the individual superficial, unreal, puny, and
temporary, limited to a very little space and time,
with corresponding disabilities. The sensible child
to which the mother gives birth, being but a mode of
herself, to call either of them a distinct individuality,
as if they comprised two persons, is to contradict the
science of psychology. They do not comprise even
one person. They are only two out of an indefinite
number of the experiences of one person,—the absolute *ego*, though, as we have expounded, they symbolize two different persons.

A final objection is that all the good of the universe
is on this theory accidental. There is good developed in certain conditions; and these conditions
come and go with the same indifference as opposing

conditions, and all are equally legitimate, and neither are any more an end than the other. With certain physical changes, all attained good passes away remorselessly and irrevocably, because it was a mere accident of physical conditions, just as all evil is. It is, therefore, utterly void of all moral significance, just the same as lightning, mildew, and springing flowers, which are temporary consequents of certain physical interactions simply.

Limitation of Psyche-morphic Changes.

Let it not be overlooked that these psyche-morphic changes are only partially relative to their subject. They do not comprise the whole being, not the absolute *ego*, but only the local and organic *ego*, which changes by changing interaction with the environment; which environment is the extra-organic and pre-organic subject, which first generates and then endlessly modifies the organic *ego*. In the mean while, the inorganic *ego*, or universe, is constantly changing in its forms and in the relative motions, force, and effect of its parts; and it is these changes which modify the organic world, which again reacts on the inorganic world. These organic forms and changes we can trace back to their origin in the inorganic. But they are modes of the same individual through all the changes; and they have the same conscious subject as that whose phenomena constitute the inorganic and extra-organic universe, which changes comparatively little. And so our total individuality changes very slowly, while the modes of our local organism change rapidly. I—the one individual constituting the universe—exist through all time and constitute all time, because I am the subject of all known changes, all co-existence and succession.

Dignity and Significance of the Lower Animals.

Subjective evolution implies that in the whole course of times there are just as many creatures of one grade or kind as of any other (except the highest, where they stop and accumulate, if we may suppose any such rank, which we do not); for all the lower pass into the higher (unless there be some irretrievable deterioration and perversion), and all the higher were once in all the lower conditions, and have evolved out of them. This gives us an ascending series of existences of a nobler order and significance than any of which poets and theorists have ever dreamed. The lowest, the most insignificant, and the most repulsive has before it a sublime destiny possible or certain. Its goal is manhood or archangelhood or we know not what of greatness and elevation beyond. What a glorious right to be is thus conferred upon the humblest creatures! and what a persistent power to be is theirs, also, for their organic destruction is only a psyche-morphic change, which is preliminary to a first evolution somewhere by birth, in perhaps a nobler form! For each and all, not for a few late comers only, is this grand and endless destiny. The oft-raised question is now answered: "What did God make such things as these for?" He made them that they might be men, and better and wiser men than those who captiously ask the question. In the mean while, they have their own enjoyments, and subserve unconsciously many purposes of importance as they move on their unknown way to the higher stations which they are destined to attain; and, above all, the whole vast and grand chain of progressive existence discloses a teleology far surpassing any that theologians have ever endeavored to expound.

Reality and Thoroughness of Subjective Evolution.

Subjective evolution is thus complete and universal. It is the normal privilege and law of every individual organic being to evolve itself from the lower to the higher evermore. Objective evolution, on the contrary, is accidental, partial, and limited. All animals, including man, die to live no more; for at death their individuality is forever extinguished. Even where there is said to be an evolution from the lower into the higher, that means only the extinction of one individual and the beginning of another and a higher, —a new individuality as well as a new order or species. No one individual itself ever evolves into a higher order, except it be from the embryonic and preliminary and amphibious state into the subsequent developed condition. There is a succession of rising (or falling) orders, and no more. On the other hand, according to the scheme of subjective evolution I have briefly described, each individual existed in every order, the same individual in every preceding order, and the same will exist in every succeeding order. Death is but the ending of one form, and birth the beginning of another. Each individual is immortal, and an endless duration in an innumerable succession of mortal lines is the heritage of each. The general outline of the past history of those who are now men we are getting quite able to trace on the pages of palæontology; but what are to be the evolutions of the future and the duration of each is beyond our power even to imagine, except in a faint degree, as an inference from our present intellectual and moral life and action. But here Spiritualism may possibly help us some time.

Universality of Evolution because Subjective.

Objective evolution is also limited, in that it is confined to particular points where only the ascent takes place. It searches for the forms in an order which makes the closest approach to some of the forms of another and higher order, and then says that here, and here only, was the ascent made. Here is the narrow and crooked stairway up which nature climbed to the next landing place above. At all other points, the order or species remains unchanged;

and none of its individuals ever pass beyond their present rank. This is a scientific necessity with objective evolution, because it proves evolution (in distinction from creation) only by showing gradual approaches of the antecedents as a sign of naturalistic transition to the subsequent of a higher order. It has no other proof, and it can claim evolution only so far as it can show a close structural approximation of antecedents to certain subsequents of a superior rank.

With subjective evolution, the case is entirely changed. The egoistic unity of the universe is immediately found by an analysis of consciousness, and all space and time and their contents are concentrated in the ego. I can transcend myself only by a sematic inference, never by experience or the action of any natural force or influence; nor, therefore, in any wise can I be brought into contact or association or connection of actual proximity or natural influence with any other being. Hence, it is impossible for one being to be evolved from another. All action and interaction, all succession of cause and effect, are only between the different modes of the same one individual which is the subject, the cause and effect, antecedent and subsequent, of all change and evolution in the same universe from the beginning to the end of its transmutations. This is a logical necessity, and we need not adduce close physical connections to prove this general proposition. And now, as no individual can be evolved from another, the later states of each may be and must be evolved from its earlier states. This is the only evolution that is possible, and this necessarily prevails from the beginning of the world onward and without end. Every successive state of the same individual or universe is necessarily an evolution from its predecessors, whatever they may have been; and this can never for a moment be brought into question by any alleged unlikeness between the succeeding and preceding forms known to us; for here, in the same subject, there is no possible room for the supposition of the creation of a new species. This, therefore, is true of my local ego, which has certainly evolved from precedent and lower forms of my universe, or absolute ego, whether I can give a scientific verification of the points where the transitions took place or not.

But, as there is a phenomenal order of succession, which is symbolical of transcendent realities, it follows that what is true of me is true of all,—all other individuals and universes which transcend my own. And as, in this symbolical universe, there is a succession of species, with birth and death for all, it follows that there is a succession of evolving states for all individuals, each from itself.

One more question still remains on this vast and almost awful subject,— a question which, if it were overlooked, would be asked by others with a laugh, as if they had found in it a refutation of our doctrine. As we have concluded that men have probably many successive human lives — how many I know not — as successive psyche-morphic mutations, we now want some rule or principle to determine when shall cease this process, if it ever shall, when men shall pass beyond the human rank by evolution into something permanently higher, with no more earthly reincarnations. There is nothing in the mere order of things as successive phenomena to help us determine this. The degree of intellectual advancement might be interrogated on the subject, but the response is equivocal.

There is a higher principle than mere intelligence. It is the moral and religious power and quality. These are certainly peculiar to civilized men in the extent of their development and in many of the forms which they assume and develop, whether they differ in essential kind from the faculties of the brute or not. I hold that the moral faculty is, in a degree, a supernatural power, and that, as such, it belongs to all beings in a state of moral probation, so that it is always in the power of such a being, without any change of circumstances or antecedents or subjective state, to do either right or wrong. And therefore, on that account, all such are for a period in a state of moral probation, since such a power is necessary to such probation, and necessitates it, until they have determined and fixed their character for good or evil. The development and proof of this theory belong to another connection and topic. Here we take it for granted that we may use it in answering the question under consideration. This moral probation is the highest possible end of man as man; and through it every man must be supposed to go, and enjoy every possible advantage and opportunity it implies and involves, and to the utmost extent, until he has fixed and sealed his own fate for the future, and, perhaps, forever. Then his human career is run. There is no more call for his existence in this probationary form. He now enters upon another state, in which he reaps by self-inheritance what he has here morally sown. With the good there is, then, fixity in good; and all after that is a course of education, while the certainty of an everlasting ascending series of felicity and glory is before them. With the bad — well, we'll leave them. It is neither as pleasant nor as clear on this side as on the other. They have taken the dark path, and it is difficult to follow them. We know there are animal deteriorations, but will leave it to others to draw conclusions. Indeed, all this discussion as to the future, and the passage of men from the ranks of men, is quite theoretical, with little in the way of positive indices to guide us. Only the indices of a future existence, unequivocal, and the psychic change it involves, should, in the normal course, be a progressive evolution beyond the present kosmic form and order.

There is a dualism which imagines that the body comes by natural generation, and that, at the moment of the gestation of the human body, God creates for it, in each separate instance, an individual soul. Thus, the fiatism of creation is still going on, only God now creates infant souls for infant bodies, instead of a manly soul and a manly body, as in the legendary Adam. Some who affect to despise fiatism seem to believe that the soul is different from the body; that it is not the product of any known antecedents, like the body ; that it is not subject, as to its origin, to the law of evolution and correlation ; and that it comes we know not how or whence.* The only alternative is either the old fiatism or an evolution of the soul, according to the unknown laws of an unknown spirit world.

A thorough-going evolution dispenses with all this. It refuses to assume an infinite fiatism, contingent on the sexual action of the animal world. It knows nothing of the duality of body and spirit, and of one as naturally engendered and the other as supernaturally introduced, preserved, and developed. But the new doctrine is here beset with another difficulty of its own creation,— the self-contradictory miracle of a new human soul and life, absolutely originating as a series of links in an unbroken chain of sequences. It is a stupendous and incredible marvel that such a being as man, with all his spiritual capabilities, should absolutely begin his existence in the womb as the natural product of certain physical antecedents. This can never be widely received by the human mind. Hence, the foremost evolutionists, like Spencer and his followers, here make an unscientific hiatus, and declare the actions of the mind and body concomitants, and not correlatives ; and they relegate the origin and cause of the mind to the Unknowable.

But philosophy cannot be content with anything like that. It demands intellectual completeness and unity. This is attainable in accordance with our doc-

---

* John Fiske.

trine of Philosophical Realism. According to this, all births are but changes in the old and common life of the universe,—the subjective ego; and every birth is the symbol of an evolution of some subject from one condition into another and, perhaps, a higher condition or form of existence,—a psyche-morphic change in the individual or spiritual being, which exists in all the successive forms, so that the change is an evolution strictly, not the destruction of one individual and the beginning of another, but the unfolding of higher powers and the attainment of a higher form by the same one individual.

The doctrine of metempsychosis will probably be offensive to some, on the assumption that it is not Christian. It is not taught in the Bible, but it is not opposed to the Bible, as we know that many of the Jews who revered the Bible rather leaned to the doctrine; and they thought that John was Elias metamorphosed, thus fulfilling the prophecy that Elias must first come,—before the Messiah. Allowing the name of Adam to the first man, like the Jews, that does not debar his sons from any number of transmigrations, whether, to begin with, they inherit his depravity or not; and it affects not in the least man's relation to Christ or the Holy Spirit. But, if any have not had an adequate moral probation in one life, they may have it in a second or third here in this world. This would remove some objections to the Scripture doctrine that probation is confined to this world. It allows that every one may have in this world every possible advantage for the determination of moral character. Against the doctrine here propounded, neither the Bible nor the councils nor the creeds have uttered a word.

XIII.
HUMAN INTERCOURSE.

Collateral Testimony.

IF on this subject there is a babel of voices, there is an unrecognized unity of thought. Against Idealism, Dr. Reid argues in the following terms: "It seems to take away all the evidence we have of other intelligent beings like ourselves. What I call a father a brother, or a friend, is only a parcel of ideas in my own mind ; and, being ideas in my mind, they cannot possibly have that relation to another mind which they have to mine, any more than the pain felt by me can be the individual pain felt by another. I can find no principle in Berkeley's system which affords me even probable ground to conclude that there are other intelligent beings like myself, in the relations of father, brother, friend, or fellow-citizens." (*I. P.*, Es. 2, c. 10.)

It is characteristic of the human mind that we are ever apt to think opinions easy and clear when familiar to us, and to think that all that is repugnant to these is obscure and beset with difficulties. This is a sufficient explanation of Reid's trouble on the matter under consideration. To all who are not prepossessed with Reid's view, it will be easy to show that his doctrine on this point is at least as obscure and thorny as ours.

How does dualism, whether expounded by himself or Stewart or Hamilton, hold intercourse with or attain the knowledge of other men? Certainly, not directly by the senses. By the eye, a dualist sees nothing but color; by the touch, he immediately knows nothing but organic impressions or sensations; and so, through all the senses, he knows only some impulse of air or combination of light or peculiar muscular pressure. Will he allow these disjointed phantoms to be his father, brother, friend? The real father, brother, friend, are hid behind all these phenomena, and are entirely unknown by the senses. It is, therefore, evident that he can really know them only at second hand by the help of some medium, which has never been clearly conceived, much less expounded, by any of the Scottish School. In accordance with their theory or notions, the medium can only be some "instinct," or "an inference without reasoning," or some "fundamental principle of human belief," or a "mental impotency." The Philosophical Realist has as much right as they to assume such things, if he needs them; but he needs them not, and not one of them would he accept.

Berkeley explains the method as follows: "I perceive several notions, changes, and combinations of ideas, that inform me that there are certain particular agents, like myself, which accompany them, and concur in their production" (*Princ.*, § 145). He might better have been more full and explicit; but he is as clear as his critic, and more relevant to his own theory as it is a partial explanation of Idealism, while it is entirely foreign to the needs of a genuine Natural Realism, as described by Hamilton, which, after all, has no real existence. For all theories are virtually idealistic, however disguised; and they all equally need a bridge from the ego to their friends and all other non-ego. They have constructed bridges, which have all given way under the pressure of criticism. Constitutional conviction of immediate perception was surrendered by Hamilton, and he never attempts more than to tell us how the objects of muscular tension are known. He allows that we do not know other men by the eye or ear, or even the common sensation of touch. All this is generally overlooked by the English readers of his works, and by nearly all his admirers.

Conditions of Mutual Intercourse.

Several of our prominent writers have given brief utterances which show that the intellect, seeking to get beyond itself, is beginning to discover, though dimly, that the only route is that which we have described. Prof. Huxley writes: "It is wholly impossible absolutely to prove the presence or absence of consciousness in anything but one's own brain, though, by *analogy*, we are justified in assuming its existence in other men." Herbert Spencer writes: "Each individual is absolutely incapable of knowing any feelings but his own. That there exist other sensations and emotions is a conclusion implying, in the first place, the reasoning through which he identifies certain objects as bodies of a like nature with his own body, and implying, in the second place, the further reasoning which convinces him that, along with the external actions of these bodies, there go internal states of consciousness, like those accompanying such external actions in his own body." Prof. Clifford says: "I have absolutely no means of perceiving your mind. *I judge by analogy that it exists.*" I am aware that these had no such notion proper as I have expounded, and that, in penning these very sentences, they were submitting to the usual illusion of considering external organisms as non-egoistic ; yet they all clearly affirm that only by analogy and sematism can they attain other minds and their thoughts.

Demand for a Method or Medium of Intercourse.

If it is agreed that every animated being is a universe of itself, numerically different from all others; that every soul is absolutely shut up to itself always and forever; that it is only by sematology that we can scientifically justify any one in asserting the existence of aught but himself; that, by this principle, we have proved not only the existence of other living beings, corresponding to the phenomenal world of men and animals, but also their mutual relation in action and influence,— it behooves us now to inquire respecting the possible condition or medium through which this relation is maintained. Such a medium must be something on which each can operate by natural force and law, and through it on each other. If there is no medium, and if no medium is possible, then the intercommunication in question, if there is any, is not a natural process of cause and effect, but a supernatural appointment. This question is, therefore, of very great importance, and philosophy must endeavor to determine it with scientific precision and logical rigor. The reader will easily see that the proof of the *fact* of this interaction and influence, and the proof of the *method* or process or conditions of the interaction, are two different things; and it is the latter which we are now to endeavor to ascertain. The fact of the intercommunion we assume to be already proved. The mode or condition or law of its action we have yet to furnish.

The Method not explained by Sematology.

Sematology explains and scientifically justifies itself; and, at the same time, it justifies our affirmation of the existence of conscious beings, which answer to the extra-organic phenomena of our consciousness. It is on the same principle that we have affirmed that, between all these living beings, there is a law of action and reaction, so that the action and experience of one are changed relatively to others. The argument for both is precisely the same. But, while it proves the intercourse, it does not show the means or natural conditions of that intercourse, as of this it says nothing.

No such Medium in Non-egoistic Matter.

We therefore inquire if such a medium can be conceived in a supposed non-egoistic matter. This is a question never before considered. It is entirely different from the question whether matter is the cause or condition of sensation,— a question which we have already answered in the negative. We are inquiring for the cause or condition of intercourse between two or more universes or minds.

Since matter, as known to us, is sensation, self, it follows that non-egoistic matter, if there is any such, must be unknown, or not the direct object of our knowledge. Hence, it cannot be the medium sought. We cannot be conscious of our operation on such a thing, nor of its operation on us. And, as we can use only that which is known, and whose laws are also known, we cannot have any guidance in the use of such a medium. Accordingly, in point of fact, it is only in relation to the known that we ever do act. The supposition, therefore, of an unknown medium explains nothing, but introduces another incomprehensible element.

Such a medium would also involve all the logical difficulties, on account of which we have been compelled to reject hylatic dualism and sensism, and kindred theories which assert a non-egoistic matter, known or unknown.

Further, whatever is non-egoistic is, by the very hypothesis on which we are proceeding, utterly incompetent to serve as a medium, since we have agreed that we can never transcend ourselves in immediate action and knowledge.

Nor in the Forms of Sensible Matter.

Shall we, then, suppose a medium composed of the forms of sensible matter? That is to say, that we are ourselves the medium, which contradicts itself, because the medium sought is something between me and others. Besides, there is no medium, if we operate only on ourselves; and, as we can operate on nothing else, all media are impossible.

An Impassable Gulf between Different Minds.

Therefore, so far as concerns natural force and law and their operation, there is an absolute gulf between one being and another. There is no known or conceivable natural force nor means which can span that gulf, and no intelligence can throw over it a bridge constructed out of natural elements and forces. It is a gulf which reaches from the confines of all knowable nature to an unknowable, but inferred, nature beyond. It is a gulf which natural science has never contemplated, which is entirely and forever beyond the range of scientific investigation, because beyond the universe of phenomena, with all their connections of cause and effect, of antecedent and consequent.

It can only be by Supernatural Appointment.

There remains, therefore, but one possible conclusion,— that the connection that obtains between the action and utterance of animated beings is wholly supernatural; that is, it follows a law which transcends nature or the universe. All admit, as they must, this connection. All must see that it is a natural impossibility. Therefore, it must be a fact which transcends nature. We have thus disclosed to us a supernatural agency, which has appointed certain correspondences between animated beings (that is, between all beings), and made the action and passion of each to have a fixed relation to others, as certain and regular as if it were a process of natural causation, which (natural causation) the reader will bear in mind is confined to the natural universe, knowable, ourselves.

The magnitude of supernatural agency thus demonstrated is unutterably, inconceivably stupendous. It regulates in detail the relative action of a countless number and variety of universes, with absolute and unvarying precision. How vast the power and intelligence which all this involves!

Pre-established Harmony.

We have, hence, a striking picture of the perfect isolation of every living thing; that is, of everything. No one ever knows aught or affects aught but itself, and all things constitute a sublime system of Pre-established Harmony. Whatsoever is is a living monad, a unit of force. But every monad is a whole soul, which is always a whole universe. The *natural* action and influence of each are confined to itself; and its parts, so called, are only modes of the one. And each universe is sufficient to itself, and by its action on itself is the source of its own development or decay; and within each individual or universe causation is real and vast. But each develops or decays, and variously operates, according to fixed laws of relation to others, by the appointment of a supernatural agent.

XIV.

THEOLOGY IMPLIES PHILOSOPHY.

WE have thus suddenly, and by a singularly original route, been brought face to face with the supernatural; and that subject is now fairly forced upon our attention. And, through the vast mound of mental excreta which the abortive thought of past ages (and the present age) has built up before us, we will as fast as possible make our way. And we will first utter some protests and caveats concerning the method, without a better understanding of which the problem cannot be solved or intelligently attempted.

Theism and Agnostic Deism.

To confound one thing with another, and to assume that one is proved or admitted because the other is, is a procedure which is but too common in the history of thought and dialectics. In all ages, some Christian divines have been guilty of it; and they still keep it up. All the admissions of the anti-supernaturalists concerning what is called Deity, they appropriate to themselves as equally good for themselves. All unite in making the divine existence a postulate instead of a logical conclusion from known data. Some of these are scientists, and others are theologians. The authors of the "Unseen Universe" say, "Let us begin by stating at once that we assume, as absolutely self-evident, the existence of a Deity who is the Creator of all things." As confirming and coinciding with this assumption, they quote the following from Herbert Spencer: "We are obliged to regard every phenomenon as a manifestation of some Power by which we are acted upon. Though omnipresence is unthinkable, yet, as experience discloses no bounds to the diffusion of phenomena, we are unable to think of limits to the presence of this Power, while the criticisms of science teach us that this Power is incomprehensible." These writers ought to remember that Spencer's ultimate and incomprehensible Power is not the "Creator of the world," is not even discriminated from the world, but identified with it, and as devoid of consciousness, purpose, and will, being in every essential particular opposed to the standard theistic conception of God. That such a power as this which Spencer affirms exists is incontestable, since to affirm it is simply to affirm that there is a known universe which we do not fully comprehend. This is not a mere postulate, though it is called a postulate by Spencer. It is a logical conclusion from known data, and as such is deduced by Spencer.

God's Existence to be Proved, not Postulated.

It is wrong to say that "the existence of God is the common *postulate of all religion and all philosophy,*" if by God is meant the Creator of the world, or as aught else than the world itself. There are great religions and philosophies which deny, and indeed most of them deny, creation proper. It is unhistoric for a creationist to affirm that in this he occupies the common ground of all religion and all philosophy. Religion postulates a supreme power; but whether creative or not, whether mundane or supra-mundane, it does not say with united voice.

On the other hand, philosophy does not properly postulate anything. Its essential nature and office and object are exposition and comprehensive intellection. It is therefore bound to prove the existence of

God, and show his character and agency, not to postulate them. And any affirmation without such proof, whatever else it may be, is not philosophy. Whether nature is all, or whether we can have any proper proof of a supra-mundane Deity and Creator of the universe, is the greatest philosophical problem of the age; and as a problem it should be treated, and not assumed as a postulate unproved.

Penumbral Metaphysics No Refuge for Theology.

In apology for their inability to give us satisfactory exposition and logical defence of their systems, theologians have frequently pleaded that "no difficulty emerges in theology which had not previously emerged in philosophy." This is, indeed, in substance the entire argument of Butler's celebrated *Analogy* against Deism. It is very valuable as a thoughtful comparison on some points, chiefly the darker points, of nature and revelation. It is, however, not only without value as a positive argument for revealed religion, in which all are agreed, but it is also of less force as a shield against assailants than its admirers have supposed. To say that nature has as many and as serious difficulties as revelation is to say very little for the latter in the estimation of most people, including the majority of divines, who generally harp much on nature's defects in order to enhance the need and value of revelation; and even Butler himself, in the chapter on the "Importance of Christianity," follows to some extent the same track. To say that metaphysics is just as obscure and chaotic as theology would sound like a satire on theology, if we did not know the assurance and seriousness with which it is uttered as an effective rebuttal of the weightiest objections. Yet this rebuttal is simply a confession that theology is just as unreliable as metaphysics,— a confession which, in the estimation of almost everybody, divests theology of all value; for nobody greatly values any metaphysics, except it be some theory of his own. To endeavor to shelter theology under the defects of philosophy is a wretched subterfuge. It is analogous to the bad man's plea for his sins, that he is as good as his neighbors. To one who has no system of metaphysics except that, no satisfactory philosophy of things is yet attained or appears to be possible; and that the universe gives no evidence of the existence of an infinitely perfect Being, which John Stuart Mill and many others affirm, there is on this principle no answer. Theology is bound to have a philosophy, while philosophy is not bound to have a theology, and may possibly forbid it. Theology must be logically consistent and philosophically tenable. Where it is wanting in either of these two points, it is wrong; and we should correct it instead of defending acknowledged inconsistencies, under the plea that its philosophical supports are equally bad.

XV.

Method of Conceiving and Proving Creation.

Conception of Deity.

THICK and manifold are the metaphysical cobwebs which have been woven over the face of Deity, yet I hold that he is not wholly hid from all human conception as an Infinite Personality. In the first place, this conception is perfectly clear and distinct as the conception of a Being who is above all knowable nature,—that is, strictly supernatural, relative to the universes ; and this is the logical correlate of finite nature and finite personality, so that the two are equally clear and distinct, as defining each other. Nature is necessarily conceived as limited in space and in power. It does not comprehend itself, its processes and issues, which is a limitation ; and this we cannot distinctly conceive without conceiving its logical counterpart, illimitation on all these points, which is an infinite personality. People are, therefore, under no illusion when they affirm that it appears to them perfectly easy to conceive and believe in a Being who is superior to all nature, who comprehends it in whole and detail, who has brought it into existence, and whose will prolongs its existence, who gives to it its essential force and direction, and intelligently controls it. To assert that such a conception is not possible to man is metaphysical trifling.

Surely, those who affirm know their own thoughts better than anybody else, and are as competent as others to analyze the contents of consciousness with accuracy, besides being able to affirm that this conception is a logical implication from the affirmations of their opponents.

Besides, as all knowable nature is ego, which is conceived as limited, though we can never define or know its limits, the supernatural Infinite is that which is superior to ourselves and to all other conscious limited beings, taken together; and all beings are conscious beings. I myself constitute all nature knowable to me. By the law of sematism, we have inductively proved that there' are countless myriads of other beings of various forms and orders, each one of which constitutes a universe or system of nature. The Deity of which I speak is simply a Being who is numerically different from each of these separately or all of them taken together, and who is without limits in the various ways in which all these are limited. The action of such a power, we have already seen, is implied in the universal assumption of harmony and intercourse between different spirits and universes. We are compelled to conceive and also to recognize a power indefinitely superior to all these separately and collectively, entirely apart from them as other than they, whose action is a condition of their regular interaction. Our doctrine of the subjectivity of all nature and of our individuality, as commensurate and identical with all the universe, therefore, furnishes not only the conception, but also data for the proof of the existence of a supernatural Being, who is virtually infinite as the Author of the universes.

In the second place, the Infinite is the conception of a personality. By personality is not meant that old vulgar notion, which is begotten of sense, which implies form and outline and, therefore, limitation, against which there is a violent, misconceiving outcry, on the supposition that it is the only notion of personality, and, therefore, the one held by Christian philosophers. Our known personality is simply a limited power to think, feel, and will,— a power which is super-sensible and non-spatial. The Infinite Person is precisely that same power, without limit or infinitely perfect. Personality is the highest form of being. It is the highest conceivable definite, coherent differentiation, and the upper sunlit antipodes to the pre-animate, which is, therefore, not only limited, but exceedingly limited, compared with a supernatural personality, even though this may not be strictly infinite.

In the third place, we conceive this Personality as of infinite perfection and excellence. By this, I mean that he is able to do whatsoever does not involve a self-contradiction. This is my definition and conception of the Infinite Power and Person. This is clear and definite as a conception. There can be no higher power, because the supposition of such power contradicts, and so nullifies, itself. Not to be able to work a self-contradiction is no limitation, because the contradictory in thought or action is self-nullifying; and to be able to do everything but this is to be able to do everything real. And that is power infinite. To say that personality always involves limitation begs the question. That assertion, we allow, is true of human personality; but that it is true of all possible and conceivable personality is the point in debate. And, in proof of this, no argument has ever been offered, except the fact that human personality involves limitation, which is surely no argument at all. What! Is it impossible for us to conceive anything above ourselves in degree? And, if we can, where shall we limit the degree? There is no conceivable limit till we reach the point we have described as the nullifying self-contradiction.

The term "consciousness," as the chief synonyme of personality, is turned about in every possible way (but one) to show its implication of finity, which, relative to our experience, is very true. But that is trifling. By consciousness, we mean knowledge, and nothing else; for it is nothing else, and all *our* knowledge is limited. But, in affirming this, we imply a conception of its logical opposite,— unlimited knowledge; and this implies an omniscient Personality. Does limitless knowledge imply limitations of said knowledge? Do limitless goodness and power imply that they are limited? That is only the same as saying that *all* consciousness (or knowledge) implies limitation; for, if all is conceived as limited, the limitless is so conceived.

To say that the alleged notion of the Infinite is only negative and empty, and that to bring it within conception and definition is to limit it, is an assertion which is good for those who so think. Spinoza, who is quoted in support of this, himself defines the Infinite. With him, it comprises all substance and all quality. Nothing could be more clear, distinct, and definite as a conception; and on the assumption that this notion of the Infinite is not negative and empty, but positive and pregnant and definite, most of his writings are based. My definition differs from his in being apparently smaller, but really larger. With him, the Infinite is nature. With me, it is a personality which does not include nature, but which is above nature, and infinitely greater. His Infinite cannot create or destroy, cannot increase or diminish, the sum of Being; and mine can. So mine has a power of supremest quality which his wants, and many other such powers are implied in Infinite Personality.

I will add that Spinoza explicitly and constantly teaches not only the *conception*, but the *knowledge* of the Infinite. He says, "Understanding or intellection, whether finite or infinite in act, must comprehend the attributes of God and the affections of God" (*Ethics*, Part II., Prop. 30). "The human soul has an adequate knowledge or cognition of the eternal and infinite essence of God" (*Ib.*, Part II., Prop. 47). In another proposition, he tells us that this knowledge is the supreme good and highest virtue of the soul. As, with him, God and nature are one, the knowledge of God is a necessity, where there is any knowledge at all. With the theist, God is only known by inference; and there is, therefore, here room for possible doubt and for opposing arguments as to the existence, but not the conception of God.

Finally, the denial of the notion of infinity overlooks one of the first laws of thought,— the law on which the doctrine of logical opposition is built. That law is that we think in doubles, so that every thought is incomplete, except so far as it includes a duality of logical counterparts. Thus, whole and part, subject and object, true and false, fair and foul, good and evil, right and wrong, more and less, are so many examples of terms which express a dual unity of thought. Neither term of the pair can be truly thought, except as both are thought. To these might be added many others. I know not how many. But it is certain that finite and infinite belong to this class; and, therefore, it is beyond dispute that, if we have the conception of finite intelligence, power, and goodness, we have also the conception of infinite intelligence, power, and goodness. And they are equally clear as a whole. Such a Being is a personality of infinite perfection; and it is not any one of these attributes which properly constitutes his infinity, but all together as a total unity.

It is along this line that I am happy to coincide with a fundamental position of Hegel, whom, on the whole, I regard as unsurpassed among philosophers, because, with faculties equal to any, he inherits their bequests, and uses them as he only could.

On conceiving Creation.

In these days of unprecedented progress, men have discovered not only new capacities, but new incapacities. The philosophic world is now afflicted with a very general inability to conceive creation. It is said that a Newton approaches no nearer to the peculiar power of the Creator than the lowest savage, and that we should have to say the same if Newton's powers were indefinitely exalted and augmented, because the power of creation is not among these powers possessed, and no higher degree of these would bring that in. He could so much better comprehend, expound, and use the things that are; but he could not add an atom to their sum total or detract an atom from it. This is the analytical statement, to which modern thought has attained, of an intellectual hiatus in the philosophic mind of all ages and lands. It really never has formed a clear, definite, and consistent conception of creation; and what it has designated as creation it has always described as if it were evolution. It is well that this has come to be recognized, and the notion of creation discarded as a phrase without any meaning, except that of evolution; for, till the thought is developed into definiteness, it can never be refuted, however erroneous. This developed denial enables us to show that it is the product of three definable errors.

(1) The statement that progress in degree would never result in a higher order or kind is not justified by human experience. All experience, all science, now utters a different note. It is the essential principle of naturalistic evolution, in whose interest the denial in question is made, that higher forms, species, genera, and orders are evolved out of the lower forms and orders of existence. Man has kinds as well as degrees of powers, physical and mental, which do not belong to the polyp and ferns and gases. It is, therefore, conceivable that a very high development of human powers might result in the power of creation.

(2) At all events, this comparison of kinds of powers brings into bold relief the contrasted concep-

tion of a kind of power to which man has *not* attained. By what right and with what significance can we say that man cannot create, if we have no notion or conception of creation? We use words, in such a case, without meaning. We describe evolution as a change in the form of a pre-existing and perduring force; and we say that this is exemplified in all experience, that it is not creation, that creation can be nothing less than an absolute contrast to this, — the absolute beginning of being and force as well as of phenomenal forms. No one who develops articulately his whole thought can escape this; and this is the distinct and definite expression of the conception of creation, in contrast with the conception of evolution. Indeed, the two are the logical contradictory correlatives of each other. Neither can be definitely conceived, except in contrast with the other; and the proper and adequate conception of either, analytically developed, involves the conception of the other, just as good and bad, light and dark, high and low, heavy and light, must be conceived together, if truly and fully conceived at all.

(3) While it is true that the difference between the philosopher and the troglodyte is chiefly one of intelligence, this is not the only power man possesses. He has a will power which is peculiar and striking, if not wonderful and awful. Education and culture in art and science do not necessarily develop this in proportion to the intellect. But we know that it exists in different degrees of power in different men, that in the lowest as well as the highest its action often, if not always, generates a new order of phenomena and sequences, both internal and external. Will is thus universally recognized as a power of changing to some extent the forms and direction of the forces of the world. True, it cannot increase or diminish the sum of these forces. That were to create and annihilate, and to say we cannot thus create is to express a definite conception of creation as well as

to deny that it is within the power of man. We can conceive of a Being who can do what we cannot do, who can do for essential force and being what we can do by volition only for the form and order of temporal phenomena in some degree. As my puny volition can set a vast train of forces in operation in a determined direction, so my mind can conceive of a Being whose will *may* have brought these forces into existence, and who can increase or destroy them at his pleasure.

The old allegation, that Infinite Power would become finite as soon as there were aught besides itself, contradicts the presupposition on which it is made,— that the Infinite is immutable and yet a power that can create or increase the sum of existence. Its own nature is not changed by the act, else it would not be immutable or infinite or creative, all of which are contained in the presupposition which the allegation in question seeks to invalidate. If you define infinite as the sum of all existence, then, of course, it cannot create anything which is not a constituent of itself; that is, it cannot create in the sense of adding to the sum of being: it can only evolve new modes of itself. But that definition assumes the point in debate, while the definition we have given does not. The Infinite is the immutable Power which is competent to do whatsoever does not involve a self-contradiction. All are obliged to admit no less than this, and none can go higher. It now remains to inquire whether creation is inconsistent with this. I claim that it is not, because it leaves the Infinite the same; and it is not a self-contradiction to say that he can add to the sum of being indefinitely. Therefore, this power must belong to him, else he is not able to do whatsoever does not involve a self-contradiction. Such a power is of the highest rank, and, if it does not exist, there is no Infinite Being; and, if this creative power does not exist and operate, the term infinite is only a name for the indefinite, the finite.

Equally false and illogical is the declaration that Creative Power must work under conditions which prove its finity, since the conditions are limitations. Primarily and ultimately, the Infinite Creative Power cannot work under finite conditions, because, to begin with, or before creation, there are none; and, after creation, they are infinitely subordinate, and are therefore of no account in the calculation. The only conditions, therefore, under which the Creative Power works are the qualities and laws of his own being; and, as he is infinite, the alleged conditions are infinite. They are not conditions at all, in the sense of limitation, but only as modes in which Infinite Perfection operates with infinite freedom, which is the action of Infinite Power, self-approved.

The creative act needs no explanation in a higher law and power, because it is itself the action and expression of the *Highest* Power and Law,—the Infinite Nature itself. This Being is absolutely and supremely a law unto himself, because he is infinite ; and conformity to this law is at once perfect freedom and absolute necessity, else he would not be infinitely perfect. As there are no objective conditions before creation, God is the creator, not only of all finite things, but of all finite conditions and relations, so that there is here no logical obstacle in the way of creation.

While God is shut out of the universe so far that he is not identified with its forces any more than with its forms,—so that the universe is an automaton,—it is not to be confounded with the old deistic mechanism, the violability and inviolability of whose laws have been so much debated. So far as known to us, mechanisms do not sustain and repair themselves, while the universe does. The universe is a living organic whole, not as the organism of Deity, but as the working forms of the human spirit, as the absolute ego.

If this leaves nothing for God to do,—as some may

regretfully say,—so much the better, I should say. Why should we be anxious to find work for God? Cannot he be supposed to be worthily employed except at some task we have given him? Besides, what is the value of that product of his creative power which cannot do anything except as he works it? The more it contains *in itself* of an elemental force, manifested in ceaseless, various, and progressive action and unfoldment, the more nobly does it bear the stamp of the divine wisdom and power. Such is the universe, the mind of man, the soul of the world. It is a superficial and logically antitheistic philosophy which assails the created product as a mechanical contrivance which dispenses with its Creator, shutting him out from all action in the world unless he interfere with its laws, which would confound science and dishonor his own work and plan. It is possible for the kosmic mechanism to have been so planned as to require extra agency all along the route of its action or at intervals here and there. As this is conceivable, it is enough, because it is the conception of the universe which we are considering.

Further, for an extra-natural agent to act on nature and use nature, or in any wise modify nature's action, is not a violation of its order. The human volition thus operates on organic nature, and thence on the external world; and any superhuman volition may do this. And, if such agency is invisible or supersensible, so that we see its effects only, whether these appear through the organism of a human being, as in prophets, or directly in the changed phenomena of nature, it becomes a miracle, a wonder, a "sign" of said agency. This does not in any wise imperil or impair either science or religion, because science itself observes its own boundaries and nature's fixity, together with the interactions of the higher forces. All that we need here is due proof of superhuman action in relation to nature's action and forms; and this we can know by knowing Nature's own regular and necessary action and the difference of its action in all such superhuman interpositions, so that all through it is a scientific observation. It is not the mechanical construction of the world which is here the source of our trouble, but the *mechanical notion of human and superhuman action* relative to nature as a mechanism, as if that action interfered with the nature, plan, and laws of the mechanism, as scientists assume sometimes.

The Church has never been much divided on the question of the immanence and emmanence of the Divine Being relative to the universe; and very few Christian divines, if any, have held either view to the exclusion of the other. For all alike hold that the universe is finite and other than God, as well as infinitely less than God. They therefore all hold that, in every possible meaning, God must transcend the universe. They must also logically allow, as they do,—the Greek as well as the Latin,—that the created universe is really something, that it constitutes some complexus of forces, so that of itself it can and will do something, or else what is the wisdom of creating it,—a thing utterly powerless and useless? They also claim, with united voice, that this created universe is not to be worshipped, because it is not God, but that it is yet a thing of such grandeur, glory, and power as to be worthy of the creative fiat of the Infinite. They only differ in that some of them more than others vaguely identify or unite the agency of God with the agency of nature. And the Greek Fathers, perhaps, do this more than the Latin, —not always; for the Gnostics and Platonizing Christians, who were far the most numerous among the Greeks, made matter an eternal force other than and independent of God (and, indeed, so did Aristotle and some of the Latin Fathers and theologians down to a late date). But, whatever their minor differences, all the Christian Fathers and theologians have equally been at an infinite remove from the kosmic philosophers who merge God in an eternal universe, conscious or unconscious. No writer should confound these two systems of God and the universe, and attempt to advance the latter view in the name of the former, as some are doing, which is a discredit either to their perspicacity or equity.

The kosmic view, so far from exalting, as its advocates claim, degrades the notion of God. Though it may allow that God is more or less a sort of mentality as adumbrated by our own, yet, as it confines his action to nature and conscious finite beings as the modes of his agency, it limits him, because these are limited. Metaphysicians may affirm the infinity of space, if they choose; but the assertion of the infinity of its contents is a self-contradiction, unless all space is absolutely filled, which no one can affirm. Further, this notion degrades Deity to the rank of the lowest organic and even inorganic beings, and does not raise him anywhere above them, for that were to transcend the universe; and, if that were allowed, we could assign no limit to his possible varied action, whether in accordance with or in counteraction of some natural forms and motions or irrespective of them.

Finally, this kosmic notion furnishes no advantages in relation to science and natural law. It does, indeed, secure by necessity regularity of nature's action; but so does the conception of the world as a created unconscious complexus of forces. It has, indeed, the peculiar distinction of keeping its God constantly occupied, like a blind Samson grinding in the prison-house to keep the mill going,—a form of activity we do not court for God or man relative to their creations or inventions. It keeps God always at work, without ever being able to effect an achievement. According to the counter theory, he is able to achieve some works at once,—to speak, and it is done; to command, and it stands fast. Kosmic theism says that God is the universe and no more. Christian theism says that the Creator infinitely transcends the universe, and is able to vary it at will, and also to work with infinite variety in ways transcending our imagination, which is limited by our experience; and we suppose he is so working, as implied in his infinity.

The theory of a kosmic deity immanent in the universe, if pondered a little more deeply, will disclose a new and more startling aspect. The advocates of this theory hold, for the most part, to the doctrine of modern psychological science, that all phenomena are subjective states; and these states include all the known and knowable universe. Hence, immanence in the universe is only immanence in the individual sensible ego.

It is evident that writers, in the course of their exposition of divine immanence in the universe, have forgotten the proper modern scientific meaning of the word. Their thought has slipped down to the old pre-scientific and still vulgar notion of the universe as non-egoistic. In unfolding their theology, they have entirely contradicted their psychology. They think only of one universe as all-embracing, vast, and boundless, fit area for the Infinite Presence, and affording scope for the exercise of his infinite energies. Hence, in close connection with the subject, they dwell upon the proofs of the unity of the universe, which are utterly needless to those who keep in mind that all phenomena are modes or states of one subject, which implies that the universe is not only a unity, but a conscious unity, of which doubt is impossible.

Now, if we recollect the great dictum of psychological science, that the universe is a complex state of consciousness, it becomes very obvious that the immanence of God in the universe is only his immanence in me and in others like me; and all will allow that it does not take much of a deity to fill the immensity of the sensations of a human being or any number of them. A God confined to such a domicile will never command much reverence.

If, as is often alleged, this immanent Deity operates all the universe, he operates my sensibility and no more. He is thus made the subjective energy of all my sensitive being and experience, and so is identified with me. He and I cannot be discriminated. From psychological science, I learn that I am the immanent subject, active and passive, of all my own conscious states, and that these include the whole universe. From the theology of kosmic theism, I learn that this immanent subject-agent of all my sensitive conscious states, or the universe, is Deity. God is thus but another name for self,—certainly, a practical truth often exemplified.

Kosmic theism appears to no better advantage in arguing from cause to effect, or from effect to cause. Contrary to all the affirmations and implications of modern science that matter is not dead and inert, but contains all the quality and potency of life, they unwarrantably pronounce that its energy is a foreign element which pervades matter, shapes, animates, and directs it; that all the material sciences show only forms, colors, and relative local changes, not the action of any force; that the recognition of force is extra-scientific and supersensible, so that it is not material; that this force is persistent through all material changes, the eternal and almighty factor of all things. What is universally in all other connections called material force is called by kosmic theism God. The God of kosmic theism is material force.

But this persistent force, this god almighty in the material world, can never be discriminated from the material world itself. Matter and its force are never known apart, and never can be. If the force is not a sensible phenomenon, it is not immediately known, but only inferred. And the question next arises whether we are to infer that it is intrinsic or extrinsic to known matter; that is, whether or not it is matter as one with matter. The simplest inference is that they are one; that matter is intrinsically forceful, and the simple is to be preferred, as there is no reason for the opposite. Now, we have an intelligible unit of perception and conception; and matter is competent, for aught we know, to be the sole author of all the forms and motions that the universe unfolds. We, therefore, need, so far, no other god; and kosmic theism is good only for those who are pleased to split matter into form and force, and to call the latter god, and to forget that the form in which this god is said to dwell is the conscious sensitive ego. The theism of Jesus and Paul and of Christianity is of a very different character, and must have a very different support.

The Logical Method and Demands in Proof of Deity.

The popular heisenism or objective evolution begins its investigations with the senses and the outer world. This is the way philosophy began among the early Greeks. A loftier method and scope were given to it by Plato and Aristotle. In this age, a very numerous and conspicuous party return to philosophic juvenility, and proclaim it loudly and with absolute assurance to be the acme of philosophic procedure. And it is of eminent service in working a fruitful field, which is only one sphere of consciousness. It is possible to begin our inquiries with our inner consciousness instead of our senses; and, in that case, we must analyze the senses and their objects in relation to consciousness. This is the correct and most thorough method; for we are not thorough with the senses till we have gone as far in our analysis as consciousness and its logical implications justify, and we cannot justly go any further. As all philosophers admit, the phenomena of the outer world itself are all resolvable into sensations; that is, modes of consciousness. Consciousness should be our starting-point, as this method is the most comprehensive and profound and ulterior. Still, to meet sensism on its own ground, we have commenced with the senses, and have analyzed them into forms of consciousness, or have supposed this to have been already done.

If the analysis of the facts of sense or consciousness then compels us to identify the objects and subjects of sense, and so to accept some form of heisenism, that form will be subjective, the outward world being but a mode of our subjective being, the evolution into consciousness of our intrinsic, subconscious force, which first evolves the inorganic world, and then, successively, the organic forms of life, including what I call my own organism.

The process and result of this subjective heisenism are pre-eminently individualistic and personal. The cosmic world known to each person or individual being himself is numerically different from that known to any other individual, just as the individuals are different. Hence, the universe, as known or knowable to each, begins with his own conscious existence, if this had a beginning.

The operation of the law of natural causation, by which naturalism maintains itself, to the exclusion of all supernaturalism, is confessedly all confined within the kosmic universe, as thus knowable to each individual, which universe is often styled "Nature." Hence, they are precluded from applying their principle to the connection of one mind or individual man with another. Hence, also, if men have a beginning, universes have a beginning; and naturalism cannot account for this. And natural force and law have here no place or operation. Such beginnings are supernatural, and must have a supernatural cause. On the theory of subjective heisenism, if we can prove the commencement of our individual existence, we shall prove that the kosmic universe, known to us or knowable by us, had a beginning, and that it is the product of a supernatural agency. A supernatural Being, as the Creator of all knowable things, will thus be demonstrated.

This being attained, all subordinate supernaturalism necessarily associated with theism may be easily vindicated. A Creator and creation being proved, we have gained the great point of religions, supernaturalism; and subordinate forms and varieties of supernatural operation and manifestation may be proved to be reasonable and proper.

The Positive Method must supersede the Old Metaphysical Method.

Positivism is normally religious, because it is inevitably impressed with religious phenomena, which it cannot ignore, though it may not be able to explain. The old metaphysical method invented certain essences and quiddities,— an abstract substance or noumenon or absolute as the explanation. Positivism prefers to do without the explanation for three good reasons: First, the explanation does not explain; second, we have no proof of the existence of the things alleged, because they are beyond the sphere of any possible experience; and, third, because they are, therefore, in themselves, confessedly incogitable. Admit such things, and we may as well admit anything; for all sensible and all logical barriers are broken down. The admission may then defeat the object for the sake of which it was made. The mediæval theologians distinguished themselves by these admissions in support of Orthodoxy; and, in modern times, these have been the most prolific source of heresy in high intellectual latitudes.

The old metaphysical distinction, for instance, between substance and quality cannot be made by Positivism, because such substance is unknowable. The only substance it can affirm is that which is identical with the known, with quality or attribute, which is the doctrine we have advocated, and must insist on.

Had this principle been fully grasped by Spinoza, how different would have been his speculations and the course of modern thought! His *Ethics* is based and carried out on that old and incogitable distinction of substance from quality. If substance is different from all quality (and even from essence), as he affirms, there is nothing to distinguish one substance from another, and no reason for asserting more than one; and, with logical rigor, he affirms only one, and all quality and essence as its modes. This notion of substance helped to seduce Leibnitz into his doctrine of monadology, as it furnished, verbally at least, a possible unity at the base, where he was made even with Spinoza, whom he dared not own. The same distinction, with different terminology, has had an equally conspicuous place and power in all systems and in popular apprehension, down to our own time, save where the recent spirit of Positivism has shed an effective light. While I hold to the unity of the knowable universe, I object to such a method of proving it. Intrinsically false, it is certain, everywhere, to be obstructive to all true science and philosophy.

If our exposition is correct, Positivism is more profound and thorough than it claimed to be. If substance and quality, force and phenomena, cause and effect, are one, then, in getting a thorough knowledge of either, we have both; and our knowledge, if sufficiently comprehensive, is ultimate and perfect,— the true and final philosophy.

This implies a rebuke of Agnosticism, which deals so largely in the intrinsically unknowable, in distinction from the phenomenal. It is either one with the phenomenal or there is no unity; and, if there is any such unity, it is a unity of force, of which all phenomena are so many modes. And, if there is anything beyond this unitary force or quality, it is useless, since forceless, and can be dispensed with, and must be, since it is only a word.

Positivism, however, is intrinsically averse to supernaturalism in the spirit of its votaries, but not in its essential method. Its glory is that it is a method, and the correct and perfected method to which the other and imperfected methods—the theological and metaphysical—were not only preliminary, but ancillary. Now, if the method itself should ever be found to lead to the supernatural, of course that is properly the end of all aversion to such a conclusion, and the legitimate end of pure and exclusive naturalism. Besides, in any case, Positivism is bound to be consistent in its procedure and conclusions. If, in following its method faithfully, it is obliged either to contradict itself or infer the supernatural, it must do the latter, or it violates its fundamental law and destroys its own method, and its glory is departed. This is the alternative forced upon us in the present chapter. We have tracked and analyzed the varying phenomena of sense till we have classified them all as modes of the ego. We have then seen that we universally act on a system of sematic symbolism, on which we assume the existence of other beings beyond our universe, answering to the extra-organic forms of our experience. On the basis of this symbolism, we next infer that they and we act and change with lexical regularity relative to each other. But for this correspondence there can be, it is plain, no natural cause. Here the original Positivism, in its crudest form, comes in and says: We have nothing to do with that. We do not seek causes, but only related phenomena. But a wiser and more mature representative of the method approaches, and speaks as follows: It is true we invent no metaphysical or abstract entity which can never be known by experience in explanation of the phenomena of experience; but we may infer what we do not experience and actually never can experience, else logic or reasoning and even intellectual intuition were of no use. The great body of science is largely made up of such inferences. Now, if by common consent we enter on a certain line of reasoning on admitted facts, we may not stop arbitrarily along the route where there is just the same reason for advancing as there was for taking the first step. Here, without being conscious of the vast movement, we have crossed a gulf such as was never before contemplated, vaster and more vacuous than the awful chaos crossed by Milton's fallen arch-fiend in his primal passage from hell to earth. This gulf we have passed on the wings of induction, which are the great and lauded powers of scientific locomotion through the universe. In the case under consideration, they have carried us beyond the known universe to other universes. This passage is made by all, every day. We affirm the existence of such universes, and that they are like our own. But we never saw them. No one ever saw any but his own. He induces them on the basis of the sematic principle. In so doing, we have, for some of our experiences, inferred a cause and explanation which transcend the known universe and all possible experience; and it is very arbitrary and irrational to stop here and refuse to answer on the same principle the irresistible question, Whence comes the harmony which we so confidently affirm between other men and us; that is, between unknown universes and our own? And Positivism will not be true to its better self to utter this refusal. It would become the victim of a self-engendered and fatal atrophy, and be speedily superseded by a more robust philosophy.

XVI.

ORIGIN OF MAN.

Not Known Directly.

THAT our individual existence had a beginning has never been questioned, and to go about with much ado to furnish the proof of this universal postulate will appear to most men ludicrously superfluous. But to be assured of a thing, and to be able to give a scientific account of it, are far from being the same; and it is the latter we want and which we are bound to furnish, and the question is not so simple as it at first seems. Neither our senses nor our inner consciousness can inform us of the beginning of our own existence, since we are already in existence when these powers come into operation. So Milton represents the rebellious angels doubting their creation because they know nothing about it, and arguing that they may have always existed.

We see other children born; but those visible children are only secondary qualities of matter, mere affections of sight, modes of our own conscious selves. In the same way and with the same result, we may go through all our sensible experience respecting the birth of children and the beginning of human existence.

Our proof of the beginning of our own existence is inferential, an induction from the facts of experience; and we make this induction on the principle of analogy and sematology. This organism of ours, pronounced to be ours because of its special and peculiar sensitiveness relative to ourselves, resembles those forms which we call the bodies of other men; and, as we know from consciousness that ours is the outward embodiment and impersonation of a living conscious being, we infer by analogy that those other bodies are signs of the existence of other beings who are, in endowments and circumstances, as much like ourselves as these bodies are like our own, and that, as our bodies undergo certain changes in concurrence with certain conscious changes in accordance with fixed laws, we infer that the changes in those other bodies (which are only modes of self) indicate certain other changes in the conscious beings which they represent. As we can often observe the changes in many of these bodies more than in our own in some respects, the knowledge of them may help us to determine respecting ourselves what we cannot directly learn from consciousness.

We can be conscious of being, though we cannot be conscious of beginning. We can be also conscious of the anterior end of a train of recollected states of consciousness, which affords a presumption of the absolute beginning of such states. By the law of sematology, on which in some way we are always acting, from infancy to old age, each knows that others had a beginning as organic forms before himself, that our parents preceded us, and that they had parents. By the same law, they know that other human beings are all the time commencing existence as organic.

Our Alleged Parents not the Cause of our Existence.

No being can be strictly the offspring or natural effect of anything in the same universe, because all the alleged products or offspring of each are himself or modes of himself. The child that is immediately known to the parents is the parents; and each parent, and all others, know or see and hear and feel a different object, which they call the same. As all immediate percepts are egoistic, no two persons can have the same immediate percepts; and the objects of each sense are peculiar to that sense. No sense cognizes any thing or object cognized by any other sense. The one child is, therefore, a different child for every person and for every sense of every person. This egoistic child, so called, which is immediately known because it is egoistic, is a sign or representation of a conscious being, which holds a very sublime and mysterious relation to those who are called the parents of the phenomenal child, and by whom it is considered and appropriated as theirs in a peculiar sense. The real child—the spirit or conscious being—is known to them immediately only through the egoistic sign-child.

The sign-child is from the parents, because it is the parents; and the alleged parent is also the child. The real child or spirit is not from the recognized parents, but from some other source or cause. These parents are not the natural cause of the non-egoistic or real child, because it does not belong to the cosmic system to which they belong, or, rather, which belongs to them, and which they constitute, and with which only they are or can be immediately acquainted. Natural causation, as recognized by science, is only between the objects and forces of the same one kosmic system. But, as every conscious subject has a kosmic universe of its own, absolutely egoistic and numerically different from all others, so the child, the real child or spirit, has no universe in common with the parents. Natural causation is, therefore, as before seen, impossible between any two human beings, so far as that causation is immediately known or knowable, which is the character, we repeat, of all natural causation heretofore recognized. Recognized natural causation is always between antecedents and consequents that are or may be immediately known as objects of consciousness. But we can thus know only the ego. Therefore, natural causation is always limited to the ego. Hence, parents are natural causes, not of real children, but only of sign-children, which are modes of self.

The declaration that there is no *recognized* natural causation between different men and successive generations will strike many as absurdly wrong. They will, in refutation of it, confidently point to obvious facts of life and history, the unity of the social fabric, and the manifest evolution of all things. But this is irrelevant. All these phenomena and their changes are purely subjective states. So far as known, they are simply the evolutions of thought and feeling and volition, modes of the individual life; and all the interaction here spoken of is only that which obtains between these modes of the ego. While admitting the egoism of all sense percepts, Positivism can only be positive for the subject, which is all it positively knows. The subject is the sphere of all phenomena, of all succession, and of all action and interaction that we ever directly know. The known action and interaction are of phenomena, which include what are called men, women, animals, and inanimate forms and forces; and all these, in every case, are *one* man. If there is any causal interaction between *that* one man and any other intelligence, that action does not belong to the phenomena of the known universe. If there were those who preceded us and had an agency in our production or generation, we never knew them and never can. They never had an existence in the universe to which we belong. Those forms which are called our parents and ancestors are our own very selves, and not our natural authors or even predecessors. All times, all spaces, are included in the vast capacity of my small individuality. It is, therefore, a logical impossibility that anything in the universe should be the cause of my existence; for, since all that universe is myself, I should then have to be my own creator, and act with creative energy before I had an existence. The universe is the cause of my organic existence; but that is only to say that I have evolved this as one of the many modes of myself.

Knowable Nature not the Cause of Man.

As our recognized and sensible parents cannot be the source of our being or the cause of our existence as individualities, so neither can the knowable world called Nature be such source or cause ; for the reason that all Nature, so far as known to each of us, is his own nature or self only. The universe known to me could not exist before me and generate me, any more than I could exist before I existed, and be my own creator. It is, however, possible, on the other hand, that I existed before the known universe, and that I am its author as I am its subject. And the universe having been created by God (or, less probable, engendered by myself), it generates organic forms.

Universal Symbolism of Successive Changes.

We have already seen that human and animal forms are symbols of living beings beyond our universe, which correspond with us as these correspond with our organism. We shall now be permitted and logically obliged to extend this symbolism, so as to make every birth the symbol of an unknown creature entering on a new state of existence, corresponding to the form and state of the body born ; and every death the symbol of such a being leaving the state in which it has been existing, and entering on another which, perhaps, is not symbolized to us. This symbol'sm is familiar to modern thought, and it is only the formulation of it which is really novel. It therefore needs no proof or defence. All acknowledge that human bodies are not other men, yet all agree that the birth and death of these bodies are proofs of the beginning and ending of distinctly organic human lives ; and this is justifiable only on the basis of the symbolism which I have expressed. We make this system of symbolism perfect by making it strictly universal, extending it to all lower organic changes, whether modern or ancient or fossil. It is thus we read the past record of our own and countless other universes with assurance.

Creation in the Lowest Condition.

The theory that every birth denotes there and then an immediate creation is not favored by Sematology. Sematology seems rather to indicate that all organic human beings have evolved from inferior pre-existing conditions, extending in a receding series back to the preorganic world, the source of all organic forms and organic life. Because such is the fact concerning the men and animals of the phenomenal world.

This, however, does not necessarily invalidate the argument for creation ultimately, but only for the immediate separate creation in every instance when a new form appears. While it allows that evolution is of vast extent and marvellous variety, it also implies that the original being, which at first is very low down in the scale of existence, and which admits of all this evolution, is endowed with a very marvellous capacity. This evolution, be it remembered, is not the successive extinction and generation of new beings, but only the evolution of new forms of the same being. The whole known universe is a substantive unity, and that unity is the one subject and no more, so that every evolution of an apparently new life is the evolution only of a new mode of the same life or subject. In the capacity for this evolution from the lowest organism and preorganic form up to man, and perhaps indefinitely beyond him, is seen the wondrous power of the original endowment of the one subject. And each of these, if created, is the creation of a thing with all this power of development, which is not less wondrous than the creation of the power fully developed. And, if all this is forethought and planned, it is far more wonderful.

It is the primitive and still popular opinion, and favored by objective evolution, that the world of inorganic matter preceded man and all organic life. But how can that be, if it have no existence except so far as it is perceived? This question, raised by the theory of Berkeley, Berkeley met by saying that it was seen by angels before the creation of organic life. But that answer is fantastic, besides travelling beyond the domain of philosophy and obtruding into that of theology; and, even then, it is good only for his own solitary notion that all sensible phenemena are non-egoistic, while all modern psychologists have affirmed that they are subjective states.

So far as they are subjective states, they cannot precede their subject; and, so far as they are organic affections, they cannot precede the organism. But modern psychology, with great and growing unanimity, affirms the subjective and organic character of all sensible phenomena. And yet it is universally assumed, inconsistently, that the organism, if not the conscious subject, is evolved out of the sensible world, which has been already declared to be an organic affection, which must hence be evolved from itself, which is its own refutation.

To evade this, resort is had to the assumption of a sort of unimaginable as well as unknowable mind-stuff, out of which the known world, organic and inorganic, is evolved. That is equally blind and unwarrantable by any principle in science or philosophy, a mere invention without any conception of the thing invented, so that it is only a verbal process.

Besides, it is ineffective at the best, so long as sensible phenomena are pronounced to be organic affections, because it cannot dispel the conviction or annul the fact that the inorganic world is preorganic and the source of the organic, which it cannot be, if it is itself only an organic affection as well as a subjective state. Our organism is posterior to the sensible world, arises from it and returns to it by dissolution ; and thus the world exists after as it was prior to the organism.

The solution of this knotty problem is to be found in conceiving all sensible phenomena as subjective states, but not as organic affections. Some of them are organic affections, and some are not ; and we need to discriminate the two classes of subjective states.

All visual phenomena except the visible organism are extra-organic. Their occurrence and recurrence are conditioned on some conditions and relations of the organism, but they are not the organism nor any affections thereof. The earth, the houses, the rivers, mountains, and ocean which I see are all beyond my organism, though they are subjective states. They are extra-organic modes of my own existence. All men see them as extra-organic ; and psychologists discern them as subjective states, and have thence erroneously concluded that they are also organic states, which is the source of all our confusion here. While muscular contraction is an organic affection, the stone wall which resists its action is extra-organic. In touch (without special resistance) there is a twofold sensation when we touch our vital organism ; and this is wanting when we touch anything beyond the organic periphery, and this is the recognized sign that the object touched is beyond the organism, an extra-organic conscious state or affection.

This extra-organic world existed before the organic. It existed as it does now as a subjective state, without its present lexical relations to the organism and its affections. These relations it establishes as fast as it evolves the organism; and they vary as vary the forms and stages of evolution, both organic and inorganic. Thus, while the world preceded all organic life, as all sense and science affirm, it did not precede ourselves as a conscious being, because, as known to me, it is me, the sub-organic modes in which

I exist and operate and express myself. Hence, the creation of the world is the creation of a conscious spirit, the whole knowable universe one such being, and the universes therefore just as numerous as individual spirits or souls.

It is perhaps possible that these several universes or individuals are uncreated and are eternally undergoing a process of successive evolution and involution or deterioration. But the very marvel of evolution in the facts of which we have already taken cognizance renders that supposition extremely improbable. As each individual constitutes a universe, and as these have no connection of natural cause between them, and as they are each evolving themselves in lexical connection with all the rest, as shown by sematology, we hence see how vast and various and all-seeing is the supernatural agency which secures this lexical harmony and sematizes it to all. It is easy to see that such a Being can be better employed than in the labor of an eternal balancing of evolution and involution, or progress and deterioration, and that the better employment would be creation. It accords better with our higher intuition as well as with the phenomena of science that under the dominion of such a Power there is an absolute progress, and not merely the everlasting rise and fall successively of the two ends of a beam.

If we look at the history of phenomena, we shall find no ground for a theory of an eternal balancing of evolution and involution. Deterioration is infinitesimal, so far as known to us, compared with progress. Kosmic collapse and re-evolution do not here enter into the calculation, because they are unknown, are only conjectural and without any sure or strong evidence. And, if they were known, they could only indicate what is common to the race, not the elevation of some and the depression of others ; and a new kosmic cycle might introduce an order of creatures far superior to any we know, including man. So vital decay in old age and other cases may be preliminary, as in the supposed worn-out world, to entering on a new and higher career. Certainly, the various forms of weakness preceding death are no proof of coming degradation in the next state, else there would be no progress or evolution anywhere, which contradicts all phenomenal indicators. The only evidence of an eternal balancing of progress and retrogression is to be sought in a comparison of progressive organic evolution and deterioration. Here the case becomes clear. There is organic deterioration where it is not a process of dissolution or a sign of transition, but a comparatively permanent state and propagated by generation; and this deterioration compared with progressive evolution, so far as we can judge, is almost infinitely small, so that, to keep up this progression, a successive origination of lower creatures is necessary.

Proofs of Creation summed up.

Now let us in conclusion sum up our evidence in favor of creation. We have already proved the existence of a supernatural Being, whose power and intelligence are of vast and unknown extent, as the great relative regulator of the mighty clock universes, so as to make them keep time with each other, and to guarantee this as the foundation of the sematic proof of the existence of other men and of our practical intercourse with them, which is all supernatural, because transcending nature. The very existence of such a Being makes creation probable; for, as he is thus superior to all nature or natures, it is but natural and easy next to suppose that he is their Creator. And, further, it would seem that their creation, with certain specific capacities relative to each other, were necessary, in order that they may work in accord with each other. Then let us bear in mind the further fact that, so far as our knowledge extends, evolution is very vastly in excess of deterioration, which makes creation necessary in order to keep up the process, because there can be no common stuff out of which it has heretofore been supposed they are or may be evolved, and all existence is individualistic, and all evolution is self-evolution, the same thing evolving itself into other modes of the same thing, never into other things.

Then, having followed the order of lexical mutations back and down to the lowest conditions, we must ask an explanation of that condition, why and whence. And the most rational answer is, Creation. Else we must suppose an (almost) infinite number of individualities existing unchanged from all eternity, and yet endowed with powers of developing into various successive universes, and then begin a course of evolution in marvellous and absolutely inexplicable supernatural yet lexical harmony with all other evolutions. That were far more astonishing than creation, especially now that we have already found a Being who, for aught we know, is competent to create, and who, it seems, must determine their original endowments, relative to all others, in order that they may evolve themselves in accord with all the rest of the great general class to which they belong; and it would be hard to distinguish this from creation, since original quality or force is the only being or substance. Finally, let us remember that the creation of each individual is the creation of an incipient universe, and, therefore, that, in every birth, we see the sematic (inductive) proof that such creation has preceded said birth as a precondition of its occurrence, and that the process of such preorganic creation is still going on always, and promises to continue to do so without end.

Our Creation in the Preorganic State.

Here let us guard against a natural misconception, atomic and rudimentary : When I advocate creation, I do not plead for the creation of a human organism, nor any other organism, high or low. That is evolved from the world. Nor do I plead for the creation of the human soul, to be put into the developed human organism, as some hold. The organically conscious human soul is one with the organism; and, as such, it is evolved from the world. Nor do I speak of man's origin or creation in time. Man himself includes all time and times, and time begins and ends with his conscious existence. The question, therefore, as to when man began his existence is utterly unmeaning. Each man began his existence at least as early as the universe known to him began to be, if there ever was such a beginning; for this universe is he or it, the ego. Of this beginning, we can have no demonstrative proof; but I think we have some probable evidence, which, to me, is quite satisfactory.

The hasty reader may object that we know the sensible world only in connection with organic affections; that to destroy the organic sense is to destroy for us the sensible world; that, therefore, we should conclude that we had no preorganic knowledge of the world; and that we have no knowledge or memory of our own preorganic existence; and that we know ourselves only as organic, or as related to the organism. This is a specimen of a very natural but unscientific way of thinking and reasoning. There is truth in it, but the truth is rendered false by its isolation from other truths with which it is vitally connected.

By implication, it contradicts the doctrine of the subjectivity of sensible phenomena, because, as before noticed, if they are subjective states or modes of ourselves, and if we had no existence before the organism, then the sensible world, which exists only in us, as our various feelings, had no preorganic existence, which contradicts both all science and all common sense. Let the reader consider this, and be consistent. Let him deny, if he can, that the sensible world is a subjective state or mode of self, or that it had a preorganic existence, or else he is logically bound to affirm that its subject existed before the organism, and that the external world thus preexisted as its subjective states or modes. The science of psychology impales him on the first horn of the trilemma. All the physical sciences and common thought unite to impale him on the second horn. And, hence, the forceps of logic seizes him, and pitches him on to the third.

How comes it, then, that we know the world only through organic affections? If we knew it before we had an organism, before we were born, why do we not know it now independently of any of the senses? Whether we can answer this question satisfactorily or not, that does not affect the value or verity of the above exposition and argument. It is possible that we were once able to do what we cannot do now, though we cannot duly explain either the ability or the inability. We know that modes of knowledge and action have changed in the history of the life of our planet, and that new forms of knowledge and power have been continually relegating old ones into desuetude and oblivion. Stubborn solid facts do not liquefy and flow off, because impotency bids them in vain to explain themselves. Yet, in this case, the facts are not wholly inexplicable, because we see them in their connections of time and place, which is, for the most, all the explanation that science claims to give.

There is also an explanation to be found in the very existence of the organism, such as it is. The fact that it has come into existence especially by natural evolution implies that, so long as it exists as such, it establishes and maintains relations with the world, so that only or chiefly in such relations is the world henceforth known. These relations cannot be ignored so long as they exist. And, as the organism is only a mode of self and the external world another mode of self, their common subject simply knows both in their mutual relations. If we falsely conceive ourselves as not only identified with the organism, but as confined to it, we may then suppose that we know the world only through the organism, and only on that false basis.

What is called sense perception is not an organic perception or the organism perceiving. The organism and the extra-organic are perceived by a super-organic and a super-material power, of which both these are perceptive acts or subjective states. It is not the eye that sees or the ear that hears. They are seen and known by the supersensible ego. As before quoted from the Greek poet,—

"Mind, it seeth; mind, it heareth:
All beside is deaf and blind."

This supersensible power discerns the external world usually in certain relations with the organism; but that is only a temporary fact, and not a necessity.

Nor is it a universality of human experience. There are numerous and indubitable proofs that the mind often has knowledges which do not come through any organic media. Clairvoyance and clairaudience and trance perceptions are proofs of this. Things are seen and heard at distances of time and place, and the soul can give no organic explanation of its knowledge. Cases of this kind are so numerous and clear and well attested, and the prints in which they are found are so accessible, that it were superfluous here to give examples and proofs. It is enough to refer to them, and especially to such publications as those of the London Society for Psychical Research, the London journal, *Light*, the American journals, *Mind in Nature* and the *Religio-Philosophical Journal*, of Chicago.

A still further, but more questionable proof is furnished by the apparition and manifested agency of disembodied spirits, which all ages have believed in, and which in these days have received a study and a faith unparalleled in more credulous and less scientific ages. Doubtless there is a nucleus of fact in the mountain of illusion and imposture which constitute modern Spiritualism. And, if we live and know the world after the body is dissolved, we may have done it before the body was formed ; and here and there, all along the course of our organic history, we may rise above organic conditions.

Creation and Evolution distinguished.

What I have described under the name of creation is to be understood as creation strictly in contrast with evolution, which is what philosophers usually mean when they use the word "creation." I mean by it the absolute causation of existence, not merely the causation of a new mode of an old existence, which is evolution. One of the most pious and nearly orthodox of our recent philosophers is Herman Lotze; but even he is open to the charge of describing only evolution under the name of creation, when he says: "Nor, again, is it out of nothing that the soul is made or created by the Absolute; but, to satisfy the imagination, we may say it is from itself, from its own real nature, that the Absolute projects the soul" (*Metaphysics*, p. 246). This may satisfy the imagination; but it does not satisfy the pure intellect, whose satisfaction only we seek in metaphysics. And here there is no sphere for the imagination. As the Absolute projects the soul from itself, "and so adds to its one activity—the course of nature—that other which, in the ruling plan of the Absolute, is its natural completion," there is, in all this, no addition made to the sum of being, nothing but a modal change or evolution of the eternal. This is panheisenism very clearly, whether or not it rise to the dignity of pantheism. On the other hand, I advocate a theism and creation, proper and pure, in which man and the universe are not conceived as the modes of God's being and action, but the created effects thereof, and absolutely other than himself in mode and substance. If we are a projection from God, we are either one with him—an integral element of deity—or he is diminished by our projection; and neither of these presents us the God of Christian theism.

Man an Intrinsic Force, Individualistic.

I also claim that this creature, whether called nature or soul, is an individual power, which, being once created, can run its course without extraneous aid from any source whatever. It is an intrinsic energy, which not only can act, but must act, according to the nature and degree or extent of its energy. Lotze justly argues that an organism is also a machine; but he claims that God's machine will not run without him, as a man's machine will run without the inventor, because the human inventor finds the forces and laws of nature as pre-existent and independent, relative to him; while God, on the contrary, makes the forces and laws of his machine, and so constitutes their constant and perpetual operator, the very agent of all their action, the real essential force which they seem to exert, the only and immanent energy of all the universe, of all existence.

Now, philosophy ought to be able to see that it is a higher notion of God to see in him a power which can create another power or set of powers, or intrinsic and essential energies, which, from their very nature and from the moment of their creation, are themselves centres and sources of causation, and always operative, without any further agency on the part of God, who can, however, modify their action at will or leave it unmodified, and without any further influence.

Divine Immanence in Nature.

It is a pity, too, that so good a thinker as Lotze, writing at so recent a date, was not able to discern and remove the veil which incompetent philosophy

has thrown over the doctrine of the divine agency in
the universe. If God is the name for the only power
and agency, if he is the immanent sole operator of
all action and motion, then let us, *if possible*, henceforth avoid speaking as if we had any finite individuality, because this is false. Our force or quality of
every kind is God ; and so we are God, simply modes
of the infinite agency. Herein, Spinoza was thorough ; but he was not able to be consistent. He
talks, all along, as if he were not God, while arguing that he is, that there is but one substance and
being, whose attributes are thought and extension.
This one being of thought and extension we who
are thought and extension, ought to worship,—worship ourselves as " not ourselves."

Philosophy ought not to overlook the meaning of
its own words. What is the universe ? In its fullest
meaning, it denotes both the conscious and the unconscious worlds. In this sense, God's active immanence in the universe, as its sole operator, excludes
all individuality of souls or spirits, except as modes
of divine action, as deity so and so, existing and
acting.

If the word "universe" is used only for the unconscious worlds, and if the absolute immanence and
sole agency are limited to this, allowing an intrinsic
individualistic force to conscious beings, we require
a reason or principle in justification of the distinction.
Why should God be identified with the unconscious,
and not with the conscious? If he has created one
form of quality and force as other than himself, why
should he not create another ? Having thus created
the greater, why not also the less ? The implication
of these questions is indeed allowed by philosophers,
and their procedure is based upon it. They disavow
or ignore this distinction. They have but one kind
of creation, whether of the conscious or the unconscious,— the projection or evolution of the absolute
or eternal power into that form or those forms of

existence and action. No distinction of the nature of the creative acts has ever been made between the conscious and unconscious worlds. They are the same in kind.

Immanence in Nature is Immanence in the Ego.

It is high time, surely, for philosophers to see the logical connection between a subjective universe and divine immanence in that universe, which is immanence in the subject. With all metaphysicians of our times, Lotze affirms and elaborately argues that all the known world is a subjective state; and, of this universe, he, with others, says that God is the immanent and exclusive force. This makes God to be immanent in me, as the sole and direct operator of all my sensible experiences. In that case, he cannot be discriminated from me. At the best, it leaves me only a forceless, passive puppet of infinity, abhorrent alike to logic and sentiment and the universal consciousness.

Creation Instantaneous, not Continuous.

I hold that creation is instantaneous and final, not continuous. A continuous creation is a self-contradiction. The continuous is unbroken existence. Creation is the causing of that to be which before had no existence, and a continuous creation implies continuous annihilation as its condition. For how create what already exists? And how create what is continuously annihilated? for that never begins to be. It is a logical self-annihilation all through. Nature is not a mode of the divine agency, but a created effect thereof. A mode of God is God; but nature is a mode of me, who am an effect or creature of God, who made me utterly other than himself, but in his image. Continuous agency is evolution. Creative agency is instantaneous, once for all.

The Soul evolves its own Organism.

The sensible universe, as well as the body, has an organic as well as a dynamic relation to the spirits which is their subject. The spirit it is which moulds the universe, and then moulds its own special organic form of the human body. Against Stahl, who asserted that the soul moulds the body to its own ends, Lotze objects that "the formation of the body, in its most essential and irreversible features," is fixed before consciousness is attained, or when it does not know enough for this (*Metaphysics*, p. 230). But this is inconsiderate, as our exposition shows. We have no evidence that the soul is ever unconscious. Ages indefinite and vast, it existed as a conscious being before the body or any special organism was evolved. According to the laws of this preorganic being, as seen in the material universe, and therefore according to its own ends, it evolved at length the special organism, so that we are, in every case, organically the product of our own preorganic agency, of our own spirit, which is always acting throughout the universe, which is itself. This universe, our spirit, molds the body.

The Soul's Transcendence of the Material Universe.

But the soul transcends the material universe, since it looks upon that universe as only its lowest modes, sensations, in humble contrast with its higher intellections, emotions, and volitions, instinct with the higher life. Hence, philosophers like Lotze and others contradict their own doctrine of universal subjectivity, when they say, "The soul is confined within the limits of nature." This nature or universe is contained in the soul. Their views are very small, as well as inconsistent. They make the universe commensurate with God, and call it infinite. I make it immeasurably less than man, the lower parts of his ways; and man is finite, very.

XVII.

ETIOLOGY.

This subject, after being for ages supposed to be forever settled, has been reduced to chaos, which is preliminary to a new evolution in a higher form.

Designing and Undesigning Causes.

There are designing and undesigning causes. Objective evolution excludes the first from the kosmos, while subjective evolution proves it, and thence proves the supreme action of a supernatural power, God, and thence, probably, proves creation. I have not before mentioned the argument from design, because it was needless and unavailable; but it will hereafter come into legitimate operation on the basis of our new proof of Deity, as an inference from it.

Causes in Science and in Philosophy.

Cause may be considered relative to science only, or relative to philosophy. In science, cause denotes uniform antecedent, for which it is a short expression. All the purposes of science are attained when we have attained the lexical connections of phenomena. This is the positive philosophy, and all the philosophy possible in the estimation of many. But we cannot be content with that. We must ask whether there is any force in these phenomena which makes them what they are or do what they do, or whether they are forces or operated by forces behind them? These are questions for philosophy proper; and the discussion of them is philosophical etiology, which is our present subject.

Etiology relative to Matter and Force.

Etiology is obstructed by a prevailing distinction between matter and force, because this makes all matter forceless and all force immaterial. Though it is held that these are in fact inseparable, yet to suppose them distinguishable involves us in just the same logical difficulty as if they were also separable. The distinguishable are different, however united; and, if there is a difference between force and matter, neither of them is the other, so far as the difference extends. The difference is qualitative; and they are, at least, of different quality. And this leads us to see that the distinction is self-contradictory. All force is quality, and all quality is force, so that the two terms, comprehensively taken, are of the same meaning; and to distinguish between force and matter is to make a distinction between quality and the qualitiless, an intellectual and unconscious blank, which is no distinction at all. Neither matter nor anything else can be distinguished from force, because it is only force or quality that can have any mark or distinction, either internal or external. Nothing is manifestable or conceivable except as force. Forces or qualities we can distinguish from each other, but not all force from aught else, whether we call that other by the empty term matter or spirit.

The subtle and sceptical intellect of David Hume is the source of the modern metaphysical confusion on this subject. He said the senses give us only successive and coexistent phenomena or impressions, and that ideas are only faded sensible impressions, so that we have no other notion of force or cause. Our modern evolutionists are, on one side, sensationalists, and so are disposed to deny that the senses reveal force or cause, or that matter is itself force or cause. On the other hand, they cannot do without force. It is necessary to them as inseparably connected with matter, else the theory of evolution were impossible. So they must have force connected with matter, but not itself matter, not material, not an object of sense, but an inconceivable thing which we are obliged to infer or assume, in order to explain sensible experience. But nothing can ever explain how our senses discern and discriminate as coexistent or successive the qualitiless or forceless, or how none of all the qualitative forms and motions of the material universe are quality, or how without power they are powerful to act as symbols of an unknown force. According to this theory, we know the forceless, but can neither know nor conceive the forcible, —just the opposite of the real fact and the logical necessity. Make all phenomena force, and all difficulty is removed.

Alleged Forcelessness of All Creation.

Theologians, after a long period of futile endeavor to refute Hume's sceptical conclusion on cause, adopted it without acknowledgment, and with a little twisting have turned it to their own supposed advantage. The sensible world being forceless, they argue that there must be a supersensible Power who actuates and directs it. This appears to be equally acute and just. The world cannot act without force, intrinsic or extrinsic; and, as it has no intrinsic force, it must be operated by an extrinsic though immanent force. To the objection that, having no notion of force, their argument is meaningless, they answer that volition gives them the notion of force, of will force, which must be in kind that of the Creator and Operator of the world.

This effort to flank scepticism is a failure. There is no more evidence of force in the will than there is in the external world. Volition is an experience, and conation is an experience with relations of succession and coexistence, just like all sensible experiences; and on the point in question there is nothing to discriminate the two classes of experiences.

Further, force is verified only by its overcoming opposing force. If conation meets no force from without which it overcomes and modifies, it is not a verified force. It does nothing, and there is nothing it can do. There is in will no need of force, and there is no reason for asserting its existence. Either sensible phenomena are forces or volitional phenomena are not forces, or at least not proved to be forces.

A theistic theory that God has created a forceless universe defeats itself. It makes creation a nullity, because utterly useless and worthless, since only quality or force can be of any use anywhere. To think of exalting the Creator by belittling his creation is a strange device. The opposite course is the only path to such an end. The mightier and more various the effect, the more nobly it argues for its cause. If God is the sole power and worker, he has nothing to oppose and overcome, except within himself. If there is anywhere jar and confliction, it is all within himself or of himself; and his own nature, and nothing else, appears to be a boundless range of chaos, anarchy, and war.

I hold that all things, sensible or supersensible, are force ; that, therefore, all things are causes ; that all changes spring either from an internal cause or an external cause ; that, therefore, if anything begins absolutely to be, it must be caused by some power existing before it and numerically different from it. This is intelligible and consistent, and I believe it is ultimate and comprehensive of all that the case logically involves. We thus dispense with all assumptions and postulates, and all appeals to blind, inexplicable, alleged psychological necessity. We accept the notion that all being is force, because, otherwise, self-contradiction ensues, and, by accepting it, we secure consistency of procedure and result, and the use of an ultimate principle of great power and universal application; and we have now a philosophical etiology, which we are entitled and obliged to use in all discussions relative to changes and their origin, whether the changes be substantial or only modal, and which, therefore, must be in perpetual use in the ulterior inquiries of philosophy and rational theology. This is our procedure and underlying principle in arguing from the known to the unknown, from the empirical to the metempirical, from the natural to the supernatural, and from the universe to its Cause, and exhibits and justifies the course I have pursued and shall pursue.

Paralogisms of the Common Metaphysical Principle of Causality.

The more belauded metaphysicians of Germany, France, and Great Britain have contended for a principle of causality as a primal element, necessary and spontaneous, of our constitution. It is therefore claimed by theists to speak with the authority of our Maker,—a claim which is true and indisputable. But the question is inevitable, Who is our Maker, and what is his authority? and the answers may be various. If we assume that a Being of infinite perfection has created us, then its authority is supreme, and its decisions are final and peremptory. But, on the other hand, with those who hold that our Maker is nature-force, which has finally evolved itself into this shape, the case is essentially altered.

Hence, we see how illogical it is to use this principle, with its origin thus explained, in proof of God and creation, because it is of authority only on the assumption of the divine authorship of our constitution; while the argument is good only for those who admit this origin of it. With all others, it is without authority. There is also a circular motion made very widely, with this law of causality as a constitutional endowment. It is first adduced in proof of the existence of God as the great First Cause, to which we argue from the world considered as an effect. Then, in answer to those who question whether we are justified in applying it beyond the limits of experience, we prove human perfection from God's perfection. We say that our constitution utters the principle as absolutely universal and limitless, and that thus we must accept it or charge our Maker with falsehood. In addition to this manifest circle, there is here also presented the absurdity of making an appeal to the godly reverence of a party who are in the very act of questioning the divine existence. It must therefore be quite clear to the reader that an examination of the use of this principle and its associated principle of design in their application to the world, conceived as a non-egoistic object, in numerical contradistinction from the conscious subject, will show their universal futility and self-refutation; while, on the basis of Philosophical Realism, as already expounded, they not only become effective, but show the power and wisdom of Deity in a light so strong and vivid and varied as entirely to eclipse all previous expositions of natural theology, besides leading to new and important proofs of supernatural agency.

There is force which is known and a force which is unknown. The known force is the whole sensible universe and our inner or supersensible experiences. If the sensible universe, external to our organism, were non-ego, it would be all the force we could ever know or would logically need to know; and, in that case, there would not be, in a large meaning, any unknown, much less unknowable, force. If the external world is non-ego, it is known as the source of our organism and our individual and conscious personality, and is, apparently, as a force, indestructible and eternal, though mutable as to its forms, in every form being force and nothing else, and always the same force. Thus, the all-sufficing, all-operating, and all-explaining force of all things is familiarly known to us all. There can be no proof of anything else. There is no scientific or logical need of anything else. We can *conjecture* that the sensible universe had a beginning, and that, therefore, it had a cause in an unknown but inferred Power. This is the conjecture and inference of many, but they are purely gratuitous.

But the sensible world is ego; and it is, I think, quite probable that the ego, with all its universe, had a beginning, and therefore had a beginning in the creative action of an unknown but inferred Power of vast, if not infinite excellence,—a personal Power it must be *conceived* (whether it is so or not), because a being of self-conscious intelligence and will is the highest form of existence known to us.

XVIII.

Etiology and Objective Evolution.

OBJECTIVE evolution rests upon the unity and autonomy of the universe, and these are demonstrable; and the theory is true all through and scientifically unimpeachable, if the universe is non-ego.

Nature's Panheisenism.

The unity of the universe is growing evermore apparent. There is no absolute individuality in the world. No object has a fixity and unity which is indissoluble and irresolvable into any other. Constant transformation of force is the universal fact. Every form is continually becoming something else, and their reciprocity shows their substantial unity or unity of being and force. All in one, and one in all, is nature's teaching. Each part is what it is by virtue of antecedents; and, by the same law, it will determine others, so that they are all one force indissolubly connected, always different, yet the same,—many, yet one. This is true of pure nature, both inward and outward. If there is a supernatural will, this, of course, does not belong to nature; and we are here speaking of nature, real and proper, as indisputably known to us.

The laws of space and time point in the same way. To the eye, all colors and shades join on to each other without any line of actual separation; nor can the mind conceive how such mark of separation is possible, because the supposed mark must be either joined to or separated from the objects which it isolates. If it is joined, it appears as identified; and, if it is separated, the hiatus must be filled up with some shade or color, and thus again unite it. Everything in nature is thus joined on to another; and they are inseparable, even in thought. Both mind and sense thus unite and identify all things immediately knowable.

If space is an objective reality, it must, as was argued by Newton and Clarke, as well as Spinoza, be identified with God, because it is self-existent, immutable, and eternal. But, as all sensible phenomena are spatial, they must therefore be modes of space, and be identified with space, and so with God. It will thence be very easy to demonstrate that all the phenomena of mind are also modes of the same one being. (See p. 92.)

Here, however, we are met by a new species of dualism, which denies the correlation between thought or consciousness and material phenomena. These answer to each other, it is said, only by a law of coincidence, not correlation. Neither of them ever becomes transmuted into the other. Each set of phenomena has its own total unity, within which only the law of correlation holds; but each set operates and changes with perfect regularity in correspondence with the other, yet without either having any causal action on the other. It is a case of causeless harmony, if not pre-established harmony, pure and simple.

(1) This is not a correct statement of facts. It is very certain that there is such a thing as organic consciousness, and that this consciousness is generated and modified in and by the transmutations of inorganic and extra-organic phenomena into the constituent elements of our organic consciousness. Our organic life is a conscious agency evolved from the external world.

(2) The distinction between thought and things is superficial and fundamentally false. Every phenom-

enon is equally a subjective state, a mode of consciousness, so that the alleged duality and intervening hiatus between the two (thought and thing) have no existence.

(3) Hence, we find a fundamental unity in the common subject of all phenomena,—the conscious ego,—all of whose modal changes occur in lexical relation to each other.

(4) On the theory of the duality in question there is no law or principle by which an ultimate unity is attainable. There is no logical consistency in the affirmation that the alleged duality of thought and things have the same origin. The kosmic or synthetic theory of evolution knows of no force apart from the kosmos, apart from which we know nothing, not even ourselves; and we know of nothing but the kosmos as the cause of ourselves as organic or as organically related. Therefore, if there is, as is alleged, any thought or thought power which has no such origin and correlation, we not only do not know its cause, but we have no data whatever on which to affirm it or describe or define it, except that it must be something extra-mundane; and this is neither a synthetic nor a kosmic philosophy. Further, we are entirely in the dark as to the method or law or principle of the operation by which this super-kosmic cause produces and develops these numerous and successive thought powers. The doctrine is vague and empty, and inconsistent and unscientific, and in conflict with admitted facts.

Immutability of Gravity.

Our simpler theory is rendered still more probable from our ability to point to familiar facts which reveal to us a force and law in accordance with which an endless series of kosmical processes may be possible. One of the most conspicuous and potent of these facts is weight or gravity, as one of the properties of all tangible bodies. Of this property, science traced the law, which is called the law of gravitation. Weight never wastes or diminishes or passes over into aught else; and its law never changes, so far as we know. As weight has a power of producing heat without being wasted or diminished or in any wise changed in the process, it has an absolutely exhaustless and endless power of producing heat; and as heat has the power of producing, if it does not constitute, molecular motion, which is one of the main conditions of all kosmic evolution, we seem to have here, and in associated facts, all that is necessary to an endless succession of cycles of chaos and kosmos, without the aid of any designing or any extra-mundane force.

Dissipation and Equilibration of Heat.

The argument that heat always tends to equilibrium, that in equilibrium it is powerless, that the equilibration of the heat of the whole universe must be finally attained, and that then the wheels of the universe must forever stop, without the interposition of an extra-mundane power, appears conclusive merely because it embodies only a portion of the facts of the case, and presents them in a confused shape.

In this discussion, we should not fail to note distinctly the difference between the dissipation and equilibration of heat. Equilibration is the passing of heat from hotter to colder bodies, till they are all of equal temperature in every part. Dissipation of energy or heat is the passing of heat from all sensible bodies into insensible space. Equilibrium, universally attained, would be the stopping of the wheels of the universe.

But gravitation renders that equilibrium either impossible or exceedingly improbable; and, if it were even attained, gravitation, which always remains unchanged, operating in various ways (some of which we are able to conjecture), would be very sure always to generate fresh heat and fresh inequalities of heat. Thus, perpetual kosmic changes for evolution and involution are clearly possible, notwithstanding the acknowledged law of equilibration, and even if it were, at length, everywhere fulfilled.

But the law of "dissipation of energy" forbids that universal equilibrium should ever be attained. Dissipation goes on faster than equilibration, which will create a constant inequality, because space is generally colder than bodies, and the outside space is colder than that between bodies. Hence, the exterior sides of the universe will always lose their heat faster toward empty space than the interior sides can lose their heat either toward space or toward other bodies of inferior heat; and the peripheries of bodies will cool faster than their centres. Equilibrium, therefore, can never be attained until all the heat of the universe is drawn off into space. But this appears to be impossible, because friction is a constant generator of heat, and the constant action of gravitation (and other forces) necessitates the constant generation of friction and fresh heat; and, as the force of gravitation never wastes nor the weight of things ever diminishes by the process, it appears to follow that the perpetual generation of fresh heat, not equilibrated, and thence kosmic life, are a necessity.

On the other hand, the tendency of heat toward equilibrium is only a part of the law of heat. Its converse is equally true, that, in comparative equilibrium, it tends toward inequality. When the smith brings his iron, white hot, out of the fire, it is of nearly the same heat in all parts, only perhaps a little hotter at the surface than the centre. But it will cool faster at the surface, and so will soon be much colder there than at the centre, especially if it is a large body. So, if all the matter of the universe were brought together into one sphere, of equal temperature throughout, it would not retain that equilibrium. The surface would cool enormously more rapidly than the interior. Kinetic energy would at once be generated, which, according to known laws and in conjunction with known forces, would or might eventuate in all the known kosmic evolutions.

If the exterior cooled and hardened, it has been asked why it would not, as fast as it solidified, sink through the more fluid body toward the centre, instead of staying there for a while, and then, at a convenient time, flying off on a tangent? To this there are two possible answers, which are entirely sufficient. One is that the lighter bodies would naturally be at the surface, and would float on the other, so that, when hardened, they might not be readily able to penetrate the dense mass below. Another is that, as films float on liquids and as sheets of iron (not too thick) will float on water merely because pressing equally an extended surface, so would the cooling film float on the surface of the globular universe; and, further, as it extends all round, it forms a self-supporting arch, till it gets broken. This arch becomes gradually isolated from the interior matter, which prepares it for tangential projection into separate spheres and satellites of their original source. The mere possibility and conceivability of this are enough in the absence of positive proof on the opposite side.

Autonomy and Eternity of Gravity.

It has been argued that, if the law of gravitation were other than it is,—that if the attractive force had varied as 1 2 3 instead of varying according to the squares of these numbers,—the kosmic order would be impossible; and, because the law of gravitation is the one which admits, if it does not necessitate, this order, it has been inferred that this law is imposed upon the universe solely by the will of God. This inference is unwarranted. Before this is at all admissible, we must know that there is a God, who has a will, and who is the Creator of the universe. Then we shall know that his will has imposed on the universe its laws. At present, we know only the universe itself as a congeries of forces, and that, of these forces, gravity appears to be immutable and the ultimate source of all others, so far as we can trace their origin ; while, of gravity itself, we only know that it exists. We have no evidence that it, and the simplest quality or qualities in which it operates, ever had a beginning. We as yet know nothing to show that gravity is not an eternal force, which, from necessity of nature, follows in its operation the laws which science has ascertained and defined. This is the view which is favored by the facts, as far as they are yet known and admitted. It is the simplest possible construction that can be put on these facts, and for this reason is the most philosophical. This dispenses with creation and a supra-mundane Deity.

That the law of gravitation is what it is, and not otherwise, is surely no proof that it ever was otherwise or was not always what it is. Of course, if it were such as to render the kosmos impossible, there would not be any kosmos ; but the simple fact that it is compatible with kosmos and the possible generator of the kosmos is no proof that it is not eternal. Such an argument would disprove the eternity of its inferred Creator. If he were possessed of certain qualities instead of those he does possess, he could not create the world ; and, therefore, the existence of those creative qualities proves that they had a designing Creator.

"These truths avowed, all nature shines at once,
Self-potent, and uninfluenced by the gods."

Doctrine of Chances.

It has been argued from the law of chances that they are almost infinite to one against kosmos resulting from chaos by natural processes alone. That would be of some logical authority, if we were agreed at the onset concerning the nature and extent of the kosmic force or forces; and that is just where we are not agreed. We know nothing about that, except what we see. We see that kosmos has followed on chaos; and I think that was inevitable from the nature of the forces in action, because I have no evidence to the contrary. All alleged opposing probabilities are based on opposing assumptions, which, to say the least, are no better than mine, and are infinitely greater.

XIX.
Etiology and Subjective Evolution.

Subjective and Objective Autonomy of the Universe.

THE unity and autonomy of the universe, which have been exhibited in the light and interest of objective evolution, are at least equally true and pertinent relative to subjective evolution. Indeed, here they are more strikingly evident and important,—are, in fact, a logical necessity,—because the ego is certainly a unity; and, if all the universe is ego, all the knowable must be one and self-animated, so far as that is true of the ego,—and that is supposed to be true throughout. This unity and autonomy are therefore now to be considered as settled both for objective and subjective evolution, more emphatically for the latter, which, equally with the former, exhibits an advancing process from the lowest and simplest conditions of existence to the highest known. Objective evolution shows no proof or need of any supra-mundane agent, and thence is justified in denying the right of any one to affirm it. It is possible there may be such an agent; and, therefore, objective evolution does not positively say there is not, but only that we have no reason for its affirmation or that its affirmation is irrational. Thus, it excludes all miracles and all supernatural interpositions anywhere. On the basis of subjective evolution, all this is radically changed. Here there is no one great all-inclusive material universe, out of which evolve and on which subsist all living things, which are infinitesimal in magnitude, power, and duration, compared with the universe, their parent source. Compared with it, they are like shooting stars in the light of the eternal and illimitable stellar glories. Subjective evolution, on the other hand, exalts each individual up to the height and grandeur of all the universe, or brings the universe down to his level, according as we may choose to conceive and express the identification of the universe and the ego. As it will doubtless be conceded, as it always has been, that the ego had a beginning, of which we have furnished reasonable proof, and as its beginning is the beginning of all nature, its cause must be supernatural; and he can never more be confounded with nature or man. Still more obvious is supernatural agency relative to the intercourse and interaction between one being and another, all of which is supernatural, because each man comprises in himself the whole natural universe knowable to him, so that there is no natural media or possibility of intercourse or interaction. A good probable, not to say necessary, proof of a Supernatural Being having been once attained, this Being becomes the great mental figure, infinitely transcending all others, personal because all known beings are personal (or rather the only one, for only one we directly know); and, as the peculiar and distinguishing excellence and glory of this Being is his supernatural quality, all 'the universe and all universes being infinitely beneath him,—his creatures and dependants,— it follows that this supernatural quality and agency should be made conspicuous, and as conspicuous as possible, consistent with the reliability of nature and the moral and spiritual needs of man. Henceforth, instead of a pre-exclusion of supernatural agency along the route of the world's movement as impossible or infinitely improbable, the logical course is just the reverse. We must everywhere expect it, and the effects and signs of it, because it is always and everywhere more or less probable or necessary. If it is good to know nature (ourselves), infinitely better must it be to know God, nature's author and upholder ; and, as his existence and characteristic quality and excellence as supramundane could be known only by supernatural manifestation, that quality demands perpetual exercise and perpetual expression, alike from the necessity of his own nature and the need of his creatures. The old probability against miracles rightly conceived and all supernatural interpositions is now turned in their favor.

Relation of Science to Supernaturalism.

The only legitimate question that can now be raised is, "Where and when and what are the signs of this supernatural interposition?" Here science has a just right to step in and insist upon an inductive investigation that conforms to its best and most approved principles and method. Thus, science has its place and right and duty as an investigator relative to the supernatural as well as the natural. If it can tell what conforms to nature, it can tell what does not conform to nature, and is therefore supernatural. If it knows what is a natural cause, it knows by logical necessity what is not a natural cause. Religion and science are therefore neither opposed to nor exclusive of each other. A religion which cannot be supported by science is irreligious. I am sorry to reflect that this condemns a large proportion of even modern thinking in the interests of religion, and that by some of the ablest men of our age, as, for instance, James Martineau. If there is a "God over all blessed forever," there must be a rational unity in all things; and true science can neither be opposed nor indifferent nor silent relative to him. All our conclusions must be based on facts scientifically certified. This is the support I claim for Philosophical Realism.

Unity of God.

Philosophical Realism gives to the doctrine of the unity of God, as disclosed in the unity of his works, far higher and more striking illustrations than any which it has had heretofore. In the past, philosophers could only consider this unity as exemplified in the known universe. Now, we find that the area and objects showing this unity are indefinitely expanded and multiplied beyond the universe, so called, and unexplored regions for the discovery of the same are now open to us; and, in our exposition of sematology, we have proved as a whole this newly conceived unity, and it will remain for future laborers to exhibit it in detail.

Unceasing Creation.

Jesus said, My Father worketh hitherto. Not a "lazy God" was his. A God inactive were inferior to a stone,— no God at all. And the true God must be active in his peculiar and supreme quality and potency, one should suppose. Hence, some theists have argued that God is always creating somewhere; while others, in order to keep him in adequate and steady employment, have given him *all* to do directly, arguing that everything else is and must be powerless, and therefore unable to do anything. Philosophical Realism shows everything to be intrinsically, essentially forceful, and ever active and effective; and, at the same time, it indirectly shows a Deity in constant supreme action, since, wherever there is a birth, there is implied, as its precondition, a creation, although the creature thus symbolized by the birth was created long before, and in a far lower form of existence.

Importance of the Supernatural.

The doctrine of the supernaturalness of Deity is of prime, of supreme importance. Its logical implication is vital and pregnant with vast logical issues, of paramount practical value and force. It involves an all-comprehending system of creature privilege and obligation and moral prognostication. It is obvious that, if there is a Being of such awful reality as to be eternal, and the absolute Creator of all worlds and all their forces and contents, it becomes at once an inquiry of the utmost importance, What is the actual and possible relation I may sustain to him, whether I have under his supremacy any responsibility for my future, and, if so, what; and how am I to secure his favor? Thus, a knowledge of his character and of his will concerning us is the first and great pursuit of the human mind.

There are, perhaps, minds so thoroughly secular that they would reply to this that our wisest way is for every man to proceed in a steady performance of the duties of his station, as this is sure to meet the approval of a just and wise Superior. This is true, if we are correct in our judgment as to what are the duties of our station or lot in life. But that is the very question which we are raising,—a question which is impregnated with an awful significance by the doctrine of the existence of a Creator. There must be duties and responsibilities growing out of our relation to him, and we ought to use reasonable efforts to know and do them.

Importance and Moral Need of its Manifestation.

Hence, we see the importance of the divine manifestation of himself as supernatural. The supernatural being his great distinctive characteristic, and the ground to man of all his weightiest responsibilities and regnant hopes, this characteristic must be made conspicuous in God's manifestation of himself. As God exists, he should be known; and he can be best seen in supernatural phenomena. Supernatural operation is hence the normal method of God's manifestation of himself to his creatures. Supernatural revelation, in some way or other, is a perpetual necessity of the divine nature. Of the times, forms, and degrees, we cannot be the *a priori* judges. But we can see that, on the foundation on which we stand, they are a logical necessity ; and the only question to be raised concerning the reality of any alleged revelation is whether its claim is properly supported by evidence.

As nature is fixed and uniform in its operation, it involves serious and innumerable evils. It is reckless of all consequences. It never turns aside to conserve any human interest, however important, or to spare a pang to weakness, innocence, or virtue.

This, without qualification, cannot please God. God, being supernatural, cannot be represented in his works by nature alone. It appears reasonable that he should have supernatural purposes and, in part at least, follow supernatural methods. And, if his purposes are wise and good, he must thus operate in favor of virtue. Hence, all religion has, in the past, believed in a supernatural Providence, in conjunction with nature's operations. This appears to be a logical necessity from theistic notions. When and where and how and how far this Providence operates, we cannot now inquire, much less answer.

Nature, within us as well as without us, is very often forceful for evil both to ourselves and others. This evil force and tendency are often beyond our control. We need help, and men are often powerless to help us. We need supernatural aid. Here is a vast and important field for the exercise of the supernatural grace of God. A supernatural Deity, if good and able, must meet the moral demands of our inner being. Our theism therefore renders it probable that God gives supernatural spiritual help, in answer to the prayer of those who are struggling against temptation, and gives it variously, according to the dictates of a wise spiritual economy.

XX.
Teleology: Its Presuppositions.

TELEOLOGY is the most discussed subject of modern times, if not of all times. But, because of its importance and vitality, it can never become trite; and it must emerge in every general philosophical discussion, till its proper function and authority are agreed upon. And it is now forced upon our attention and consideration.

Its Relation to Etiology.

Teleology presupposes etiology, and consequently its validity depends on the validity of its presupposed base. Both teleology and etiology have been used to prove a personal Deity. Marks of design in the world is Paley's great argument for the divine existence; and Mill thinks this is in some degree a valid line of argumentation, and the only valid one. In distinction from this, etiology can have no object but to prove a Primal Cause, irrespective of design. As soon as it attempts to prove anything more, it attempts to prove a Person; and a person is a designer. But such a proof may be attempted on the basis of other phenomena than those of design,—from the general phenomena of personal consciousness, on the supposition that a conscious effect must have a conscious Cause, so that there must always have been at least one personal conscious being.

There is another argument, however, which now for the first time is developed under the tutelage of

Philosophical Realism. It comes under the doctrine (also virtually new) of sematology, by which, while we prove the existence of other men, we also at the same time prove a supernatural, personal, and purposeful agency,—not from phenomena considered as marks of *design*, but as signs of a vast combination of *effects*, which must have a purposeful, personal *Cause as supernatural*, and are therefore designed.

Teleology is one particular form or species of etiology. It argues from a particular class of phenomena as effects to a particular kind of antecedent as cause. It presupposes a doctrine of Causality, which it appropriates and uses in this special line, to the effect that a certain class of phenomena must have a Designing Cause.

Design proves not Creation.

This argument may be considered under two or three different degrees of extension and comprehension. It may be considered as proving that the Designer is the Cause of only those *forms or modes* of nature's force and substance, and not of the force or substance itself; or it may be considered as proving both. The proof of both has been thus sought; or, rather, it appears to have been tacitly assumed that the proof of the former carries with it the proof of the latter. But it does not. Indeed, some of the first minds of the world in all ages have held to the eternity of matter, and that God is only its former or fashioner. This view has obtained even among theists and Christians, of which Milton is an illustrious example in comparatively recent times. Teleology, therefore, can never prove a creator of the world, even if it is allowed that the world bears marks of design, which prove only a designer.

Design proves not Supernaturalism.

Again, supposing there is a designing intelligence operating in nature, this can appear only as nature's own force, as a power identical with nature, nature's phenomena being its modes and exhibitors. In this case, not only have we no proof of creation (for nature cannot be its own creator), but we have only nature and evolution, naturalistic evolution. For whatever appears in the course of nature cannot appear as anything else than nature; and, therefore, signs of design, admitted in nature's course, only prove something concerning nature. And what is thus proved is the next question. It does not take us a single step toward supernaturalism. It only elevates nature, which is the tendency of modern science and philosophy. It would simply endow nature with a power which is not usually attributed to it,—conscious, purposeful agency.

Design not Manifest in Nature.

But the great subject of inquiry and debate is whether nature shows any good evidences of design. These are supposed to be found in kosmic and psychological order and adaptations. But if these phenomena can be accounted for in a simpler way, in a way that involves no assumptions, or the least possible, the telic inference is scientifically superseded. This is now easily done. All phenomena are forces, whose degree and kind are known by the uniformity of their subsequents, whence it follows that all kosmic order and psychological adaptations are the effects of precedent phenomena. We are, therefore, logically precluded from going beyond nature to account for any of the phenomena of nature.

Besides, it is conceded on all hands that Nature cannot be anticipated, and that we can assign no ultimate reason for her combinations, except so far as she herself has preinformed and enlightened us, so that from her past course we may judge of her future.

Where anticipations are raised on the basis of what we know of Nature, she often disappoints us. Prof. Tyndall has well said: "Nature is full of anomalies which no foresight could predict and which experiment alone can reveal. From the deportment of a vast number of bodies, we should be led to conclude that heat always produces expansion, and that cold always produces contraction. But water steps in and bismuth steps in, to qualify this conclusion." If it were not for this exception in the case of water to the prevailing law, nearly all water would be ice except in the torrid regions, so that the exception is a vast and manifest advantage to living things. It is hence inferred that this is proof of design. But this would prove too much. It would prove that whatever turns out to vital advantage, and nothing else, was designed by God, which is more than doubtful.

As all specific natural causes of this or that are determined only by the uniformity of their recurrence as antecedents, we have no power to anticipate them *a priori*. We have no foundation on which to base a pre-judgment of the nature or form of the cause of any particular effect. If the effect whose cause we seek is analogous to some other effects whose cause is known, we may form a conjecture based on this analogy. But this is only conjecture, not knowledge nor a final judgment of science; and it is of value only as a guide or prompter in our investigations. And, even in this aspect, it must not be much relied on, else it may lead astray or prevent the acquisition of the truth. Our discovery of causes is never made till we have discovered antecedents that are constant; and, when this is attained, it should be the end of doubt and debate. Where an antecedent is known, but not certainly known to be uniform, but which is uniform so far as it can be tested, the cause is probable in proportion to the extent of our knowledge and its harmony with other known and analogous phenomenal connections. But, whatever the degree of probability, whether of the slenderest kind or of the most convincing force, we are never entitled to bring any objections drawn from the supposed or required intrinsic nature of the cause, because of this we know nothing. We know, *a priori*, that all phenomena are substance and force; but what is the force of each, uniformity of connected experience only can determine.

Nature a Designless Combining Power.

While it is true that man designs, this is no proof that all interacting power is a self-conscious designing power like ourselves, or that nature may not have power to perform complicated operations without design or consciousness, and without being directed and controlled toward definite ends by a personal Deity.

Nature will necessarily operate in accordance with the kind and degree of force that it has or is, whatever that may be. It will operate always the same in the same forms and combinations, and differently in different forms and combinations. Thus, for instance, the eye is the means of vision in the light, but not in the dark; and, if always kept in the dark, the eye, without any supernatural agency, and merely by the action of natural force and law, will lose all visual power, and undergo a change of structural form and cease to be an eye proper. Hence it is that we find eyeless fishes in lightless water caverns of the earth.

If nature is admitted to be of any force at all,—that is, to be anything at all, and to be a force to this extent,—where shall we limit its force and by what principle shall we determine its limits? If it can destroy faculty without any conscious design, why may it not be supposed to be able to organize, generate, and develop any faculty without any consciousness and design? We know that new faculties are generated and developed; and we can trace the law of their development, and thus show that they take place according to natural law, and so give no evidence whatsoever of being the effect of any supernatural power. We know that by natural force, because, according to natural law, every faculty we possess is developed and improved by exercise and favorable natural circumstances. We also know that adults have certain faculties which infants have not, and which are developed by natural law in the course of life. We can even trace back our organism to the womb and its inception there, and show all through that there is no evidence of aught but the operation of natural force, because all takes place according to natural law. Thus, all our faculties, and our very existence as organized and conscious beings, seem to be the product of merely natural force without design or consciousness; and against this there is absolutely nothing, not a single supernatural phenomenon or sign. It is therefore certain and indubitable that Nature does do all this. Whatever be the source of her power, it is clear that she has it, and uses it as steadily as time.

Designless.

This power may be the gift of God, ordained to these ends; and so nature may be the blind instrument of the Divine Designer. This is the proper theory of theism. But, before we can know its truth, we must know that there is a personal Deity,—the Fashioner, if not the Creator, of the universe; and of this, therefore, the argument from teleology itself can furnish no proof. The argument from design is good to show the divine attributes, *assuming the divine existence*. If we already know that nature is a creature, we know it as a manifestation of the character of the Creator, who must act according to his nature and character. But, if we do not otherwise know that the universe is created, no study of its natural phenomena can prove anything but its own natural forces. If there is an Infinite Personality, He must have a design respecting all things; and this design may be proximately collected from nature. But there may be no such Being, and Nature's force may be absolutely her own and eternal; and this we must assume till it is disproved, because Nature we know immediately, and God is thus unknown.

Now suppose that there is no supra-mundane deity, that nature is an eternal force of indefinite magnitude and unknown quality, and capable of unfolding itself in an infinity of various forms, processes, and results, in an inflexible order according to its nature, we should then have, so far as we can now see, just what we have in the actual kosmic phenomena. Let there be certain unconscious forces, and they must operate so and so. They may have affinities and capabilities for certain combinations, and incapabilities for certain other combinations; and, according to all these, certain results will follow, and all processes will move steadily toward these results. A kosmos of a certain kind thus becomes necessary, partly in spite of and partly by the aid of incessant and countless jarrings and antagonizing complications,—partial chaos everywhere showing itself in the midst and alongside of partial kosmos. It is, therefore, entirely unnecessary and unreasonable to affirm that these phenomena are the product of a personal will and purpose, or to affirm anything more than what we know,—the existence of a vast and mighty complexus of natural force, unconscious in some of its forms and conscious in others, all forming one great and mysterious unity. These are the facts; and they form their own explanation, so far as explanation is possible or necessary.

Variableness of Volition.

The alleged marks of design are only supposed or inferred to be such, because certain phenomena are regular and systematic in their occurrence and recurrence, and have observable affinities and repulsions which co-operate to achieve or oppose certain results. But this supposition may be false; and, as it involves an infinite and supernatural inference from natural phenomena, it is entirely unwarranted. Besides, as Mill observes, it is improbable from the very regularity of these phenomena. They lack one of the chief characteristics of the action of an intelligent will as known to us,—variability relative to given ends and circumstances. The human will is perpetually breaking in upon outward nature, and making it assume new forms and enter on new tracks toward results which otherwise would not be attained. It seems so strange that they are not frequently thus deflected, if there is a good and wise will behind them. It is by this very variability and deflection that we distinguish a living thing from a mere unconscious object of nature. It is true that, on the theory of theism, we can explain all this. But we have not proved the truth of theism, but are considering the logical value of the argument from design as an alleged proof; and we see afresh that it presupposes, instead of proving, theism, while the inflexible method in which the alleged design is carried out is an argument against theism and against the assumption of conscious purpose and design.

The standing arguments for design and a great Designer can seem good and forceful only to those whose spiritual faculty obscures the logical and scientific. We have great respect for the *disposition* thus evinced, but not for the intelligence. We have no doubt of an infinite, supernatural, designing Agency, whose creative purpose works from original endowment in all nature; but we can no longer posit our faith on telic phenomena. Before the argument from design can be made good, we must prove that nature is not competent to do what is attributed to design. This can never be done so long as all our data are natural phenomena. Archimedes was well aware that he could move the world only when he should have a fulcrum for his lever outside of the world. Equally necessary are supernatural phenomena to prove an agency which is beyond nature, and which predetermines its forms and operations and results.

PHILOSOPHICAL REALISM 247

Adaptations, Good and Evil.

The adaptations of nature which are adduced as proof of design are themselves nothing but natural phenomena, whose laws we can trace with more or less precision, and whose powers we determine by what we see them do. They do not themselves furnish us a particle of evidence that what they effect in their various combinations is not done solely in virtue of their intrinsic nature as forces, which, because they are such forces, are ever acting and thence evolving by necessary law new phenomena and new combinations, and thence necessarily varying their action with the varied combinations, and so forever adapting themselves to the new situations, and working different results therefrom or the same results in the same connections. To assert that there is here anything but nature, either as cause or effect, is unwarranted by the data on which the assertion is made, since these very data are confessedly only nature.

This action sometimes results in good, at other times in evil; sometimes in what appears to be fraught with art and wisdom, at other times in confusion and chaos, in useless or even injurious products of various forms, misery, ruin. Allowing that these forces may not be blind, they certainly do not adapt themselves always to the attainment of ends that are clearly wise and good. The ends which are often actually attained are what would seem diabolical, if perpetrated by design; and, hence, divines have often introduced the devil as the cause of earthly evil, as in the affliction of Job. The laws of wealth readily tend to make the rich ever richer and the poor poorer, relatively. The tempest is adapted to wreck the ship, the cold to freeze the poor and needy, marshes to create malaria, the solar rays of the tropics to produce sunstroke or nervous paralysis; while gravitation is often adapted to the breaking of bones and the destruction of life. All of nature's forces are in various connections adapted to do very great evil; and they do it, and that so often and extensively that a high authority has described the world as at times full of lamentation and woe. These evils are not annihilated by asseverating that good preponderates and that good often comes out of evil; and, besides, as J. S. Mill observes, evil often comes out of nature's good by its adaptations to pervert and misdivert the good. In short, the end attained, which must be the end sought, if any, very frequently appears absolutely without any sign of goodness or reason.

XXI.

TELEOLOGY.—ITS SPHERE.

Foundation of Teleology.

WE have expounded causation as the action of force or power, so that all being is causative according to its nature and connections. This is not the dictum of a psychological necessity merely, but it is a logical obligation from the very nature and rational conception of being. Causation is change and productive of changes, which is possible only to force or power. Therefore, whenever we see change, we see the action of power, causation; and it is not merely by some physical or mental proclivity inherited as a mental instinct or bestowed at creation, but by a normal operation and fundamental logical law of rational, self-comprehending intelligence as such that we pronounce that all beginning and change have a cause, whether the cause be internal or external. We need no universal postulate, no psychological law, no assumption whatsoever, to enable or entitle us to affirm this.

On this ground, we have affirmed a causation in all phenomena, that the whole universe is a system of causes and effects, whose parts are under a perpetual process of mutual modification.

And, on this ground, we have affirmed that the whole universe must have a cause if it have a beginning; and, as the universe is ego, which is inductively proved to have had a beginning, it had a cause, transphenomenal, beyond the universe, beyond all nature, supernatural, a Creator. It is logically possible the world never had a beginning, and so never had a cause. The fact may be questioned without self-contradiction, but not so the principle. Whatever is, is cause; and whatever begins to be has an extrinsic cause,—that is the principle, a logical necessity from the notion of being. That the world had a beginning is the alleged fact, which may not be true, though I think it is.

Here the logic of Hume is blinking greatly. He does not discriminate between the intuition of a principle and the cognition of a fact. Because actual specific causes of this or that in nature are sometimes known only by repeated sensible experiments, he argues that the notion of cause itself is from the senses, so far as we have any such notion, and not from reason, because reason is perfect at first utterance; and he concludes that, as the notion of cause cannot be derived from sense, we have no such notion. He says: "From causes which appear similar, we expect similar results. This is the sum of all our experimental conclusions. Now, it seems evident that, if this conclusion were formed by reason, it would be as perfect at first and upon one instance as after ever so long a course of experience." He gives as an example "eggs varying in taste, though having the same appearance." The properties of an egg or of any other substance can be known only by experience or observation. But we need no experience to tell us that all natural properties must operate uniformly according to their nature, or that similar causes will produce similar results in similar connections. It is impossible to learn this from experience. The supposition is self-contradictory, because we can learn their properties or similarity of cause only on the preassumption that they operate according to their properties or nature. This is a general principle, and contains no assertion of particular concrete reality, but only a law for all natural properties,—that in like connections they will produce like effects, because they will always operate according to their nature.

To deny that the principle is an utterance of reason, because many experiments are necessary to discover some exemplary facts, is just as wise as to deny that the idea of virtue is an utterance of reason, because we cannot always tell at first sight an honest man from a thief. It is to say that, because we may not be able to tell from the ruins of a city what was the cause of its destruction, we know not that its destruction had any cause at all! It requires years of careful scrutiny to discover some causes; but the very investigation and every experiment assume not only the notion of a cause of known phenomena, but also the principle that all natural phenomena have natural causes of uniform operation, else they could not be determined by their subsequents and their connections in space and time, and thence all search would be blind and useless.

Teleology Relative to Other Men and Animals.

We know ourselves by consciousness, and other men we know by sematology; and, by sematology, we are able to compare their actions and motives with ours. We are conscious of our own motives and of their effect on our action. On this ground, we judge of the motives of others. The actions which we see are signs of the motives which prompt them. As we never act without a motive and end, we assume the same of others. The signs being the same or relatively different, we assume that the motives and objects are the same or relatively different. By the law of sematology, we also extend our judgments of this kind to the actions of brute animals. We know not only what certain of their actions tend to, but also what they aim at, or what the animal designs in many cases.

Teleology Relative to Nature and God.

The unconscious world has not the signs which belong to or spring from our conscious designing mind. Nature has marvellous method; but this method may be merely the inevitable effect of unconscious property, and, while we cannot think of relative change without thinking of relative adaptation, yet *purposed* adaptation is an act of consciousness, and, if nature is devoid of consciousness, it is devoid of purpose and plan. But, on our theory, the doctrine of final causes has a legitimate place and force here, since we know that nature is the agent or creature of a Power behind it, who must be self-conscious, and have an object and method in creating.

Now, theism need no longer be jealous of the attribution of force to matter or to any creature. It cannot now be supposed to affect in any way or degree the divine dignity and prerogative. The kosmos being known to be his creature, its attributes, whatever they may be, are a tribute to him and a reflection of him; and its limitations are determined by him. We know also now that it is no eternal, immutable, self-sufficient force, capable of independent, endless cycles of successive evolution and involution. Its duration is commensurate only with our sensitive consciousness, and no doubt had a beginning.

Creation is the opposite pole of unconscious evolution. It is the self-conscious and intentional exercise of volitional power. Indeed, Philosophical Realism knows nothing of impersonal and unconscious powers or things, though they may exist. These are the fictions of pre-scientific ignorance, as alleged objects of knowledge. All known realities are personal, of our own person; and, whatever these symbolize, beyond them is some living thing with at least a power for conscious development. These all act from or develop into feeling; and, the higher they rise in the scale of being, their feelings are more developed and, perhaps, differentiated, till in man, the highest known, and really the only known being, we find distinct self-reflection, intention, and volition, in view of ends desired and proposed. Still more emphatically must this general law apply to a being superior to man, and especially so much superior as our Creator must be. With him, the self-analysis must be forever perfect ; with us, imperfect. All his action must therefore be intentional, volitional, and absolutely comprehensive both as to ends and means. Therefore, design must run through all his works, and there be made manifest. The argument from design is therefore now validated by the demonstration of creation. Before this, we could not surely tell whether, prior to man's action, nature contained any design. Now, we know it must be there, and that all things are everywhere the effect and expression of design ; and all that has ever been done in tracing the marks of this is now supplied with a philosophical foundation.

These marks of design are exhibits of the divine purposes and character, of which they are the offspring and expression. Now, the heavens declare his glory, and the earth and firmament show his hand-work, and all the things which are made indicate his eternal power and Godhead. We shall need a moral and scientific discretion in our researches in God's works for the traces of his intentions. They are not always easily understood, and false and superficial conclusions may do much harm. But, prosecuted with caution and reverence, such labor will always be healthful and edifying.

Exalted Place of Design in Philosophical Realism.

Myriads of times indefinitely, in power and in variety and distinctness of impression, is the proof of design augmented by our exposition of Philosophical Realism. Design and adaptation become more striking in proportion as multiplicity is shown to contribute to unity, and in proportion to the reconditeness of the parts, and the ease and simplicity and thoroughness with which they work into each other and conspire toward the common end. Heretofore, phenomenal adjustments have been supposed to have a boundless spatial region beyond the ego. Now, a new wonder comes in, of measureless magnitude, by the discovery that all possible forms and operations, and all directly discoverable footprints of the Creator and fabricator of all things, are within the compass of the human individuality. What a marvellous exhibition of wisdom and power is here! How are forces so many and so mighty, and all their known multifarious operations, made a part of our own selves? By what forethought and detailed comprehensiveness of intelligence are they in their vastness and diversity and multitudinousness made to work and co-operate and develop within my own sole consciousness? Tremendous power, combined with my weakness and constituting an integral part and element of my being! Boundless magnitude, combined with my little limitations and the modes thereof! Infinite multiplicity an element in my individual simplicity! Here are ideas unfolding fields of contemplation sublimer than any that man has ever before essayed to explore, and a new method of research, and a more inspiring prospect to guide and stimulate future explorations in natural theology. Heretofore, adaptations and collocations and adjustments have been considered only in reference to one universe, it being supposed there is only one. Now, these universes are found to be as numerous and as various as are conscious individuals. Directly, we know only one. All others must be phenomenally to us an eternal blank. We have inferential proofs of their existence and of their interaction with our universe. Like so many clocks, they are constructed to keep time with each other and, in certain forms and degrees, to work together, and each, and the parts of each, to be indicators for others. Here, the complexity is again indefinitely augmented, combined with an element which is awful in its sublime reconditeness,— the transcendence of our action and influence beyond the phenomenal and knowable universe into universes which are beyond all times and all spaces, and their contents as known or knowable to us. Yet all these are adjusted to each other, and all working relative to each other, while yet all are unknown to each other; and so occult and profound is the great plan that the most general conception of it is as yet above the attainment of nearly all the highest minds of the human race. What a gulf celestial is here opened up to us! What boundless campaigns for intellectual racing, treasure-filled labyrinths, with clews to guide the brave and bold! Henceforth, let the phenomena of our life be investigated not merely in reference to ourselves and our universe, but also relative to other universes, as indicators of adaptations heretofore unconceived, and as marks of a wisdom and design as great as they are at this day novel.

Limitations of Teleology.

But, while we know that there is a design in all things, we may not be able to ascertain what is the particular design in all particular events. Our knowledge here is always only probable, and often the probability is of the very faintest degree. In this, however, there is nothing peculiar to one class of facts. Concerning the proof of all facts, there is always a possibility of the intrusion of error. From this, none of the physical sciences are exempt. But telic causes behind facts are more difficult usually to determine than the facts themselves from which we reason. While we know that all facts have a special mission, they do not tell us what it is; and by no skill or cunning of cross-examination can we always extort from them an unequivocal utterance. This holds equally of human and divine purposes, and neither can be known except by teleology. Even human language and gesture are significant only when considered as telic phenomena; and, as we often need much care to interpret aright the purpose of human language and action, much more must it be so concerning the action of God. Sacred teleology is therefore of very limited scope and doubtful application, beyond a few broad and universal principles of supreme importance, which we may be sure are acted on in all the divine operations.

XXII.
ASSIMILATION OF SCIENCE.

Tests of a True Philosophy.

A TRUE philosophy will be consistent with itself in every part, will answer every self-consistent and significant question,—that is, every real question,—till no more can be raised; and it will thoroughly assimilate all the indisputable facts and principles of science. This is the threefold power and characteristic of a real and genuine philosophy. By these must be tested all claimants for recognition as the true system and fundamental exposition of all things real or possible. Whatever meets this test is true, and all that fail here are so far false; and, in one or more of these three points, all theories have hitherto more or less failed. I now propose to show that Philosophical Realism, after fulfilling all other requisitions, also assimilates all the great lines of phenomena which constitute physical science.

Assimilation of Kosmogeny.

In entering on this subject, let us remind ourselves afresh of the necessity of consistently thinking in the light of the egoistic nature of all the knowable, and also in the light of the law of sematology, which is the primary principle of all inductive inferences and of that great inference from self to various altruistic existences, and the only scientific route to that goal, though most people go by another and forbidden track.

It has always been conceived that our kosmic system began with chaos, a loose mass of incandescent gas; and, in more recent times, we have conceived gravitation as generating chemical differences, affinities, and repulsions, whence ever-multiplying forces advance the kosmic condition till its present comparative perfection is attained. To all this, I assent. But it requires some exposition. Most of the propounders and advocates of this theory use its leading terms, such as the phrases "planetary systems" and "incandescent gas," and their equivalents, on the assumption that these describe non-egoistic phenomena.

They forget that all the planets and the original nebulæ, and all the processes of evolution, whether in our planet or beyond it, are, so far as known, only modes of self. By means of one sensation or complexus of sensations, as the telescope, we generate others, which are called by different names, to designate their likeness and difference. All these, as visible objects, are secondary qualities, so that, on any theory of psychology and philosophy, they are only sensations or modes of the ego. Here all are agreed, when contemplating simply the psychological facts. Hence, the only real ground on which there can be any difference is inferential. The objective evolutionist, in stating what he calls his theory, ignores all this, and goes on to speak of these phenomena without any misgiving, as if they were non-egoistic. The whole theory assumes this, in contradiction of all the admissions of its advocates and the plainest and most widely recognized facts of psychology. Now, we fully admit this phenomenal evolution. About this there can be no reasonable dispute. It is only the self-contradictory assumption of their non-egoistic nature which we dispute. They only repeat on a false assumption what we have already agreed to on a true foundation. In other words, their theory consists in saying, on the basis of the assumed non-egoistic nature of phenomena, what had been previously said and granted on the opposite assumption. All the kosmic phenomena are so related to each other as to be properly described as an evolution, an evolution of the later from the earlier. But we hold fast by what we have already proved, and which has been so generally though reluctantly confessed, that all these kosmic phenomena, all these worlds and their changes, are nothing but various sensations or modes of self. All known and knowable evolution, therefore, as before expounded, is an evolution of self. On any theory, this must be recognized as a regnant truth; and whatever else is said must bear it in mind and be in harmony with it.

Now, the question arises whether there is any other evolution than this of self; and does this egoistic evolution indicate for us anything beyond itself? To this, the popular or objective evolution has no answer, because it has no place for aught but a sensible world, which it has failed steadily and persistently to recognize as egoistic. Our answer, based on our doctrine of sematology, is that these kosmic phenomena are symbols of facts beyond them, and beyond the universe of our present personality and knowledge. They show man's prehuman and subhuman conditions, and symbolize an order of successive states and sets of experiences before organic man was developed. Thus, also, the known universe, —ego,—by the law of sematology, indicates to us the existence of similar universes beyond us and prior to our *human* existence, and shows that these universes are related to other sentient beings as our universe is to us.

There is one noticeable point of similarity in the method of supporting our theory and that of objective evolution. That theory makes the known phenomena to be signs of what took place before man existed. These phenomena, however,—the known heavens and earth,—being only sensations, can exist only while we experience them. These heavens and earth, therefore, did not exist before man. They begin and end their existence with our experiences; and, with these experiences, they vary, because they are nothing else than these experiences. The utmost, therefore, that the objective evolutionist can say of them consistently is just what we say, that they are signs of certain forms of existence anterior to man *as man* and as an organism. Thus, when he sticks to the facts of psychology and the egoistic nature of all things visible, which he has confessed times without number, he stands just where we stand; and the method of his procedure from these facts is the same as ours, and his conclusion is necessarily the same. The method and principle are the same, though he inconsistently starts from the assumption that visible phenomena are non-egoistic, which confuses his conclusions. It is still a procedure from the known to the unknown on the principle of sematology; and, like the premise, the result is with one egoistic, and with the other it is non-egoistic.

But here there is an inevitable ambiguity in some of our terms, which will need explanation. The modern psychologist, while confessing that all phenomena are ego, sometimes conjectures (for that is the true descriptive verb) that the phenomena external to our organism are effects and indices of a material non-ego, which is the common substratum of the universe and the source and cause of all sensible phenomena, according to fixed laws; and, by these means, it affects us and thus we affect it, and through it we affect each other. Hence, the kosmological phenomena of which we have spoken, while egoistic, must be the effects of material transphenomenal changes in that common non-egoistic and non-sensible matter. This is the consistent logical statement of modern objective evolution combined with modern psychology. But these evolutionists often overlook this. They do not see their own system on all sides at once, and are blind to their own inconsistencies and vacillations.

Now there can be no doubt that the common supposition of the readers and abettors of evolutionary doctrines is that the evolution spoken of belongs to the sensible world as non-egoistic. But it is equally clear that, if the admitted psychological facts are carried out logically in the conception and development of evolution, these phenomena of sense are construed as only egoistic symbols of transphenomenal realities and processes. But this is precisely the method of what men choose to call idealism. Evolution (objective) infers a non-egoistic matter which is unconscious, and forms the real but supersensible world, which is the common sphere and source of all human and animal life. But, besides this, it has to make another inference which it has never thought of. The other men and animals of which it speaks as known are only egoistic phenomena; and these are insignificant or false, unless they, too, are symbols of real men and animals which are transphenomenal to us. Thus, they have two classes of the unknown represented by the known, the conscious and the unconscious. So far as they are consistent, they are idealists precisely in the same sense that I am, affirming the egoism of phenomena and that these are symbols of certain transphenomenal realities. They differ from me in that I infer only one class of transphenomenal realities. If this smaller inference will meet all the logical demands of philosophy, then it is to be preferred. My arguments are that my theory is not only the simplest, but that it is the only one which combines phenomenal completeness and logical consistency and ultimacy, as we have before shown. My own inference, however, includes a real known material world as a mode of the inferred conscious reality. Every such being of every form and grade is the subject of a congeries of coexistent and successive experiences, which constitute its organic and extra-organic world, as symbolized by the phenomenal organisms known to me.

A similar train of reflection and comparison applies equally to the mutability of the hitherto supposed immutable ultimate elements of matter. It has long been agreed generally that there are such elements; though the number and nature of these have never been settled, and their number has varied from the standard four of the old pre-Socratic times to the sixty or seventy or more of our own day, in which it is supposed we have quite well determined their nature and number and several functions.

But, just when this doctrine seemed to be quite well established in the light of modern science, it began to be undermined. Modern evolution and the nebular theory raised the question whether these elements have not been thus naturally evolved. Recently, the spectroscope has begun to disclose facts which strongly favor an answer in the affirmative, since we thus find that the stellar worlds contain some of the same elements contained in our planet, and that the number of these elements diminish as the stars grow more nebulous. The notion, therefore, of the fixity of these elements, is giving way in favor of the notion that their number varies with the kosmic condition of the world where they are.

A true psychology is prepared for this, and ours would have deduced it as a logical necessity from indisputable sensible or psychological phenomena. If all sensible objects are only subjective phenomena, it follows that they have no fixity except the laws of the mind, or the subject. As they are only sensations, they may indefinitely vary with lexical regularity; and the only fixity is the great mysterious force, the cause of incalculable effects, the ego.

Objective evolution was so far prepared for this as to anticipate this issue of elementary unfixity in consequence of its reference of all changes and all relative fixedness to the Absolute and immutable Unknown, the one great force which constitutes the cause of all phenomena, the immanent and constitutive essence of all things. This we are obliged to reject, because, contrary to the admission of all its advocates and of all psychologists, it assumes that the objects of the senses are non-ego. All the known is ego. This we consider sufficiently proved and conceded; and, therefore, if the unknown is identified with the known, then the unknown is also ego. This conclusion is free from all logical embarrassment; and it coincides with Philosophical Realism, which affirms that the ego comprises in its own unity all the force and phenomena of the universe.

Assimilation of Philogeny.

Philogeny assumes to compare the earlier and lower organic forms with the later and the superior, and to show the relation of the latter to the former. There are two things here, the alleged facts and the inference from them. The alleged facts, through the influence of a superficial psychology, are misconceived. We really never compare the past with the present, as is supposed and affirmed. This is only a mode of speech based on inferences or acquired perceptions. It is very proper and convenient, but philosophy must understand itself; though the common mind will forget the fact of the inference, and proceed to speak on the assumption that we *know* what we have only *inferred* and believed, because the inference is so universal and so spontaneous. Whatever we know is of the present only. We can, therefore, directly compare the past and present only relative to our own experiences or conscious modes; and, further, as a condition of the comparison, the earlier modes must remain after the later have come into existence. In other words, it is always a comparison of present modes of consciousness only, which are all we ever directly know. Hence, whatever comparison we make beyond this can be done only by inference; and all such inference proceeds on the principle of sematology. We erect certain phenomena into signs of earlier and non-egoistic existences, and others into signs of later non-egoistic existences. This is the necessary process for all: no other is possible.

It is only by the same process of sematic inference, also, that we arrive at the conclusion that some of these inferred organic existences are relatively inferior and some superior to others. We find by direct experience and intuition the relative inferiority and superiority of the phenomenal organisms, which are our egoistic modes; but it is only an inference, and a sematic inference, that these are proofs of non-egoistic organisms of corresponding relative dignities. As we know neither the past nor the non-ego, we cannot know their relative organic excellences. The fossils, of which some perhaps would inconsiderately remind us, are themselves only sensations,—sensations chiefly of color and touch. We fully allow with all science and all philosophies that these, on the principle of sematology, indicate the existence in past times of other beings, comparing and contrasting with the present existences as the fossil with the living organisms. On this basis purely, we believe with objective evolutionists that there has been a very striking and wondrous progress from the lowest forms of existence up to man's present condition.

But the later and superior forms known to me are not evolved out of the earlier and inferior forms, which is the distinctive doctrine of sensist evolution. All known or knowable organisms, living or fossil, from my own sensitive body down to protoplasm and the primeval gas, are myself. I cannot be evolved out of them. They, so far as they are known, are all evolved out of me. I cannot have been evolved out of any things knowable, because they are me. These phenomena, living and fossil, by the relation which they sustain to each other, are made the ground of a sematic induction that there has been a corresponding order of existences, the successive states of each of which have evolved out of the preceding state, according to a temporal law of progress thus indicated.

Let it be further observed that these successive orders of beings have not existed in our world. This is implied in what has been already often repeated,— that all we know is self, that each is its own world. The extreme indisposition and apparent inability to get and hold this conception make detailed and repeated exposition in this region very necessary. In our world, because it is self, no one can exist but ourselves; and we do not so much exist in it as that it exists in us, and is evolved from us. All being is spirit and life, though of different forms; and every being constitutes its own world and its own knowable universe. Hence, the beginning of any new existence, however humble, is the beginning of a new universe; and, as all known or knowable natural causation obtains only within the knowable natural universe, there can be no such causation between one being and another, so that no one can, by natural causation, be evolved from or engendered by another. Each engenders its own successive states, which is the only possible evolution. This survey shows that our philosophy not only assimilates philogeny, but gives to it a more comprehensive and ulterior explanation beyond all other philosophies.

Assimilation of Ontogeny.

A similar train of exposition applies with equal force to ontogeny, or the science of the forms of existing life. The successive forms of the human embryo, corresponding to the embryonic forms of the lower orders of animals, presents a striking coincidence with philogeny. It is not without reason, on the basis of sensism, that this fact is considered as being a strong support to the doctrine of organic evolution from lower to higher existences. Those whose intellects are chiefly of the sense will think they have ocular proof of evolution to a large extent, and that the laws of legitimate induction will carry them much farther. They will be ready to say that they know that we are evolved from our parents, they from theirs, and so on, to the beginning of our race, if not of all life. So subtle, so manifold and comprehensive are the ultimate facts of existence that it is very difficult to grasp them clearly and firmly, hold to them consistently and undeviatingly. This explains the pertinacity of those superficial and dislocated forms and habits of thought, or rather of impression, miscalled philosophies, dualism, and sensism. Suppose it is agreed that I can trace the evolution of my body up from the lowest forms of life: what have I done? How far have I gone? I have not travelled beyond myself; and I have done nothing but trace out certain phenomenal connections within the sphere of my own individuality, since all these alleged ancestors, even back to the fire-mist, are simply modes of myself, certain modes of self evolving other modes all through the whole, all these processes working and unfolding the inherent virtue or force which constitutes my being. The same holds true of what we see of the evolution of other animals or men. We never see other men or animals at all. No other man or animal sees me. What the other calls me is himself, and all the evolution which he supposes he sees is but a successive modification of his own conscious self. But inarticulately, by the law of sematology, he makes these subjective states the signs and proofs of certain corresponding non-egoistic realities; and this inference has become so established and rapid as to take on the airs of a sense-perception and to pass itself off for one, and, from oft-repeated assertions, it has come to believe it is such.

In fine, it is true that the known universe is a unity of force; and, within its whole extent, a law of evolution obtains. But this universe is ego, and only one of a countless host, each of which exemplifies the same powers and processes. Thus, we grant to evolution all it can intelligibly claim; and then we swallow it up totally and as a whole, just as the ocean swallows up the raindrop and unites it with its own vast volume, or as the whale swallows and assimilates the small mollusks and medusæ on which it subsists.

Useless Organs.

Many animals have useless and abortive members, whence it is inferred that no designing mind of infinite perfection determined their structure. Our theory solves the difficulty in consonance with theism. It admits evolution throughout the whole known universe, which is as far as any of its advocates ever presumed to carry it. This universe evolves its own forms according to laws of its own nature, which laws our evolutionists are expounding with commendable zeal and skill. But this universe had, probably, a beginning, and so was created, and is only one of very many, since it is only ego; and here is our difference from them. By the law of sematology, we find that other universes have an appointed and lexical connection with ours, so that one being comes into existence in each of its successive modes or conditions according to a law of action and change relative to other beings and its own previous states. One animal in greatly altered circumstances uses certain members much less than did its ancestors, and consequently that member is in a measure atrophied; and it is still more so in its subsequent evolved state called its offspring, and it then appears purposeless. Let us recall the truth that an animal's known offspring is the animal itself, and we shall then be able by sematology to take these known changes as indicators of corresponding transcendental existences. And there is a purpose in such correspondence, as it then gives the true "history of creation" and evolution, and of all the action and experiences of the creatures. Such a purpose is wise and high and moral.

It is here that all the practical energies, as well as the purely intellectual, prudence and moral purpose, find scope. We may hence foresee in a measure what will be the consequences to ourselves of certain lines of action; and, by the aid of sematology, we may see what will hence follow to others in joy or suffering, and we may therefore govern ourselves accordingly. The effect which follows to others from my action is a supernatural effect, meaning by others the unknown symbolized by the known, which is ego. There is thus disclosed to us both a natural and a supernatural causation and responsibility. All natural causation terminates on ourselves the known universe. All that transcends ourselves is supernatural, above nature. By the law of sematology, we are to suppose that it corresponds with the natural. This preserves a possible unity of intelligence and action and rational anticipation and self-control. Without this, all life and its unfoldings would be chaotic. Intelligence would be confounded and morals impossible. Thus, our theory again comprehends all that is true in sensist evolution, as the greater comprehends the less.

Prefossil Phenomena.

As animate forms are symbols of living realities, it will be asked, How are we to explain the geological record of a world before life, unless this was the symbol of unconscious matter? The present world, so called, of animated forms of which I am conscious is a symbol of the conscious modes of other beings, which are transphenomenal to me. The fossil geological world shows what other living beings have been in the past. What, then, do the primeval flora and rocks and chaos denote before there were any living beings? To this question, as it stands, there is no possible answer. But it is a sophism, and begs the question. It unconsciously couches a denial of our whole philosophy. It assumes phenomena before consciousness, and that there was a form of existence before there was any living being. This assumption is found in the last two words of the question, "before life." Of course, I cannot admit this. There could be no plants or rocks or clouds or gas before there was any living being; for these are the phenomena, or conscious modes, of such, and they must always imply such, and no form of question can be permitted which contradicts it, whether directly or by implication.

But the geological record places these in chronological order before fossil animal organisms, it will be replied. True. That could not be otherwise. It was a fact. The world is spirit; and so the spirit of man, before it evolves the organic mode of man, is commensurate, both in time and space, with the universe, because they are one; and, in process of time, this spirit world evolves vegetable and animal organisms.

We must also call the reader's attention to an imperfect analysis of the external world in relation to living beings and the confusion of the organisms with the living beings. The world contains organisms, but not living beings. The organisms known by any one are but modes of the one Living Being which knows them. Even the whole material universe knowable by any one is but one series of the modes of that one living being which is not contained in the universe, but contains it, being larger indefinitely. Hence, while the organic fossils of the early world are found as contained in the world, the living things they represent are not so contained. They have all a universe of their own. And every living thing itself transcends its own organism and all known organisms and all the world in which they are contained. Strictly speaking, the living thing itself is not organic, much less a mere organism. It has an organism, a relatively fixed and mutable complex mode so named. But, then, these are no more egoistic than all the rest of the universe; and it is only a partial and misleading designation to speak of the ego as organic, unless we understand the term partitively. It is organic; but it is also celestial, starry, nebulous, inorganic. Hence, it is clear that, as different living beings vastly differ in their modes, they may differ so far as that some shall be without the complex mode which is called the animal or bodily organism; and thus, again, the prefossil world, having no organisms, may represent the existence of living beings, including ourselves, without this special organism, but who have had perceptions of forms analogous to those of our prefossil world. To object to this because we have no direct knowledge of such creatures is to object because we do not transcend the laws and limitations of our own faculties. The question is whether known facts do not justify the inference that there are probably creatures which have no such modes as an animal organism, and which, therefore, are not thus represented in our material economy, and in that sense are not known to us by the senses; for we must not forget that, except ourselves, we do not know any creature directly. Some are inferred from the phenomena of animal organisms. This is admitted. And our latest point is that some are inferrible from material forms without animal organisms, and that these forms point to creatures without animal organisms, but perhaps with a faculty of material perception.

When the great work of Copernicus was first published, his all-illuminating doctrine was opposed, because it implied that Venus must have, like the moon, changing phases, which had not been yet observed. Copernicus, however, and his disciples were confident that they would be observed, if, by any means, the visual effects of distance could be overcome; and, sure enough, when Galileo directed his eyes to the umpire planet with the newly invented telescope, the required phases became manifest. Similar temporary difficulties may be expected to beset and oppose the inauguration of the reign of Philosophical Realism as "the true intellectual system of the universe." But, having abundantly demonstrated the main points, we may be sure of the subordinate details. The Venuses of this intellectual world will surely confirm the doctrine as fast as intellectual vision becomes sufficiently clear and strong to discern their real aspects and significance.

XXIII.
SUMMARY AND CONCLUSION.

The World as Sensation.

OUR primary principle in this volume, the one which is expounded and argued in the earlier chapters, is the common ground of modern psychology. It is the affirmation that all sensible phenomena are only subjective states, only a congeries and series of mortal thoughts, so that neither our body nor the world beyond has any existence, except as sensible experience.

All the rest of the volume is simply a logical extension of this principle. This logical consistency is the only peculiarity of the volume. Science should be consistent; and philosophy should go where the logic of facts enjoins, and nowhere else.

This shuts every man up within the environment of his own individual consciousness. No one ever directly sees aught but himself; for what each person calls other people is not other people, but a mortal mask of his own creation. Each of us creates a world of his own, and imagines it to be a real non-egoistic world, common to himself and all other human beings.

How this comes to pass is a question demanding answer. Is there something outside of us which is the cause of this, or is the cause to be found in ourselves?

One of the chief reasons for inferring an external

cause is that we cannot think an internal cause is adequate to such effects.

But that is an argument which judges of causes *a priori*, which is contrary to the principles and practices of modern science. This science declares that we know the nature and extent of causes only by their effects, which are determined by uniformity of connection.

Its Cause or Origin.

In this case, however, we cannot determine the question by the law of lexical sequence, because, our quest being the cause of all sensible phenomena, it must transcend these phenomena, so that we have to infer a supersensible cause. What shall that be? It must be the least inference possible. We must not bring in the infinite for a finite effect, nor a plurality of causes where a unity may possibly do, nor a thing unknown where what is known may be sufficient.

For all these reasons, we infer that the sensible world has a subjective origin. God cannot be its immediate cause. Nor can we infer that it has a cause outside of mind, because we do not know anything outside of mind, since all we know is mind. To infer as its cause what we do not know and cannot imagine or conceive is merely a blank verbal process. Therefore, sensible phenomenon, or mortal thought, is a mode and effect of its subject, mortal mind.

The oft-repeated assertion that we know mind no better than matter, and that we know it only in the terms of matter, is erroneous. We know matter only as sensations or modes of consciousness; and consciousness we know only as consciousness, not as matter in distinction from consciousness.

Now, these subjective states, these sensations, are states of something,— states of their own subject; and to that something or subject we give the name of ego or I myself. This subject is known as subject in knowing its states of consciousness. Here phenomenon and noumenon are one. The phenomena are modes or states of the noumenon or knowing subject.

When, therefore, we infer that the source of the subjective states is the subject itself, we make an intelligent inference, and the least possible inference.

Further, this inference is a logical necessity, because every noumenon is the admitted source of its phenomena; and it is only in this light that the two terms have any correlated significance.

Further, it is generally agreed that there are unconscious subjective states which are the source of conscious states. This was especially elaborated by Carpenter in his doctrine of unconscious cerebration, and by Hamilton in his exposition of unconscious mental action. Hence, it is quite possible that this sub-conscious region is the source of sensible phenomena.

How transcend the Ego.

How, then, can we ever get beyond ourselves? How prove that there is aught but ourselves? These questions we have answered in our exposition of Sematology, which cannot be well epitomized. We must be content to say that the sensible phenomenon is a symbol of a reality beyond the sphere of sense; that, as I have an organism and sensible world in my consciousness, an organism like mine symbolizes a transphenomenal being like myself, with a sensible as well as supersensible consciousness like mine; and that different sensible organisms are symbols of different transphenomenal realities.

Theistic Conclusion.

This indicates a wonderful and harmonious system of correspondences of vast extent and of infinite variety,—a pre-established harmony to which nothing could be competent, except a Being of infinite wisdom, power, and goodness, or love. His character, too, must be interpreted in the light of the highest thought and attainment and aspiration of man, because all else is subservient to this. (When we have spoken of God as a Person, we have meant by it only this trinity of qualities,—wisdom, love, and power,— not any form of any kind.)

The method by which this conclusion is justified is peculiar, and in contrast with the prevailing methods. These identify God with the world force. God is the immanent agency of the known sensible world. This is strenuously elaborated by Lotze, and it has been recently repeated by Fiske in his *Idea of God*. This immanent Deity is, as Fiske insinuates, Spencer's great kosmic Unknown. *Scientific Theism*, as expounded by Dr. Abbot, teaches the same doctrine, more consistently, on a basis of natural realism· This doctrine has the merit of bringing God and man close together,—so close, indeed, as to make them one. They differ only as whole and part, or as noumenon and phenomenon, or as common subject and various modality. That which is alleged to be immanent in the world cannot be discriminated from the world or from its organisms and their organic life. The author of *Scientific Theism* has the merit of seeing and of recognizing this fact and its logical implication, that to this extent theism is pantheism. He also sees that it implies natural realism as its basis. If sensible phenomena—that is, all the knowable universe—are only a series of my subjective states, then God's immanence in them is only immanence in me, his force my force, and indiscriminable from myself as conscious subject.

The method of Philosophical Realism, on the other hand, scoops an infinite gulf between God and man. It appropriates all the knowable universe to man. This theory has been so conceived and expounded that, with sufficient truth for the purposes of satire, it has been described as teaching that "man trundles his universe before him like a huge goitre." That identifies man with his organism. But the organism, like the mountains, stars, and milky way, is but a mode of the man who is the common subject of all. He therefore does not trundle his universe about. He only changes the local relation of the several objects of the universe, including the organism. The universe, as a whole, never moves, and cannot move. Nor does its subject and cause, the true and real man, ever move. He is always everywhere throughout the whole universe, since all this is but a portion of his various modes or subjective states. He is thus omnipresent and omniscient, relative to this universe. He himself constitutes all the knowable, and how much beyond he constitutes of what is unknowable we know not.

But we have perfect proof that he is finite. We have abundant evidence that there is a vast and indefinite multitude of finite beings. The evidence is equally good that these finites have not an infinite duration, though they may and doubtless will continue forever. They had a beginning. They had, therefore, an antecedent as a Cause. This Cause must be conceived as a *conscious and designing* Cause, because we know no other kind of cause, since we know only ourselves. Much of what we know we do not purpose, we allow; but we do not know that these are not effects of a designing Cause. That is the question now before us. No other than a designing Cause is conceivable by us, because utterly alien from all the analogies of human experience. Therefore, no other is inferable from experience. Our Creator cannot be merged in the blind forces, so called, of the material universe, since these, so far as known, are modes of my conscious mind. He must be a self-conscious mind, and his action must be intelligent and not without purpose and plan.

The moral nature or quality of this cause also must be determined from the effect. This effect must not be contemplated only or chiefly in its lower potencies, but in its higher potencies and their relation to the lower. Now, the higher potencies are seen in the noblest action of the intellectual and moral faculties; and to these all things else, it is clear, are normally ancillary and subservient. The discoveries of modern science, resulting in the doctrine of evolution, unfold this with irresistible force, which has been well set forth by Mr. John Fiske. All that is best in the present is the evolved product or result of all past kosmic agency. All the best and highest now attained, therefore, stamps with its own dignity and intent all the prior and lower agencies. The earlier and lower mean the later and higher. They are all of one piece. They show a continuity of force and a comprehending plan. Their Maker designed them all, and designed the lower as having their end in the higher, which constitute the final cause of the creation.

Further, we have shown that the lower do themselves actually become higher. The evolution is a development of the same individuals from lower to higher. Each of us was once in the lowest rank of existence, and from the first it was designed that we should undergo these successive elevations. This process is to be everlasting. By this which temporally was and is and is to come, we must judge of Him who eternally was and is and is to come.

Prospective Working of this Theory.

The incompetent will deem these high metaphysical speculations entirely barren. They think they are justified in this by the past history of philosophy, because philosophy has not yet yielded all we have sought. But this is hasty and superficial. A perfect philosophy in detail can never be attained by a finite mind, because it cannot comprehend the infinite. It can be settled in the acceptance of certain clear and indisputable principles. Under these, it can know some things; and it can be correct and consistent so far as it goes, and this it is bound to be. But who shall say *how much* we ought to know as a reward for past effort, and that the result does not justify that effort or any further labor? Surely, the very labor is a benefaction of the highest order; and its beneficial influence is telling upon all the forms of life.

This is especially true of the higher philosophy of idealism. It has always steadily pointed to God. Its logical right to do this, and its proofs that it points in the right direction, have been questioned; but its spirit and intent and large influence on the subject are beyond dispute. This is seen in the old-time argument, still cherished by some, for an infinitely perfect being from the idea of such a being. By the use of this argument and its result, Descartes reconciled psychological idealism with natural realism. God was thence a necessity in psychology and philosophy. The doctrine of pre-established harmony proposed by Leibnitz presupposes Deity. According to Malebranche, God is the subject of our ideas, the real abiding, sensible forms of the world, so that we see them in him. With Berkeley, he was their direct Cause, if not their subject. While Kant based theism on our moral nature, Hegel finds Deity in the intellectual processes as an absolutely ideal and, therefore, real result. Philosophical Realism is equally theistic. It shows that the proof of other men contains the proof of God, and his constant supernatural agency.

The new philosophy, so far as it is true, will levy tribute from all things. It has the right of universal supremacy and domination. It is heir to all the past, and enters at once on its inheritance and takes full possession. In the births of thought, the law of primogeniture is reversed. The last becomes first, as the heir of all things. This was ordained from the beginning. It is evolution's highest law. Nor does this imply that all theories must be transient. The true thought, known as such, can never be superseded. It will be always the latest. First thought on deep matters is always crude. Science and philosophy are ripeness and maturity. The intelligence which attains and discerns the correct theory will always see that it is not to be, that it cannot be, philosophically superseded. Being true and ulterior, it is all-comprehending and immutable.

Evolution is always a movement of matter toward spirit and spirituality. As a process from the lower to the higher, it moves from the inorganic to the organic, from the apparently unconscious to the conscious, then to the self-conscious or the reflective consciousness, in ever-growing degrees and varieties of supersensible power. It then rises into the sphere of abstract thought and morals and philosophical religion.

All inventions observe the same law. As they are the product of thought, they aim at the expression and communication of thought. They bring distant minds near. They shorten distances, and make intercourse more immediate, speedy, and perfect. Witness articulate speech, writing, printing, steam, the telescope and microscope, the telegraph and telephone. Spirit, as a supersensible conscious power, is thus growingly made manifest as the source and end of all things called material. Idealism, as the true Philosophical Realism, is the goal toward which all thought and action clearly tend. It will, therefore, in innumerable ways show its practical power in proportion as the world's intelligence advances; and this doctrine will be seen to be the very soul of all theories and intellectual forms, so far as they have in them any validity and truth.

Hence, it has recently been made the ground of a theory of metaphysical healing called "Christian Science," which is rapidly multiplying disciples of the very best kind of people.

EXCEPT the last few pages and some late interpolations, all of *Philosophical Realism* was written years ago, and much of it printed at long intervals in the *Index* of Boston, which is one of the most philosophical weekly journals in the world. The work, therefore, is not written from the stand-point of Christian Science ; and the form and phraseology in which the thought is put are such as may possibly mislead an unwary Christian Scientist. It is for him no guide. Rightly conceived, it is, so far as it goes, in perfect harmony with Christian Science, unless it be possibly in one or two minor details, which the author would now modify. Its great object is to show that there is no matter, except mortal thought, and that Mind is all ; and thence to unfold some logical conclusions, not to teach Christian Science, on which it is no authority whatever.

Moreover, it may be well in closing to say distinctly what is assumed in the course of the preceding discussion, that the attribution of reality to sensible things applies to them only as sensible ; that is, as mortal modes of mortal thought. They are but the fashion of a world which passeth away, and perish with the very power of sensibility which begot them, till the immutable and eternal remains alone,— the Perfect without a counterfeit.

INDEX.

Abbot, F. E., 29, 275.
Abiogenesis, 154.
Absolute and Relative, 72–86.
Absolute Ego, 117-1.0.
Absolute: the, 149; creative, 213.
Academics, 25.
Action and Reaction, 29.
Action: involuntary, 35, 36; subjective (q. v.), 142.
Acts, as subjective and objective (q. v.), 20.
Adam, 166, 167.
Adap'ations, 247, 248, 253, 254.
Adjustment, 254
Affections, organic (q. v.), 211.
Agency, supernatural, 246.
Agent, supramundane, 233.
Agnostic Deism (q. v.), 175, 176.
Agnosticism: allusions, 12, 73, 107, 108, 113; rebuked, 196.
Altruism, 137, 138.
Ammonia, 77.
Analogy, 170.
Analogy, Butler's, 177.
Analytical Processes, 45.
Anarchy, 221.
Ancient Mariner, quoted, 124.
Angels: rebellion of, 199; seeing unformed organisms, 205.
Animals: personality, 89; two in one, 128; bodies, 146; dignity, 160, 161; world of, 171, 206; teleology, 251; origin and offspring, 265, 266.
Annihilation: allusions, 55, 105, 185, 186; of self, 216.
Anomalies, 241, 242.
Antecedents, 84.
Anti-supernaturalist Claims, 175, 176.
Appetites, 35.
Appointment, supernatural, 173, 174.
Arch, 230

Archimedes, 246.
Ariel, 136.
Aristotle, 25, 189, 193.
Art, developing power, 185.
Assimilation: of science (q. v.), 257–271; of kosmogeny, 257–263; of philogeny, 263–265; of ontogeny, 265–267.
Astronomy, 28 (See *Copernicus, Jupiter, Planetary System, Stars, Sun, Venus.*)
Atomism, 59, 60, 99, 107–110.
Atoms, 76.
Autonomy: of the universe, 225; of gravity (q. v.), 230, 231; objective and subjective, 233–237. (See *Evolution.*)
Avalanche, 279.

Babel, of voices, 168.
Barbarians, 145. (See *Savages.*)
Barren Metaphysics (q. v.), 277.
Being: as force (q. v.), 84, 159, 221; supernatural and natural, 179; sum, 182; awful and real, 236, 237.
Berkeley, Bishop, 3, 24, 73, 121, 122, 141, 142, 168, 169, 205, 278.
Bible, and metempsychosis (q. v.), 167
Birth, 67, 124, 156, 159, 199–204.
Bismuth, 242.
Black Hole, 33–46.
Bluebeard, 15.
Bodies: as dual and real, 10; animal, 146; existence of, 200
Body and External World, 143.
Body and Soul, 166.
Body and Will, 129, 130.
Bone, as an index, 139.
Book, illustration, 39.
Bossuet, 25.
Boulder, 22.
Brain and Consciousness, 129, 170.

Brain and Thought, 58, 59.
Bridge, from the ego, 169.
Brothers, 168, 169.
Brown's Philosophy, 24.
Buddhism, 155.
Burns's Tam O'Shanter, 11.
Butler's Analogy, 177.

CABBAGES, 130.
Cæsar, 5.
Carpenter, W. B., 274.
Causality, 222-224, 239.
Causation: unity of, 61; changes, 148-150, 249.
Cause: of existence, 200-203; in science and philosophy, 218, 219; of world (q. v.), 273, 274; confusion as to, 219, 220; design (q. v.), 276.
Causes, designing and undesigning, 218.
Cells, 67, 68. (See *Germ*.)
Cerebration, 274.
Chances, doctrine of, 231, 232.
Change, in causation, 148-150.
Chaos, 56, 153, 158, 221, 258, 268.
Character, 135, 274, 275.
Chemical Elements, 262.
Chemical Forces, 56.
Chicago, 212.
Chicken, 63, 64. (See *Egg*.)
Children: ideas of, 145; birth of, (q. v.), 199-203. (See *Fatherhood, Parentage*.)
Christian Fathers, 189, 190.
Christianity: importance of, 177; theistic, 193.
Christian Science, 279.
Christians, view of matter (q. v.), 240.
Christian Theism (q. v.), 214.
Church Opinions, 189.
Chyle, 61.
Circle, 223.
Circumstantial Evidence, 141.
Civilization, 164, 165. (See *Barbarians*.)
Clairaudience, 212.
Clairvoyance, 103, 104, 212.
Clarke, Samuel, 226
Clifford, Professor, 170.
Clocks, 254.
Cobwebs, metaphysical, 179.
Cold, 80, 81, 247.
Coleridge, S. T., 75, 124.
Collateral Testimony, 168-170.
Collocations, 254.

Colors, 56, 169, 192, 225, 226.
Combining Power, 243, 244.
Comicality, no argument, 97, 98.
Common Sense, 71.
Community, 126.
Complexus, 189, 190, 258.
Comte's Philosophy, 44, 45. (See *Positivism*.)
Conation, 221.
Conception: of creation, 179-198; of deity (q. v.), 179-183.
Conditioned, Philosophy of the, 113.
Conditions of Intercourse (q. v.), 170.
Consciousness, 181, 182, 194.
Consequents, 84.
Constant Ego (q. v.), 99, 100.
Contemporary Review, 80-83.
Copernicus, 28, 29, 97, 270. (See *Astronomy*.)
Cosmic States, 49-53, 56. (See *Kosmos*.)
Cousin's Philosophy, 25, 26.
Creation: not evolution, 20, 213, 214; forms, 55; power (q. v.), 176, 185; method proven, 179-198; conception, 183-193; lowest condition, 204-208; proof, 208, 209; pre-organic state, 209-213; instantaneous, 216; forcelessness, 220-222; unceasing, 236; no proof, 240, 241; history, 267. (See *Cause, Evolution*.)
Creative Power, 187.
Creator, as force (q. v), 218, 220. (See *Deity, God, Infinite, One*.)
Cross-examination, 255.

DEATH, 103, 104, 156. (See *Birth*.)
Deism, agnostic, 175, 176. (See *Theism*.)
Deity: of theism, 36; proofs, 59; materialist admissions, 175; mundane, 177; conception of, 179-183; defined, 180 ; kosmic, 191; proofs of, 193-195, 218; immanent, 275. (See *Creation, God, Infinite, Spirit*.)
Demands for God, 193-195.
Descartes, 3, 20, 121, 132, 278.
Designer, 240.
Designing Causes, 218, 276.
Designless Power, 243-245.
Design: marks, 239 ; no proof of creation (q. v.), 240 ; not supernatural, 240, 241; not in nature

INDEX 285

(q. v.), 241-243; lacking, 243-245; exalted place, 253-255.
Destiny of Man (q. v.), 135, 136.
Deterioration, 208. (See *Moral.*)
Dichotomy, 110-113.
Dignity of Animals (q.v.),160, 161.
Dissipation of Heat (q.v.),228-230.
Divine Immanence (q.v),214-216.
Doctrine of Chances, 231, 232.
Dragons, 15, 16.
Dualism: repellent, 1; vacillation, 16, 17; of Leibnitz, 99; personal, 111; old, 123, 124; defence, 128; soul and body, 165, 166; expounded, 168, 169.
Dualists: demands, 19, 20; dementation, 80-83.
Duality, 10, 11; of things and thought (q. v.), 227.
Duns Scotus, 26.
Dynamic Relations, 216, 217.

EAR, 102. (See *Sound, Speech.*)
Earth: separate, 206; life of the, 211; cooling, 230; beginning, 260. (See *Matter, Universe, World.*)
Education, developing power of, 185.
Egg, 63, 64, 150, 250.
Ego: in general, 3, 6, 7, 13, 14, 18, 30, 31, 33; based on experience, 8, 9; opposed, 12; shut in, 42-46; inclusive, 43; stationary, 48; modes, 49, 50; oneness, 55, 56; relation to organism, 57, 58; independence, 58; essay, 87-98; proof, 87-89; two conceptions, 91-93; permanence and simplicity, 99-116; constant and perduring, 99, 100 ; immortality, 100-105; pure unity, 114-116; absolute, 117-120; local, 120-132; defined, 120; transphenomenal, 120-122; supersensible, 123-125; organic, 125-131; panheisenist, 131, 132: transcended, 133-147, 274; Fichte's efforts, 133-138; sematic relation, 143, 144; no waif, 159: modes, 197; immanence in, 216; of sensible world, 223, 224; of universe (q. v.), 249; of all phenomena (q. v.), 260; name, 273.
Eleatic Sceptics, 25.
Electric Energy, 53.
Elias, 167.

Embryo, 265. (See *Birth.*)
Emerson, R. W., 118.
Emmanence, 189. (See *Immanence.*)
Empiricism, 222.
English Literature, Taine on, 94, 95.
Environment: references, 29, 57, 58, 83; of ego, 96, 97, 272.
Eocene, 138, 139.
Epicurus, 99, 107.
Epiperipheral Feelings, 39.
Equilibration of Heat (q. v.), 228-230.
Eternity: of gravity, 230, 231; of matter, 240.
Ether, on the eye, 17.
Ethics of Spinoza, 182, 183, 196.
Etiology: in general, 218-224; relative to matter and force (q. v), 219, 220; and objective evolution, 225-232: and subjective evolution, 233-238; and teleology (q. v), 237-240.
Evil: from nature, 238; adaptations for, 247, 248. (See *Sin.*)
Evolution and Progress, 31.
Evolutionists, modern, 59, 60.
Evolution: objective, 1-7, 42, 72; agnostic, 12, 13; unlike creation (q. v.), 20, 21, 213, 214; individual, 47-49; complete, 56; and spiritualism, 110; subjective, 158, 162-167; vast, 204; stages, 207; new form, 218, 219; and philosophy (q. v.), 259-262; into spirit (q. v.), 279.
Excreta, mental, 175.
Existence: of God (q. v.), 176, 177; cause of (q. v.), 199-203, (See *Creation.*)
Experiences, 70, 71.
Experiential Knowledge, 132, 140.
Extension, 45, 46. (See *Space.*)
External Cause (q. v.), 272, 273.
Extra-natural Agent (q. v.), 188, 189.
Extra-organic Ego (q. v.), 125-131.
Extra-organicism (q. v.), 93-95.
Extra-organic World, 206.
Eye, 63, 64, 77, 102, 143, 170, 225, 243. (See *Light, Sight, Stars.*)

FACULTIES, new, 243, 244.
Fashioner, 244. (See *Creator.*)
Fatherhood, 168, 169. (See *Birth*).

Fauna, 49.
Fénelon, 25.
Fichte, 43, 73, 119, 120, 132-137.
Fiery Mist, 52.
Final Causes (q. v.), 80, 81, 252.
Finite Spirits (q. v.), 125.
Fire, 146.
First Cause, 222, 223. (See *God*.)
First Principles, Spencer's, 113.
Fishes, 243. (See *Animals*.)
Fiske, John, 53, 59, 166, 275, 277.
Fixity, 262.
Flavor, 77.
Flora, 49, 268.
Fœtus, 67.
Fog, 75.
Footprints, 254.
Force: egoistic, 14, 87, 101; one (q. v.), 34, 157; assimilated, 35; of sentient world, 53, 54; known, 55; cognized, 68-70; from matter, 192; man a, 214; and etiology (q. v.), 219, 220; verified, 221; all things are, 221; everywhere, 236; and nature (q. v.), 243, 244; and theism, 252.
Forcelessness, 220-222.
Forces: the humble, 32; increased or diminished, 185, 186, 189, 190; and quality, 219; unconscious, 245; blind, 247.
Fossil Metaphysics, 78-83.
Fossil World, 147.
Fossils, 264, 268.
Foundation of Teleology (q. v.), 249-251.
Fowler, J. H., 62-71.
Foxes, illustration, 83.
French Metaphysics, 224.
Friends, 168, 169.
Frogs, 103.
Fulcrum, 149.
Future, 48, 49.
Future Existence, 165. (See *Immortality*.)

GALILEO, 271.
Gas, 49, 50. (See *Incandescent*.)
Genii, Oriental, 90.
Genus, 23.
Geology, 268.
German Metaphysics, 222.
German Philosophers, 5, 133.
Germ-cells (q. v.), 127.
Gnostics, 189.
God: forms in, 24, 25; nature, 118; existence, 176, 177; left out, 187; work, 188; transcending the universe, 189; degraded, 190; mode of action, 213, 214; exclusive force, 216; sole power, 221; spiritual, 226; gravity, 230, 231; known, 235, 237; unity, 236; and teleology (q. v.), 252, 253; action, 256; immediate cause (q. v.), 273; character, 274, 275; near man, 275; how judged, 277. (See *Deity*, *Infinite*, *Supreme*.)
Godhead, 253.
Goethe, 74.
Goitre, 275.
Good, accidental, 159, 160.
Good Adaptations, 247, 248.
Good Samaritan, 127.
Grand Totality, 119.
Gravitation, 56, 227-231.
Great Britain, its metaphysical schools, 222.
Great Designer (q. v.), 246.
Great First Cause (q. v.), 222, 223. (See *God*.)
Great Unknown, 36, 54, 55. (See *Deity*.)
Greek Fathers, 189.
Greek, quotation from, 212.
Greeks: intellect, 24; idea of person, 89; early philosophy, 193.
Gulf: between all minds, 173; bridged, 198; celestial, 255; between God and man, 275.

HAMILTON, SIR WILLIAM: references, 20, 24, 73, 74; *natural*, 41; quoted, 113; duality (q. v.), 168, 169; on cerebration, 274.
Harmony: pre-established, 174, 198, 278; causeless, 226.
Health, 77.
Heat, 65, 77, 228-230. (See *Cold*.)
Hegel's Philosophy, 73, 105, 183, 278.
Height, 185.
Heir of All, 278.
Heisenism, 193, 194. (See *Panheisenism*.)
Helmholtz's Philosophy, 64-66.
Heterogeneity, 119.
Hetiology, False, 11-13.
History of Creation (q. v.), 267.
History of Modern Philosophy, 26.
Hobbes, Thomas, 59.
Holy Spirit (q. v.), 167.
Horses, 138.
Human Form, 152, 153.
Human Intercourse, 168-174.

Hume, David: references, 7, 25, 73, 92; metaphysical confusion, 219, 220, 250
Huxley's Science, 20, 59, 170.

ICE, 230.
Idealism: opposing evolution, 1; imperfect, 24; double form, 24; objections false, 30; Reid's, 168-174; absolute, 279.
Idealists, demands upon, 19.
Idea of God, Fiske's, 275.
Ideas, doctrine of, 120, 121.
Identity, 83, 84.
Idol, external world, 34.
Igdrasil Tree, 157.
Illusion, 8.
I, meaning of the pronoun, 126.
Immanence: divine, 189, 191, 214, 215, 279; egoistic, 216. (See *Emmanence*.)
Immortality: of the ego, 100-105; personal, 157. (See *Future*.)
Immutability, of gravity, 237, 238.
Impassable Gulf (q. v.), 173.
Importance: of Christianity, 177; of supernaturalism, 236-238.
Improbability, intrinsic, 15.
Incandescent Gas (q. v.), 258.
Inches, 113.
Inconsistency, 13, 14.
Index, The, 20, 62.
Individualism: of evolution, 47-49; superficial, 156, 157.
Individualistic Force (q. v.), 214.
Individuality and Personality (q. v.), 89 90, 127.
Individuality: proved, 134; subjective, 180; not finite, 215.
Individual Power (q. v), 214.
Individuals, created, 209.
Induction, wings of, 198.
Inductive Basis, 138-141.
Inductive Method, 132-147.
Infinite Being (q. v), authority of, 222. (See *Deity*.)
Infinite Personality (q. v.), 90, 179-183, 244.
Infinite Power, 181, 186, 187, (See *God*.)
Infinite, the: notion of, 182, 183; defined, 186.
Infra-consciousness, 49-51.
Intelligence: in nature, 240, 241; confounded, 268.
Intercourse, human, 168-174.
Intrinsic Force (q. v.), 214.
Inventions, 278.

Involuntary Action, 35, 36.
Involution, 207, 229.
Iron, 230.

JACK AND THE BEANSTALKS, 108.
Janet, 80-83.
Jesus Christ: theism of (q.v.),193; quoted, 236.
Jews, 167.
Job, 247.
John the Baptist, 167.
Jupiter, 66. (See *Astronomy*.)

KANT, 28, 29, 73, 78, 82, 100, 133, 134, 278.
Kinetic Energy, 230-232.
Knower, the, 44.
Knowledge: subjective, 2; direct, 79.
Known and Unknown, 55, 56.
Know Thyself, 42, 66.
Kosmic Force (q. v.), 101, 227. (See *Cosmic*.)
Kosmic Theism (q. v.), 190-192.
Kosmogeny, 257-263.
Kosmos: allusions, 16, 30, 153; collapsing, 207, 208. (See *Universe, World*.)
Kubla Khan, 75.

LABOR, of God, 207, 236.
Labyrinth, 255.
Lacunæ, 93.
Lamp, 15. (See *Eye, Light*.)
Latin Fathers, 189. (See *Greek*.)
Law, 126, 127.
Leibnitz: allusions, 25, 99; monadism, 105-107, 196; doctrine of harmony, 278.
Lewes, G. H., 20, 33.
Life-events, 124.
Life, preceded by existence, 269.
Light, 17, 65, 77, 185.
Light, a magazine, 212.
Limitations of Teleology, 255, 256.
Lines, blending, 225.
Living Being, 269.
Local Ego, 120-133.
Locke, John: allusions, 3, 72, 73, 121; *reasoned*, 41.
Logic, 140.
Logical Method, with Deity, 193-195.
Logical Points, 18-21.
London, 212.
Lotze's Philosophy: allusions, 80-83, 118, 275; quoted, 213-217.
Lucretius, 99, 103.

MACHINE, God's, 214.
Maelstrom, 27.
Malaria, 247.
Malebranche, 24, 25, 278.
Manifestation of Supernaturalism, 237, 238.
Mansel, Dr., 20.
Man: sublime representation, 56; walking, 83; not a divine mode, 156; developed from animals, 161; a universe (q. v.), 171: origin, 199-207; inclusive, 210; intrinsic force, 214.
Marriage, 124.
Martineau, James, 235.
Materialist, name, 21.
Material World, nature of, 4-7.
Mathematics: relations, 27; pure, 45.
Matter: supersensuous, 8-22; belief in, 36; cognized, 68-70; errors, 78-83; Leibnitz's view, 106; dead, 192; force, 193; and etiology, 219, 220; eternal, 240; how known, 273.
Maturity, 279.
Maudsley's Philosophy, 107, 129, 130.
Me, 125.
Mechanical Constitution, 189.
Medium of Intercourse, 171-174.
Memory, 114-116, 200.
Men, and teleology, 251.
Mephistopheles, 72, 74.
Messiah, 167.
Metaphysical Causality, 222-224.
Metaphysical Method, how superseded, 195-198.
Metaphysical Principles, 8.
Metaphysical Theory, 6, 7.
Metaphysics, Lotze's, 213, 217.
Metaphysics, no refuge for theology, 177, 178.
Metempsychosis, 148, 150, 167.
Meteor, 159. (See *Astronomy*.)
Microscope, 127, 279.
Milky Way, 276. (See *Astronomy, Copernicus*.)
Mill, John Stuart, 88, 139, 140, 239, 248.
Milton, John, 198, 199, 240.
Mind: a force (q. v.), 68; errors, 78-83; human, 168; known to itself, 170; alone, 212; as unknown, 273.
Mind-expression, as in evolution, 62-71.
Mind in Nature, 212.

Mind, Review, 22.
Minds, separated, 173.
Miracles, 235.
Mohammed, 5.
Molecular Motion, 60.
Monadism, 105-107.
Monadology, 196.
Monads, 106.
Monism, spiritual, 107, 108, 118.
Monists, 21.
Monkey, 48, 153
Monuments, 48.
Moral Economy, 157.
Moral Order, 158.
Moral Probation, 165.
Moral Qualities, 185.
Morals, made impossible, 268.
Morphism, 148-167.
Mortalism, 157.
Mortal Mind, 273.
Moss-trooper, 152.
Motion, 106; circular, 222.
Mountains, 206, 276.
Murder, 124
Mutation, 209.
Mutual Intercourse (q. v.), 170.
Mystery, a last privilege, 12.

NATIONS, 126, 127.
Natural Realism (q. v.), 169.
Nature and Supernatural, 222; known, 235.
Nature: as force (q. v.), 139, 222; and universe (q. v.), 194; cause (q. v.) of man, 203; divine immanence (q. v.), 214-216; uniformity, 238; evil in, 238; lack of design, 241-245; and teleology, 252, 253.
Nature's Panheisenism (q. v.), 225-227.
Nebulæ, 258. (See *Milky Way*.)
Necessary Belief, 36.
Need of Supernaturalism (q. v.), 237, 238.
Newton, Sir Isaac, 184, 226.
Nimbus, 107.
Nominalism, 22-26. (See *Realism*.)
Non-ego (q. v.): allusions, 9, 10, 16, 20, 26, 40, 41; unproved, 37; admitted, 65; two kinds, 121, 122; sensible, 123-125; extra-organic, 125-131.
Non-egoistic Matter, 172.
Noumena, 73, 78.
Noumenon, 274.
Now, 49.

OBJECTIVE AUTONOMY, 233-235.
Objective Evolution (q. v.): expounded, 1-7, 33; broken, 51; its exclusions, 218; and etiology (q. v.), 225-232; how supported, 259, 260.
Objective Reality, 62-71.
Occam, William, 26.
Ocean, 206.
Odor, 77.
Omnipotence, 276.
Omniscience, 66, 276.
One Being (q. v.), 88, 89, 119; modes, 226. (See *Infinite*.)
One Ego (q. v.), 43.
One Force (q. v.), 34.
One Only, 13, 156. (See *God*.)
Ontogeny, 265-267.
Optics, 130.
Organic Atomism, 107-110.
Organic Consciousness (q. v.), 226.
Organic Ego (q. v.), 125-131.
Organicism, 91, 93-95.
Organicists, 93.
Organic Phenomena, 59, 60.
Organism: real and unknown, 9; relation to ego, 57, 58; sematic, 145-147; of deity and universe, 187; objective, 193, 205; of all phenomena, 205; of souls, 216, 217; traced back, 244. (See *Sematology*.)
Organisms, two, 10.
Organs, useless, 267, 268.
Origin: of man (q. v.), 199-217; of world (q. v.), 273, 274.
Orthodoxy, 195.
Oysters, 63.

PALÆONTOLOGY, 48, 102.
Palate, 102.
Paley, 239.
Panheisenism, 131, 132, 213, 225-227. (See *Heisenism*.)
Pantheism, 118.
Paralogisms, 222-224.
Paralysis, 247.
Parents, 200. (See *Birth*.)
Pascal, 58.
Past, 47-49.
Paul, theism of, 193.
Penumbral Metaphysics, 177, 178.
Pepper, 77.
Perduring Ego (q. v.), 99, 100, 128.
Perfection, 187.
Permanence: of the ego, 99-116; explained, 148-150.

Personal Deity (q. v.), 59, 240, 243, 275.
Personality: defined, 89-91; lost, 114-116; organic, 127; future, 156; of God, 158, 179; defined, 180, 181; human, 181-184.
Person: defined, 89; a designer, 239. (See *God, Infinite*.)
Phenomena: subjective (q. v.), 2-4; nature, 6, 7; egoistic, 20, 21, 40; defined, 23; character, 48; organic, 59-61; forceless, 53, 54; one with ego, 55, 56; ever changing, 95, 96; supernatural, 104, 105; of memory, 114-116; sensible, 123-125; modes, 191; unity of all, 227.
Philogeny, 263-265.
Philosophic Realism: unity in, 16, 114-116; scope, 31; definition, 41; self in, 132; logical, 135; basis, 223, 235; divine unity, 236; new argument, 239, 240; knows no unconscious power, 252; design, 253-255; assimilating power, 256; unity, 263; reign, 271; method, 275; prospects, 277-279.
Philosophic Realists: method, 146; assumptions, 169.
Philosophy and Science (q. v.): rank, 12; identity, 28-31.
Philosophy: scientific, 22-33; implied by theology, 175-178; cause in, 218, 219; true, 257.
Physical Science (q. v.), 124; errors, 255.
Physiological Ego (q. v.), 125-131.
Planetary System, 258. (See *Astronomy, Copernicus, Jupiter*.)
Plants, 269. (See *Flora*.)
Plato, 26, 120, 121, 193
Platonizing Christians, 189.
Pluralism, 113, 114.
Poison, 128.
Porphyry, 25.
Positive Method, 195-198.
Positivism, 45, 46, 50, 195-198.
Possibility, argument from, 15, 16.
Postulates, 8, 9, 36; about God, 176, 177.
Potential Substratum, 119. (See *Tyndall*.)
Poverty, 237.
Powder, 84, 85.
Power: above, 176; inferred, 224; designing, 243-245.

Powers, 184, 185.
Prayer, 238.
Pre-animal World (q. v.), 49-53.
Pre-established Harmony, 174.
Pre-exclusion, 234.
Pre-existence (q. v.), 150-153.
Pre-fossil World (q. v.), 47, 268-271.
Pre-kosmic Existence, 154.
Pre-organic Form, 204.
Pre-organic State, 209-213, 217.
Pre-organic World, 54.
Presence, infinite (q. v.), 191.
Present, 47, 48.
Pre-visible Motion, 17.
Primal Cause (q. v.), 239.
Princeton Review, 64.
Principle of Causality (q. v.), 222-224.
Principles of Human Knowledge, 121, 122, 169.
Printing, 279.
Probation, 165.
Progress, 184, 185.
Proofs: of God (q. v.), 176, 177; of creation (q. v.), 179-198, 208, 209.
Proserpine, 18.
Protoplasm, 50, 67.
Psalms, quoted, 253.
Psyche-morphism, 148-167.
Psychological Science, and God, 191, 192.
Psychologische Optik, 64.
Psychology: of evolution, 2; modern, 47, 260, 272; important, 141; facts, 258.
Ptolemaic System, 7, 29. (See *Astronomy, Copernicus.*)

QUALITIES: as forces, 219; creative, 231.
Quality, 54, 195, 196.

RAINDROPS, 267.
Realism: ancient, 22; dictum of consciousness, 38; word, 41. (See *Philosophic.*)
Realists of Middle Ages, 25, 26. (See *Nominalism.*)
Realities, all personal, 252.
Recherche de la Vérité, 24.
Reflections on the Situation, 47-61.
Refuge for Theology (q. v.), 177, 178.
Reid's Philosophy, 24, 141, 169.
Relation, importance of, 70, 71.

Relationism, 22.
Relations: substitutes, 26, 27; subjective, 27; various, 57-61.
Relative and Absolute, 72-86, 149.
Religio-Philosophical Journal, 212.
Religious Basis, 235.
Responsibility, 126, 127.
Ripeness, 279.
Rivers, 206.
Rocks, 268, 269.
Romans, idea of personality, 89.

SAMSON, 190.
Savages, 77. (See *Barbarians.*)
Scepticism, difficult to flank, 220, 221.
Schelling, 73, 105.
Scholasticism, 22, 23, 78.
Science and Philosophy: rank, 28-31, 279; scope, 31, 32; modern discoveries, 44.
Science and Supernaturalism (q. v.), 235.
Science: strict, 11; conquests, 12; ignorance, 15; developing power, 185; cause in, 218, 219; assimilation, 257-271.
Scientific Philosophy, 22-33.
Scientific Theism, Abbot's (q. v.), 275.
Scotch Philosophers, 24, 169.
Seamen, 92.
Seed, 150.
Self-consciousness, 9.
Self-knowledge, 170.
Self-modes, 48, 211.
Sematic Inference, 264.
Sematism: in general, 138-141; between senses, 142, 143; of ego, 143; of organisms, 144, 145; what it proves, 180.
Sematology: explained, 145, 171, 172, 204, 240, 257; law of, 259, 266, 268, 274.
Sensations: relative, 27, 78, 79; phenomena (q. v.) resolved into, 193, 194; alone known, 273. (See *Subjective.*)
Sensation, world as, 272, 273.
Sense-perception, 266.
Senses, Five, 25, 56, 102.
Senses: as twofold, 57; error, 80, 81; the sematism of, 142, 143; knowledge, 169.
Sensibility, 192.
Sensible Forms, 6, 7.
Sensible Matter, 173.
Sensible Phenomena, 123-125.

Sensism, 25, 91, 92, 113, 126, 128, 194, 266.
Sensitive Faculty, limitations, 17.
Sensitive Variation, 84, 85.
Sentience, forms of, 52.
Sentient Being: a force (q. v.), 53, 54; one with God (q. v.), 54, 55.
Sentient World, 49-53.
Sentiments, 24, 25.
Sex, 166.
Shakespeare, quoted, 109.
Ship, 247.
Siamese Twins, 128.
Sight, 80, 81, 146. (See *Clairvoyance, Eye, Light, Telescope.*)
Sign-child, 201. (See *Birth.*)
Similarity, 83, 84.
Simplicity of the Ego, 94-116.
Sins, plea for, 178. (See *Evil.*)
Skeleton, 139.
Sky, 81.
Small Philosophy, 92, 93.
Snail, 83.
Snuff, 77.
Society for Psychological Research, 212.
Solipsism: essay, 33-46; defined, 42, 43.
Soul: developed, 102; and body (q. v.), 166; how created, 213; evolving organism, 216, 217; transcends universe, 217.
Sound, 80, 81. (See *Ear.*)
Source, one, 42.
Space: allusions, 13, 56, 68-70, 77, 79, 92, 106, 225, 226; infinite, 190.
Spaces, 255.
Spark, 84, 85.
Spectroscope, 262.
Speech, 279. (See *Sound.*)
Spencer, Herbert: allusions, 2, 3, 7, 20, 33, 36-40, 53, 59, 73, 74, 82; quoted, 5, 77; *transfigured*, 41; and Fichte, 43; errors, 62, 63; on sensism (q. v.), 92, 113; changes, 149, 166; self-knowledge all, 170; power, 176; unknown God, 275.
Sphere of Teleology (q. v.), 249-256.
Spinoza, 118, 132, 149, 182, 183, 196, 215, 226.
Spirit: as ego, 128; the power, 279.
Spirits: and symbols, 144, 145; intercourse, 180; manifestations, 212, 213; moulding body, 217.

Spiritual monism, 117, 118.
Stahl's Philosophy, 217.
Stars, 102, 276. (See *Astronomy, Ptolemaic.*)
Steam, 279.
Stewart, Dugald, 24, 169.
Stubble, 159.
Subjective Agent, 192.
Subjective Autonomy, 233-237.
Subjective Evolution (q. v.): real, 161, 162; universal, 162-167, 233-238.
Subjective Relations, 27.
Subjective States, 205, 206.
Subjective World: allusions, 8, 9; real, 40-42.
Subjectivism, Modern, 22-26.
Subjectivity, universal, 2-4, 210.
Substance: basis, 55; always the same, 149; and quality, 195, 196.
Summary, 272-279.
Sun, 6, 66. (See *Astronomy.*)
Sunstroke, 248.
Supernatural Appointments, 173, 174.
Supernatural Infinite (q. v.), 180.
Supernaturalism: excluded, 194; and science (q. v.), 235; importance (q. v.), 236, 237.
Super-organicism (q. v.), 93.
Super-organic Power (q. v.), 103, 104.
Super-scientific, 17.
Super-sensible matter (q. v.), 8-22.
Super-sensible Phenomena (q. v.), 123-125.
Super-sensible Processes, 17.
Supreme Being (q. v.), 156, 234.
Symbolism, 50, 69, 70; sematic; 197; universal, 203, 204.
Symbols: as forces (q. v.), 53, 64; realities, 145, 268.
Synthetic Evolution (q. v.), 227.

TAINE'S ESSAYS, quoted, 94, 95.
Telegraph, 279.
Teleology: presuppositions, 239-248; etiology (q. v.), 239 240; sphere, 249-256; form, 249-251; relations, 251-253; limitations, 256, 257.
Telephone, 279.
Telescope, 271, 279. (See *Astronomy, Light, Microscope, Venus.*)
Tempest, 247.
Testimony, collateral, 168-170.
Tests, 257.

Theism: allusions, 175, 176; of Jesus (q. v.) and apostles, 193; improved, 246; and force, 252.
Theistic Conclusions, 274–277.
Theists: allusion, 156; view of authority, 222; and matter, 240.
Theology, implies philosophy, 175–178.
Things, 226, 227.
Thought and Brain, 58, 59.
Thought and Things, 226, 227.
Thunder, 56.
Time, 56, 68–70, 79, 92, 100, 225. (See *Space*.)
Times, 255.
Tongue, 102. (See *Speech*.)
Touch, 102, 146, 169.
Transcendence of the Universe, 217.
Transcending the Ego (q. v.), 133–147, 274.
Transfigured Realism, 37–40.
Transmutation, 61, 163, 221.
Transphenomenal Being, 274.
Transphenomenalism, 120–122.
Trichotomy, 111.
Trilemma, 185.
Trinity, 275.
Troglodyte, 185.
True Philosophy (q. v.), 257.
Tyndall, John, 52, 59, 109, 241, 242.

ULTIMATE FACTS, 266.
Unceasing Creation (q. v.), 236.
Unconscious Cerebration, 274.
Unconscious Forces (q. v.), 245.
Undesigned Causes (q. v.), 218. (See *Design*.)
Uniformities, 60.
Uniformity, 142.
Unity: of philosophic realism, 114–116; abiding, 120; of ego, 130; conscious, 191; of all phenomena, 227; of God (q.v.),236.
Universality of Evolution, 162–167.
Universals, 26, 27.

Universe: external ensemble, 20; every being a, 171; organic, 187; transcended, 189, 217; unity, 191, 204; nature, 194; defined, 215; forceless, 221; autonomy (q. v.), 233–237; ego, 249; unit of force, 266, 267; trundled about with us, 274. (See *World*.)
Universes, 180.
Unknowable Absolute (q. v.), 86.
Unknowable, the, 119.
Unknown and Known (q. v.), 55, 56.
Unseen Universe, quoted, 175, 176.
Useless Organs (q. v.), 267, 268.

VACILLATION, 16–19.
Vanishing Lines, 225.
Variableness, 245, 246.
Variation, 84, 85.
Venus, 270. (See *Astronomy*.)
Vitascripts, 48.
Vocation of Man, 135.
Volition, 245, 246. (See *Will*.)

WAR, 124, 221.
Water, 242.
Wealth, 247.
Wedding Garment, 108.
Weight, 185, 228.
Western Intellect, 148.
Whale, 267.
Will: as power, 185; divine force (q. v.), 220; of God (q. v.), 230, 231.
Wisdom, in nature, 247.
Words: use, 72; flood, 75.
World: material, 4–6; different to different men, 9; so-called, 19; sentient, 53–55; term, 55; spiritual, 269; as sensation, 272, 273; each man his own, 272; cause or origin, 273, 274. (See *Earth, Universe*.)
Worms, 56.
Writing, 279.

K.

www.ingramcontent.com/pod-product-compliance
Lightning Source LLC
Chambersburg PA
CBHW031904220426
43663CB00006B/757